Coming Out, Coming Home

Coming Out, Coming Home

Making Room for Gay Spirituality in Therapy

KENNETH A. BURR

Routledge
Taylor & Francis Group
New York   London

Routledge
Taylor & Francis Group
270 Madison Avenue
New York, NY 10016

Routledge
Taylor & Francis Group
2 Park Square
Milton Park, Abingdon
Oxon OX14 4RN

© 2009 by Taylor & Francis Group, LLC
Routledge is an imprint of Taylor & Francis Group, an Informa business

Printed in the United States of America on acid-free paper
10 9 8 7 6 5 4 3 2 1

International Standard Book Number-13: 978-0-7890-3843-2 (Softcover) 978-0-7890-3842-5 (Hardcover)

Library of Congress Cataloging-in-Publication Data

Burr, Kenneth A.
    Coming out, coming home : making room for gay spirituality in therapy / Kenneth A. Burr.
        p. cm.
    Includes bibliographical references and index.
    ISBN 978-0-7890-3842-5 (hardbound : alk. paper) -- ISBN 978-0-7890-3843-2 (pbk. : alk. paper)
    1. Gays--Religious life. 2. Homosexuality--Religious aspects--Christianity. I. Title.

BV4596.G38B87 2009
204'.408664--dc22   2008038706

Visit the Taylor & Francis Web site at
http://www.taylorandfrancis.com

and the Routledge Web site at
http://www.routledge.com

Dedication

For Tom, John, and Skip, who left much too soon.
Your threads continue in this tapestry

Contents

List of Figures*

---

* Illustrations by Cameron Burr, Open Road Media, Austin, Texas

Acknowledgments

When I began giving seminars on gay spirituality I was often asked to recommend books that could help therapists and other professionals explore the intersections of homosexuality and spirituality on a deeper level. There seemed to be an increasing desire to find new ways of understanding, encouraging, and accepting clients and loved ones who were gay. As I did my research, it became apparent to me that there was little written on this topic, and I began to ponder writing a book myself.

However, such an endeavor is never a solo project. If it takes a whole village to raise a child, it most certainly takes a whole community to write a book like this. My community began with loving parents, who passed on massive quantities of love, faith, and hope for their children. I also witnessed an exceptional hospitality modeled by extended family members who not only made room for difference but have continued to celebrate the diversity of those who entered their lives. The exceptional church community where I was raised was also full of people who truly cared for each other and were often eager to learn new ways of thinking through and living the life of faith. Even today, when I visit that church I feel loved to the core, for there is a part of that community I carry with me at all times. For all these solid foundations, I will forever be grateful.

Similarly, my personal interaction with gays and lesbian spans at least 40 years and has certainly contributed to my growing unrest with the stereotypes that continue to oppress many gentle and kindred spirits. So I am very appreciative of my gay friends and loved ones who continue to embellish and enlarge my life. I also want to mention the people of Seattle First Baptist Church, who have fully welcomed sexual minorities into their community for more than 30 years. Thank you for enfolding my family into one of the most inclusive ministries in the Seattle area.

Although I had been considering writing a book for years, it really was the personal encouragement of my friends that moved me past my own self-doubts and fears to embrace this new possibility. I specifically want to thank Glen Paddock, Mike Fitzpatrick, Cheryl Storm, Shahn McGuire, and Julie and Larry Snyder for continually reiterating, "You really ought to write that book!" I also owe a debt to my friend Jim Kellogg, computer man extraordinaire, who continues to keep my computers running smoothly and has often talked me down from the peaks of anxiety whenever a techno-crisis arises.

I want to especially thank Tom "Stone" Carlson, who connected me with a publisher. Tom opened wide the door I had been staring at for ages. As a result, I entered a new phase of my life—putting words to my thoughts and intuitions on this subject, which has made this adventure a personally enriching experience.

A great deal of personal and professional support comes from my weekly consult group, which continues to provide insight and expertise that shape my worldview. This group has been meeting for Tuesday case consultation lunches for more than 25 years and consists of seven very savvy therapists who are excellent role models in our profession. Through them I have learned that compassion, fatigue, and most other professional anxieties can be cured with a few pieces of high-quality, dark chocolate! (Who knew?) We recently realized that our group averages about 20 years of full-time practice per therapist in a wide variety of clinical settings. Although I have only been part of this group for 5 years, I have grown professionally, emotionally, and spiritually in the 500 hours we have spent together. I am so very appreciative of this intentional community that has welcomed me. Special thanks go out to Peter Hunsberger, Ed.D., E. B. Vance, Ed.D., Sharon Greenberg, Ph.D., Jennifer Smith, Ph.D., Glen Paddock, Ph.D., and Kathy Wilmering, M.S.W., A.R.N.P. May shared laughter continue to fill our sails for the next phases of our journey together.

No writer can do his or her work without some constructive criticism, because after one writes for any length of time, objectivity wanes. I am particularly indebted to my friends and colleagues who read my original manuscripts and suggested much needed improvements. Their importance in the village where books are born is certainly not overlooked, and their diligent efforts were often beyond my expectations. For instance, my long-time friend Glen Paddock believed in this project to such a degree that he was motivated to continue reading mounds of transcripts in 20-minute segments after recovering from eye surgery. He is also a systems theorist like no other, whose expertise and friendship I greatly treasure. My friend and fellow therapist Ellen Sanford knows that a good friend is also an honest one, having enough confidence in our friendship to suggest that I delete whole paragraphs that did not work for a given theme. After helping me rephrase some of my edgier comments, she invited close friends to her home to meet a "wonderful new author." (Ellen is probably why California is called the Golden State.) Finally, I am indebted to my dear friend and fellow minister Bill Kettenring for his amazing ability to notice those minute details in grammar, punctuation, and phrasing that I still can't see. Bill has the eyes of a hawk and the wings of a barn swallow. I'm still wondering how he returned those corrected pages so fast while carrying his own immense workload.

I also want to thank all the people whose true stories make up a large percentage of this book. Although I have protected your true identities, as we agreed, it will have to be enough to say how honored I have been to bear witness to your lives in this way. May special blessings be showered on your lives. Thank you, "Victor, Debra, Douglas, Rachel, Jeff, Rick, Jim, Mark, Gordon, Beth, Bob, Aaron, Sam, Richard, Clint, Brett, Thomas, Patrick, Monty, Michelle, Evelyn, Lucy, Cora, Julie, Katie, Katrina, Sarah, Arnold, George, Christy, and Jonathan," for your vulnerability and trust; by sharing your life stories, others will be able to rewrite theirs.

I have also had the privilege of working with two very special artists who make this book both deeper and lighter. When I asked Dave Snyder of Chicago if he would be willing to contribute a poem or two for this endeavor, he was eager to do so and produced two poems I think are outstanding. Likewise, when I asked Austin's up and coming animation artist, Cameron Burr, to do illustrations for each chapter, he not only uncapped his black pens but also possessed an uncanny ability to take my ideas and turn them into visual images that were right on target. I was continually impressed how much synchronicity we generated as we traded emails and images back and forth across the country. I acknowledge your talents and your hearts. You two are amazing! (And just because one of you is my son does not mean I am biased!)

Finally, I am grateful for my wonderful family, who continues to encourage my creativity even when it may seem a bit out there. Thank you Carrie, Cameron, and Catie for all the wonderful times we share together; your love brings out the best in me. The way you have learned to make room for difference in your own lives is only one of the myriad ways that makes me proud to be your dad. And leaving the best for the last, I cannot begin to explain how grateful I am to Shelley, my wife of 35 years, who continues to make room for our mutual growth and development as we continue to figure out what it means to be truly human and people of faith. She has made this book possible in ways that only she and I will know, for we have shared our lives through work and play, laughter and tears, reading, discussing, and living it all side by side. To you, my dear, I give my deepest thanks.

Kenneth A. Burr
September 2008

Introduction

Welcome to *Coming Out, Coming Home*, a book written to increase the potential for spiritual growth and development in our society. I should warn you up front that reading this book is not meant to be a safe experience. People who have read it have often discovered something stirring within them as they began to see the possibilities in *Making Room for Gay Spirituality*. However, setting this book aside because you are not a sexual minority would be a lost opportunity, because this was designed for anyone who has had their beliefs and values challenged by the topic of homosexuality. It is my desire to lead readers into new thoughts to ponder, and fresh air to breathe, *in Therapy* and Beyond to the rest of their lives.

It breaks my heart when I hear young men and women say that they don't think God loves them because of their sexual orientation. I have heard numerous stories from gays and lesbians who spent years pleading with God to change them into heterosexuals with little or no success, and when their prayers went unanswered felt as if they had been abandoned by God. Some decided to reject the Divine before a religious system rejected them, while others began wondering if something was wrong with them or if they were praying incorrectly, all of which have only increased the sense of failure or shame. My conscience has compelled me to write a book that would illustrate the fact that there are members of the GLBTIQ community who have been quite successful in their spiritual growth and development.

When I have given workshops on this topic I have often heard conservative Christians acquiesce to the idea that homosexuals can be good people, but still doubt if they could call themselves Christian. Being raised in a religious culture with similar views I have great respect for some of the principles behind those statements. For instance, I love the idea of studying the Scriptures so they can be a guide for life, developing a personal relationship with God and avoiding the entanglements of sin that can certainly mess up my life. But I have also come to realize that many of those beliefs have been socially constructed and have been brewing in cauldrons of fear for generations; fear of the unknown, fear of what is distasteful or incomprehensible to them and even the fear of God's judgment for not supporting the dominant discourse. Many who hold beliefs that are dismissive of "gay rights" have probably never had an interest in or an opportunity to discuss spirituality with someone who is openly gay. They may even surmise that the "gay lifestyle" is at odds with any meaningful spirituality.

Although many books have been written and many opinions aired about gay rights and pro-gay theology, not many have focused upon providing people with an opportunity to enlarge their own belief systems to embrace gay spirituality while still being true advocates of Scripture. As you read this book it will be obvious that in doing this study, my own beliefs have expanded to make room for this issue, which is why I felt that a chapter on inclusive theology needed to be part of this discussion. From my current vantage point as a minister and a Marriage and Family Therapist, I see a growing body of evidence that homosexuals, bisexuals, intersex and transgendered people have no less vital spirituality than the majority of heterosexuals.

When I conducted interviews and did the research for this book, I was often moved by the sacredness of people's stories, and how the inner narrative of their lives greatly determined how they lived. It seemed as if these stories were just waiting to be shared with others. Every time I realized how precious a story was to a person's core identity, I thought of Maya Angelou's words, "There is no greater agony than bearing an untold story inside you," which is why I felt this book had to include many personal stories. They simply had to be told. To ensure confidentiality, I have changed identifying information of the individuals and cases mentioned in this book. The people and their stories are real, and the quotes, which have at times been edited to promote easier reading, still convey the original message.

I have also included several poems throughout this book because the poet often finds a way of telling a story that best expresses the most poignant tensions of the human heart. Most of the time, we tend to run away from this deeper world because it is too disruptive to our busy lives. I hope that you will read these poems as thoughtfully as you would someone's personal narrative because all good poetry tries to tell a story. You might even take time to read each one aloud, so the words can be empowered by your voice, resulting in a richer experience. Perhaps you will begin to notice when you feel more connected to or disconnected from the various stories and poems in this book, so that you can be more aware of how your own responses may illuminate your ideas about this subject.

And, yes, there are illustrations because let's face it: a good book is always enhanced by pictures. I have chosen to use the unique and accessible art form of cartoons, which much of America relates to on a daily basis. Sometimes cartoon art speaks to a more open and playful part of our brains that understands the language of images beyond the expression of words. Cartoonists have long used their art to address political and social issues. We saw this in Walt Kelly when Pogo ran for president in 1952, and in more recent history we also saw how Gary Trudeau drew attention to people affected by current disasters when his character Andy Doonesbury became ill and died of AIDS.

In this book you will see a gay cartoon character growing in self awareness and spirituality as each subsequent chapter unfolds.

My initial intent was to write a book to help therapists and ministers who have wondered how to encourage their gay client's spiritual growth and development. So, at the end of each chapter I have included a "*for the therapist*" section where there are questions and exercises to assist professionals who work with GLBTIQ clients. Many of these reflections are aimed at helping therapists and clergypersons examine their own belief systems that could hurt or hinder the spiritual development in those seeking their assistance. If a therapist is in the least bit disingenuous about the possibility of gay spirituality, his or her GLBTIQ clients may well experience further rejection and shame.

Because I believe this book should not be limited to the counseling profession, I have written it to be accessible to the general public. Therefore, the same reflective questions could also be interesting discussions for a group process for anyone who would enjoy the deeper spiritual connections of working through these ideas in community.

Currently many people have felt the need to split the personal from their professional lives in order to intensify their job performance and maintain proper boundaries. But in doing so, they may have also split off their soul life from their work life, forcing spirituality to go underground, which often results in tension and disharmony. Because spirituality is all about connection, we know that when people lack the opportunities and richness of deeper connections, soul healing is often inhibited.

So I am inviting you to find a deeper connection with yourself and others as we journey through this book together. As you read with all of your heart and mind, you may experience formerly rigid boundaries between God and sexual minorities begin to relax. I'm hoping you will be surprised at what you find. My own journey has led me to share my insights in this book, which in turn has increased my awareness of what it means to be marginalized or devalued by the attitudes of others.

As I sit with my fingers on the keyboard, I am looking out to a magnificent scene where the sea is teeming with diversity and the beauty of God can be experienced in every living thing. Brothers and sisters, may we all behold such beauty as we see each other with new eyes.

1

Thank God for Change!

We still condemn people who are different from us.

It is not intentional, but we just keep forgetting that many people are not born right-handed, White, middle-class, heterosexual males. Some of us were born left-handed and continually have to negotiate a world with desks that don't fit, doors that open the wrong way, soup ladles that are impossible, and scissors that are pure torture. Some of us are born as female, dwarf or giant, with red hair or no hair, with eyes of different colors, or with other characteristics that caused us to be teased or made uncomfortable at some point for being different from the norm. ("Norm," of course, is the 5'11", White heterosexual male, who is height–weight proportional, has clear skin, and is not considered a geek by the dominant group.)

Although some people in our culture still stop and stare a bit too often at those who appear different, we do seem to be making progress in making room to allow for physical differences. However, when it comes to understanding the broader spectrum of sexual orientation, it stops far short. Even people of faith who are trying to live out the ethic of love in all relationships too easily forget that according to James 2:13,* mercy is considered a higher virtue than judgment.

While many groups still tend to view sexual minorities as shameful in the eyes of God, they can do so only by overlooking the fact that each day infants are born who cannot be clearly defined as male or female, because they have the hormones or physicality of both sexes. If we have come to be tolerant of physical differences, what about variations that are hidden from our sight? Could individuals also be born with differing grades of sexual orientation causing them to be more or less attracted to someone of their own gender? Multiple theories abound as to where all these variations of human

---

* The *New International Version* (NIV) Bible isused throughout the book.

sexuality come from. Is it nurture or nature, random selection or willful choice, or some combination of all these?

When it comes to sexual orientation, the argument for biology is strong. Australian sheep herders have long referred to 8% of their sheep as "shy breeders" because they have eyes only for other males. The theory is that this is a function of differing hormonal levels in the womb. It is very likely that fluctuations in these powerful chemicals may lead to homosexuality. Scientists are also hypothesizing that there may be a fraternal birth order effect in humans; recent studies have shown that a man with four older brothers is three times as likely to be gay than a man with none. That child typically weighs less at birth, hinting that a mother's immune system or hormone production may be compromised with multiple childbirths. Other studies involving twins suggests that homosexuality may run in families. It may be possible that more than 40% of homosexuality is due to genetics (Doughton, 2005).

Many people's belief systems have not made room for the possibility that anyone can be gay, lesbian, or bisexual from birth, despite findings of current research suggesting that on average, gay youth are about 10 years old when they begin to feel different from heterosexuals (Stone Fish & Harvey, 2005), with some reporting this awareness as early as 4 to 5 years of age. This may have been underreported in the past because young children lack the vocabulary to describe their internal experience to others and have only recently been given the chance to talk about the progression of their identity as they mature.

How a person is attracted to another has perplexed humankind since the beginning of time. King Solomon, in all of his wisdom, wrote about the wonder of sexuality as something that was beyond understanding. Even the Apostle Paul spoke of the great mystery surrounding sexual unions as a spiritual allegory. Most sexual minorities, who live with inner mysteries that differ from the perception of the socially dominant members of society, will tell you that these deepest longings of their bodies, minds, hearts, and souls have been present as long as they can remember. They will also tell you that these feelings have accompanied them throughout their lifetimes. Unfortunately, so do the negative responses of a poorly informed society. Contrary to many religious views, it is the toxic response of others rather than one's natural way of connecting with people that causes most of the distress for those identifying as a sexual minority.

Where did we get the idea that being too different was not welcome? Maybe I'm going out on a limb here, but some of the answers in present society may be found in Victory Heights.

Many Beliefs Were Socially Constructed in Victory Heights

Victory Heights was the newly minted neighborhood developed all across America following WWII and was named for the optimism of an era that believed all things were possible. Most of these communities consisted of small, two-bedroom homes with full basements that could accommodate expansion for a growing family. Many living rooms had floor-to-ceiling corner windows, now among the signatures of mid-century construction, and in many of the quarter-acre yards cherry trees bloomed in the spring. Accompanying the birth of each child, silent prayers were uttered for continuing victory, stability, and prosperity for this new generation that would later be known as Baby Boomers. These suburban developments were strategically located so children could attend three levels of school with no more than a 1-mile walk in any direction. Children rode their bikes all over the city or took buses wherever they pleased with little fear regarding their own safety.

In the 1950s and 1960s, men who lived in Victory Heights held steady jobs that could support a family. There were various small businessmen who owned their own stores, salesmen who sold new inventions like blonde Emerson TVs and coral-colored Edsels, and emerging white-collar workers who were aerospace engineers, insurance salesmen, or support staff for the state university.

Moms tended to stay home and raise the kids, and this was considered to be the ultimate full-time vocation for a woman. Every family had a car, and by the mid-1960s most homes had two. My children now call my childhood community the *Wonder Years* neighborhood of north Seattle (referring to the popular TV show from the late 1980s).

If your childhood was as carefree as mine, you had every reason to believe this lifestyle would continue for generations. Although far from rich, we had everything we needed and the freedom to create ways to get what we wanted. About the only thing that was lacking was an interface with difference. We had almost no exposure to poverty, racism, or any kind of minority for that matter. What we had in Victory Heights was peace, stability, and conformity. If there were people affected by great divergence from the norm, they learned it was best to quietly blend in with the rest of the population. The climate I grew up in wasn't necessarily hostile toward minorities, but neither was it very sensitive or aware of their needs. However, other regions of America experienced much more overt hostility.

Most of Victory Heights was assumed to be Christian. We didn't use the term *spirituality* to describe our connection to God; instead, one would speak of *religion* or *faith*. Although church attendance may have been a bit infrequent, most families were members of a local church. My home was considered very religious because we looked forward to going to church every time the doors were open. For my family, church was much more than a house of worship—it was our culture and extended community. Thanks to Billy Graham and the fresh Evangelical movement, we focused our spiritual growth in the area of having a personal relationship with Christ. Jews were considered our spiritual brothers and sisters who had not yet been enlightened with the truth, and Catholics were viewed with a suspiciously raised eyebrow because they worshipped Mary. Generally speaking, differing religions of the world merited little attention except when they affected our missionary friends who were attempting to share the Gospel with parts of Asia and Africa.

Clearly, married couples were having sex back then because neighborhoods like ours were full of kids. However, the only time that topic would come up was in conversations of prohibitions. As a result, we knew two things for sure: Premarital sex was a terrible sin, and we were to save it for the one we loved in marriage! Not much was known about homosexual behavior except that it was some sort of mental illness or a sinful choice resulting from human depravity. Like other minorities, homosexuals were adept at becoming invisible for a very good reason: Personally exposing such difference could mean the loss of all things one held dear in life, including basic survival.

As long as people could line up on the acceptable side of the binary codes of ethics and popular beliefs, life was very good indeed. Societal expectations were also pretty simple by today's standards. There was consensus on what was right or wrong, dictated and enforced by the norms of the socially dominant group. People understood the hierarchy of things and adhered to their place in the pecking order, whether they liked it or not. Life was so well ordered during the years of the cold war that my family could set our clocks and moods to the air raid warning sirens that went off every Wednesday at noon, knowing we would all chuckle when the neighbor's Malamutes responded with a howling contest.

Most in Victory Heights felt blessed by God; we worked hard and had the chance to get a higher education, so we paid scant attention to the built-in advantages of being in the White middle class. Words and terms such as *heterosexism, gender bias, sexual orientation,* or *White entitlement* hadn't been invented yet. There was no lottery to win, no great inherited equities to parade; there was a well-understood value—self-sufficiency and hard work would earn "just" rewards.

By the late 1960s, America was embroiled in things that had been unthinkable in the previous two decades. We had lived through the assassinations of John F. Kennedy (JFK), Martin Luther King, Jr. (MLK), and

Robert Kennedy. They were our leaders and prophets who encouraged great dreams for the future. After Lyndon B. Johnson (LBJ) took the presidential oath in late 1963, he tried to continue the vision by casting a vision for the "Great Society," but it was quickly sidetracked by the Vietnam War.

When revolutions were erupting around the nation during the turbulent 1960s, Victory Heights was still a relative bastion of safety, but the younger generation wasn't holding to the standards of conformity of the previous generation. The views about music, meaningful worship, going to war, and sex were all changing. We talked and experimented about things that previous generations were scarcely allowed to ponder. However, because difference was not a welcome guest, we learned to keep silent in many circles, knowing we would not be taken seriously as adults unless we appeared to conform to the old standards.

Many of us conformed to a modified version of our parents' lives. We "accepted Jesus," got married, joined a church, had babies, desired to become responsible adults, but were also determined not to be as rigid as the previous generation. We wanted to remain open to life's possibilities and to new ideas.

O, the times, they are a-changing.

Bob Dylan, 1964

A Visit with LBJ

On a recent trip to Austin, Texas, I had the privilege of visiting the LBJ Presidential library and found myself moved with emotion while viewing the years of my childhood years through middle-aged eyes. Being an adolescent in the 1960s meant being exposed to the dreams of a Great Society that would lead the world to peace and promote social justice. Strolling through the library, I noted how this era initiated milestone legislation such as the War on Poverty, the Clean Air Act, Beautify America, Head Start, the U.S. Department of Housing and Urban Development (HUD), Medicare and Medicaid, the Federal Housing Administration (FHA) and the U.S. Department of Veterans Affairs (VA) loans, and more than 68 educational acts that are no longer funded.

I was reminded of JFK's challenge to think beyond ourselves when I heard his eloquent words, "Ask not what your country can do for you, but what you can do for your country," and again when he said, "We will befriend all who pursue liberty and oppose all who do not." I was surprised to realize that Betty Friedan wrote her book in 1963 that exclaimed, "The feminine mystique has succeeded in burying millions of American women alive." I got a lump in my throat when I saw the 8 mm film of MLK inspiring us with his impassioned speech in front of the Lincoln Memorial when he said, "I have a dream that one day my children will not be judged by the color of their skin, but by the content of their character."

As I left the building, I found myself profoundly saddened by our current culture, which has become so individually focused that it has forgotten some of the dreams inspired by former civil leaders. While it is true that we have made great strides toward equal rights for the disabled, racial minorities, and women, we are certainly a long way from true equality for all. How many people will continue to be marginalized, disrespected, or oppressed before we get it right?

Sexual minorities still have an uphill battle in the race for equality. They continue to lack full protection against discrimination in almost every state. The notable exceptions in the last five years have been Massachusetts and California, whose supreme courts made milestone declarations that allowed gay couples the right to marry. However, in November 2008, California voters passed an initiative denying recognition to same sex marriages which overturned the earlier state Supreme Court ruling. (Apparently people who love in unconventional ways are still considered a "threat" too much of society; which seems to point to the fact that Americans must continue to overcome the crippling effects of bigotry and injustice.) The fact is many gays and lesbians are marginalized people who feel they must often remain in the closet to keep their jobs and homes. The same day I visited this inspiring presidential library, an Austin newspaper published a story about gay Republicans who remain in the closet so they can provide an image that will yield the most power. Is this the earmark of a society where all people are considered to be created equal?

The dream of becoming the Great Society was the source of inspiration for Baby Boomers who desired to make a difference in this world by enlisting in the War on Poverty. Unfortunately, our nation encountered a distraction known as Vietnam, which drained our financial and emotional energies as we continued fighting a war we couldn't win. Hindsight is amazingly clear. We put our best efforts into the wrong war.

Although the struggle for basic human rights has been a problem for centuries, the rapid social changes made over the past 50 years are most familiar to us. The end of World War II not only freed the world from Nazi oppression, but it also reignited the dreams of possibility for everyone in America. What we failed to realize, however, is that when members of one group focus exclusively on achieving their dreams, it may blind them to the members of another group's hardships.

At this time there is a pattern that seems to grade the road to social change. After marginalized members of society endure prolonged injustice and oppression, there emerges a public outcry for justice. Activism then seeks to influence proactive legislation that advances the cause of equal rights. Public opinion and revised theologies often seem to follow rather than lead such social change at this time in our history. But it wasn't always like this. In the late 19th century, religious leaders were often those most interested in creating social change for the betterment of society.

> Life is changing faster than it ever has before, What tomorrow brings us isn't certain anymore ....

> Stormie Omartian, 1974

Changes in Civil Rights for Oppressed Minorities

Transitions in the Battle for Racial Equality

Perception and reality have become clumsy dance partners when it comes to the equal rights of racial minorities. For the White middle class that had long been the dominant social group, equal rights meant that every person like themselves should have a world of possibilities before them—but in many instances their achievements were gained by oppressing or abusing a minority group. The completion of the First Transcontinental Railroad is a good example. Although 9 of 10 laborers who built it were Chinese, none of them is pictured in the famous Golden Spike photograph in 1869. For the White privileged population, the Pacific railroad opened up the possibilities for a future of expanded business opportunities and travel, but for the 10,000 Chinese immigrants who did the most dangerous physical labor, while constantly being underpaid and abused, it did no such thing. The perception of possibilities for Whites and the reality of the oppression of the Chinese were complete opposites.

During the post-WWII years, the perception of Whites was that everyone had the equal ability to work hard and make a life for themselves. But the internal reality for Blacks, informed by two centuries of enslavement and ostracism, was psychologically paralyzing. It would take 90 years following the Emancipation Proclamation of 1865 for the African American community to rally together and force Whites to become aware that "separate" had never been equal. Despite recent advances, racism and oppression continue to flourish today.

Following the end of World War II, Black leaders began to speak up about the fears held and oppression exerted by the dominant culture. In time, legislation and courageous acts helped mitigate some of the discrimination felt by Americans of African descent.

1954: The U.S. Supreme Court ruled on *Brown v. The Board of Education of Topeka* that segregation in public schools is unconstitutional. Some 90 years after the Emancipation Proclamation, it was concluded that separate educational facilities are inherently unequal.

1955: While riding a bus, Rosa Parks of Montgomery, Alabama, refused to give up her seat at the front of the "colored section" to a White passenger. The result was a 1-year boycott by the Black community to use bus transportation until they were desegregated, which occurred in 1956.

1957: The Little Rock Nine became famous when nine Black students were blocked by an order from Arkansas governor Orval Faubus from entering a formerly all-White high school. President Dwight D. Eisenhower sent federal troops and National Guard troops to intervene.

1963: James Meredith became the first Black student to enroll at the University of Mississippi. President Kennedy responded to riots and violence by sending in 5,000 federal troops. Martin Luther King, Jr., was arrested and jailed during an antisegregation protest in Birmingham, Alabama, and wrote "A Letter from Birmingham Jail," arguing that individuals have a moral duty to disobey unjust laws. That same spring, 200,000 people joined the March on Washington as MLK delivered his now famous "I Have a Dream" speech.

1964: The Civil Rights Act, barring racial or gender discrimination in the workplace, was passed.

1965: Congress passed the Voting Rights Act of 1965, making it easier for Southern Blacks to register to vote. Literacy tests, poll taxes, and other items that were once used to restrict Black votes were deemed illegal.

1968: MLK was assassinated on April 4. On April 11, LBJ signed the Civil Rights Act of 1968, prohibiting discrimination in the sale, rental, or financing of housing.

Ten long years of intense activism and turmoil led to a societal shift in the way many in the dominant culture viewed African Americans and to legislation that would provide necessary legal protection. Today, 40 years later, although we still have evidence of racial inequality. We have elected an African American to serve as President of the United States. Public opinions have largely shifted to state that all races should have equal protection under the law, and you would be hard-pressed to find people who would believe that segregation policies ever promoted true equality.

The Battle for Women's Rights

Similarly, the battle for women's rights began in the 1850s with the Women's Suffrage Movement and continued to lobby for equality until at least 1920 when women gained the right to vote. Yet gender equality was not fully realized. This stew continued to simmer for the next 40 years, until 1963 when Friedan published *The Feminine Mystique,* addressing the dissatisfaction felt by middle-class American housewives for their narrow role in society, calling it "the problem that has no name" (p.1).

Men's perceptions of women's roles and the internal realities of women's desires were vastly different. Men took for granted their position at the top of the hierarchy, ruling the world and being known as intellectually superior beings. Given the choice, most men wouldn't have wanted to share their world of privilege with the "weaker sex."

However, after 110 years of women's activism, discriminatory attitudes began to shift, leading us toward equalizing power and opportunities for both sexes. A timeline of significant legislation follows.

1963: Congress passed the Equal Pay Act, making it illegal for employers to pay women a lower wage than men.

1969: California approved the first no-fault divorce law, which went into effect January 1, 1970. (By 1983 every state but New York and North Dakota had passed their own forms of no-fault divorce.)

1973: In the *Roe v. Wade* decision, the Supreme Court established that it is a women's right to have a safe and legal abortion.

1974: The Equal Credit Opportunities Act was passed, prohibiting discrimination in consumer credit on the basis of sex, race, marital status, religion, national origin, age, or being the recipient of public assistance.

1976: The Marital Rape Law was passed in Nebraska, making it the first state to deem it illegal for a man to rape his wife.

1978: The Pregnancy Discrimination Act was passed so that an employer could not discriminate on the basis of present or future pregnancies.

1986: Sexual harassment, a form of sexual discrimination, became illegal in the workplace.

1994: The Violence against Women Act was passed.

Each wave of change provided an opportunity for public attitudes to transition to something new. Although shifts in attitude take time, today we have a society that by and large agrees that racial and gender discrimination are no longer appropriate. Courageous activism, a broadening of empathy, and legislation have helped us evolve into a nation that is much more respectful in our attitudes toward one another while providing protection for those who may suffer at the hand of discrimination. Much of the inspiration for civil rights was credited to a growing realization that women were just as capable as men in the workplace, as well as a growing spiritual belief that God created men and women with equal status.

The Changing Status of Sexual Minorities

The first mention of the word *homosexual* can be traced back to 1887 when German psychiatrist Richard Freiherr von Kraft-Ebing published his work *Psychopathia Sexualis,* which characterized same-sex behavior as pathological. This perception persisted for the better part of the 20th century, until 1973 when the American Psychiatric Association (APA) removed it from the category of mental disorders. "The action was taken following review of scientific literature and consultation with experts in the field. The experts found that homosexuality [did] not meet the criteria to be considered a mental illness" (American Psychiatric Association). Although this news was contrary to much public opinion, homosexuals were found to have no more impairment of functionality than normative heterosexual populations. Gays were able to hold jobs, maintain relationships, and be model citizens of society; the only significant difference was the direction of their sexual energy.

Following the emerging trends toward equal rights for women and minorities, the post-WWII era also ushered in similar strivings for sexual minorities through political activism and legislation. As before, the pattern of oppression followed by public outcry and then by activism and legislation continues to promote greater equality for a minority group. Public opinion and social acceptance for the gay, lesbian, bisexual, transgender, intersex, and queer (GLBTIQ) community, however, seems to be evolving at a slower rate than the others.

The Oppression of Homosexuals

The period 1943–1953 (also known as the McCarthy Era) found thousands of people's lives in ruin when Senator Joseph McCarthy led a spurious charge against communism and anything different. To promote the orthodox view of family, he led witch hunts for "sexual perverts." Again, the perceptions of socially dominant groups did not match the oppressive realities for anyone who stepped outside the magic circle of matrimony, parenthood, and heterosexual homemaking. During this episode when national hate was targeted against difference, more than 1,700 federal employees lost their jobs due to allegations of homosexuality.

At that time, same-sex behavior was a criminal offense that often carried severe penalties. Throughout the '50s and '60s, people were arrested in routine police raids in city parks and gay bars. In the District of Columbia alone, there were 1,000 arrests each year in the early '50s. Even a simple act of affection such as holding hands in public could lead to arrest. In almost every state, the names of those charged would be published in the newspapers, often resulting in the loss of jobs. The U.S. Postal Service opened mail of people who were suspected to be lesbian or gay. Colleges often kept lists of suspected "perverts." Declaring oneself to be gay could result in admission to a mental institution without a hearing (Wright, 1999).

Science and Legislation Led to Change

1948: Dr. Alfred Kinsey published *Sexual Behavior in the Human Male,* which turned the world on its ear. This book quickly became a best seller and marked the new beginning of studies on sexuality. Kinsey revealed what Americans did not want to hear, namely, that talk about sexuality was often quite different from behavior. He was the first to address a nonpathological study of homosexual behavior and came up with a six-point scale to help categorize human sexuality, with 1 being completely heterosexual and 6 being completely homosexual. He found that many people would place themselves at various points across this scale, and he concluded that sexuality was much more fluid than previously thought and that there were large variants in sexual orientation.

1951: A small group of homosexual men organized politically to form the Mattachine Society, which was followed by a similar lesbian group in 1956 called the Daughters of Bilitis, to speak out against oppression and injustice.

1953: Eisenhower issued an executive order banning homosexual men or women from all federal jobs, which was in effect until 1975.

1962: Illinois became the first state to decriminalize homosexual acts between consenting adults.

1969: Police raided a gay bar in New York City's Greenwich Village and triggered a reaction that would later be known as the Stonewall riots. This was an event that had occurred thousands of times before all across America. But for the first time, the usual "suspects" fought back and sparked a riot. Arm in arm, homosexuals banded to the cry of "Gay Power" and left civic authorities stunned. The next night, thousands of GLBT people and their allies joined the demonstration. Homosexuals had begun to stand up for their own rights. Out of this event the Gay Liberation Front (GLF) was born (a political association that is no more), but the idea of gay power has grown continually stronger. Since 1969 the term *gay* has become synonymous with homosexual orientation of both sexes.

1970: 5,000 gay men and lesbians marched in the first organized demonstration in New York City, demanding that gays have a place in society. Gay activists also began protesting the APA's offices and annual meetings to rebuke the pathological status of homosexual orientation.

1973: The APA amended the *Diagnostic and Statistical Manual of Mental Disorders,* 2nd ed. (*DSM-II*), declaring that homosexuality was no longer to be viewed as pathology that needed a cure. However, in its place the *DSM-II* provided a new diagnosis of *sexual orientation disturbance* for people who were desiring to change their sexual orientation. This same year, Oregon and Colorado repealed sodomy laws for consenting adults.

1975: The "gay rights movement" began, and GLBT people began to refer to themselves as *sexual minorities,* seeking the same human rights as other protected groups of people. This same year the American Psychological Association supported the APA's 1973 action to remove homosexuality from the category of mental disorders.

1978: The International Lesbian and Gay Association (ILGA) formed for the purpose of demanding human rights in the United Nations for sexual minorities.

1980s: This decade saw the emergence of AIDS in America. Though the rampant spread of AIDS first strengthened antigay rhetoric to the point of calling the disease a divine punishment for homosexual behavior, it soon began a wave of compassion as thousands of young men died daily. It was nearly impossible for the general public to remain untouched by this tragedy, because AIDS now had a recognizable face. It had taken the life of people's coworkers, friends, cousins, aunts, and fathers. In the midst of this unthinkable plague, many more gay people came out of the closet. As a result, it also further organized the gay community in many ways and increased their quest for useful spiritualities. In 1980 the *Diagnostic and Statistical Manual of Mental Disorders,* 3rd ed. (*DSM-III*) removed *sexual orientation disturbance* and renamed it as *ego dystonic homosexuality.* However, by 1987 when the *Diagnostic and Statistical Manual of Mental Disorders,* 3rd ed. revised (*DSM-IIIR*) removed this category altogether, great controversy ensued.

1982: Wisconsin becomes the first state to outlaw discrimination on the basis of sexual orientation.

1987: As a result of the AIDS crisis, a new era of militancy began to resurge resulting in new political groups such as ACT UP, Queer Nation, and the Lesbian Avengers. Younger activists began using the word *queer* as an inclusive and defiant statement to describe all sexual minorities just as the early liberationists had done with the word *gay*.

1993: A policy of "Don't Ask, Don't Tell" developed. Prior to 1992, the U.S. Military policy was that "homosexuality is incompatible with Military Service ("Gays in the Military, 2007). Soldiers who were accused of being gay were often dishonorably discharged and thus were made ineligible for military pensions or retirement benefits. In his first year in office, President Bill Clinton stated his objections to this policy; however, once the debates were run through the Senate Armed Service Committee, the current "Don't Ask, Don't Tell" policy was put in place. What was intended by Clinton as a protection for gays in the military became a compromised bill that backfired. According to the Servicemembers Legal Defense Network, more than 9,000 service members have been discharged in this way. This policy is still in force (although partially overlooked), resulting in continued gay harassment and fears of potential and actual discharges.

1996: The U.S. Supreme Court struck down a Colorado amendment that would deny GLBT protection against discrimination, negating use of the term *special rights*.

1997: The American Psychological Association published a resolution about the proper psychological treatment of homosexuals, urging professionals to provide services without a sexual orientation bias and suggesting that some interventions may be harmful when treating sexual minorities. It also urged all mental health professionals to take the lead in removing the stigma of mental illness that had long been associated with homosexual orientation.

2000: Vermont recognized civil unions.

2003: This year marked the end of sodomy laws, as the U.S. Supreme Court ruled that they were unconstitutional.

2004: Same-sex marriage became legal in Massachusetts.

2005: Civil unions were legalized in Connecticut. The American Association of Marriage and Family Therapists (AAMFT) reviewed current research and issued a statement stating that homosexual orientation should not be considered pathological.

2006: New Jersey also began offering civil unions to gay couples, and Washington State passed the Anderson/Murray bill—which prohibits discrimination for sexual minorities in the areas of housing, employment, insurance, or lending—after 29 years of legislation, making it the 17th state to pass such legislation.

2007: Washington State legislature voted to allow domestic partner registration to increase the rights of same-sex couples.

2008: California Supreme Court voted to allows gays and lesbians to marry, and the American Psychological Association, after being accused of being biased against reparative therapy and not listening to the views of conservative groups such as Focus on the Family and the Southern Baptist Convention, appointed a task force of researchers and clinicians to review the current scientific research on the proper therapeutic response to sexual orientation.

Public Opinion and Belief

Although legislation has paved the way for much needed legal protection for sexual minorities, and society has become increasingly tolerant, there is still a great divide in the United States about homosexuality and traditional notions of gender: "On the one hand, there is more openness, media attention, and an older generation of openly gay and lesbian role models. On the other hand there is a greater backlash from religious fundamentalism, violence and legal intervention designed to 'protect' traditional marriages and families" (Stone Fish & Harvey, 2005, p. 1).

What is interesting about this issue is that some of the changes listed under activism and legislation were really new discoveries in the field of science. In 1948, it was Kinsey's research that led the way for a different perception of an old reality. In 1973, the APA, after listening to gay activists, decided to take a look at the science surrounding homosexuality and decided that that homosexuality could no longer be called a pathology because no mental illness was present that impaired human functioning. This landmark policy has taken some mental health associations 30 years to ratify (e.g., American Association of Marriage and Family Therapist's 2005 nonpathology statement). Although much progress has been made on this issue, there is still no general consensus embraced by all mental health professionals. In fact, even today the World Health Organization (WHO) continues to use the term *ego dystonic homosexuality* in its International Classification of Diseases, 10 revision. (ICD 10), section F66.1.

Statistics continue to show us that there are greater numbers of people coming out at an earlier age than in previous generations. Research continues to substantiate that a person's sexual orientation may be fixed quite early in life, negating the idea that being gay is always a choice. Meanwhile, sexual minorities continue to face public rejection and oppression because society continues to distrust or fear what is different. Apparently, external change and legislation are not enough. Legislation has made it more acceptable for people to express their difference, but that is not the same as claiming one's place in the community. Coming out and coming home are very different processes; one is a person's right to be equal and respected for their differences, and the other is a gift society gives to those who are different by offering a place at the common table.

Spirituality and Sexuality

It is refreshing to see that some great faiths have at times been ahead of legislation on this topic. The first organized religious program for gays began in 1969 when Father Patrick Nidorf, an Augustinian priest and psychologist, formed a ministry as an extension of his work. Father Pat later noted that "the name *Dignity* just came to me as appropriate since one of our basic goals was to bring dignity into the spiritual and social lives of some very special people" (Dignity, 1969). Other progressive individual churches began to band together under the umbrella of their respective denominations. For example, while the American Baptists were forming American Baptists Concerned in 1972, the United Church of Christ began Coalition. Episcopalians began Integrity in 1974, and the following year Friends Committee for Gay Concerns emerged. Independent Presbyterian churches began More Light in 1978 (formalized as More Light Network in 1992); the National Gay Pentecostal Alliance was formed in 1980. The United Methodists began the Reconciling Congregation and the Evangelical Lutherans started Reconciling in Christ Congregations, both in 1984. Christian Science began organizing Emerge International in 1985.

Although the Metropolitan Community Church was organized as the first church for homosexuals in 1968, the United Church of Christ was the first mainstream church to fully identify itself as open and affirming in 1985. This has not been an easy battle for many independent churches that are associated with larger denominations. In fact, some find themselves continually swimming against a current of opposition. For instance, after 23 years of intense discussion, the American Baptist Churches USA passed an antigay resolution in 1992, stating, "the practice of homosexuality is incompatible with Christian teaching" (Association of Welcoming and Affirming Baptists). This left progressive Baptists who felt a calling to minister to the GLBT community with no choice but to establish a new ministry outside the doors of their founding denomination. As a result, the Association of Welcoming and Affirming Baptists (AWAB), was formed in 1993 to continue the expansion of the work begun by others in 1972.

Changes in Psychology and Sexuality

The psychotherapy profession has also experienced change since WWII, achieving greater public acceptance and increasing its areas of research. As a result, our knowledge of how sexuality and spirituality affect human behavior has been greatly expanded. The question remains as to whether such knowledge constitutes news that makes a difference. How we choose to accept and act upon new revelations in the field of human science could greatly affect how we relate to each other in the future.

Where the use of spirituality in therapy was once dismissed, new dialogues are beginning to include spirituality at the forefront of personal growth. Spirituality is often a tremendous resource for comfort, peace, security, and healing. When clients come to a therapist's office discouraged, confused, and feeling a loss of hope, spirituality can be a powerful tool. Why should such an important resource be left out of the clinician's tool kit?

Spirituality can also be useful in the area of decision making in a culture that is conflicted about how one is to live his or her life. It is increasingly important to help people navigate their lives with an internal compass because society has evolved from valuing the input of a community to esteeming individual choice: "From expecting people to cooperate and be interdependent, contemporary society looks for people to be self reliant and learn to decide for themselves" (Carlson & Erickson, 2002, p. 14).

Since my work as a marriage and family therapist has grown out of a former career as an evangelical minister, I am very glad to see this transitional shift in attitude. For me, it has always seemed natural to connect the dots between spirituality and psychotherapy. Science without spirituality lacks purpose, and religion without science can become arrogant and blind. Psychotherapy provides an opportunity to amplify the human experience, and, given the interactive process that takes place between therapist and clients, it can easily become a place where both counselor and client can realize the sacred elements of our lives. Rather than sidestepping issues of spirituality, I believe it is time for people working in the field of mental health to learn to engage in conversations that "make room" for the spiritual in every person they seek to heal.

Sexuality Defined

Before our discussion proceeds further, I believe we need to define some of the terms that will aid our common understandings throughout this book.

Sexuality is a relational term. It is much more than simply our maleness or femaleness. Although it may include sexual behavior, sexuality is not necessarily limited or determined by one's actions. It is also a term of connection. Sexuality is based on the deep desire to reach out beyond our own internal world to that of another. It is what attracts us to each other from across a crowded room. It is the look of the eyes, the flip of the hair, and body language of which we may be unaware. We see it in the smiles of acceptance and in the frowns of rejection, as we choose with whom to converse each day. When we speak of a person's sexual orientation, we are talking about the direction of a person's erotic desires, which could consist of showing interest in a person of the same or opposite sex. Sexuality is part of the expression of our identity that desires to connect with the world.

Terms of Sexuality

Although I use the term *gay* in the title of this book, I am actually writing about the larger entity of sexual minorities often referred to as the GLBTIQ community. Each letter of the acronym categorizes the diverse makeup of people who are considered sexual minorities. Figure 1.1 provides an illustration.

Figure 1.1   Postal confusion.

Gay: an inclusive term for men and women alike but most often refers to men who have a sexual attraction to other men.

Lesbians: Women who are attracted to women.

Bisexual: Persons who have an attraction to both sexes and may therefore find their sexual orientation is more fluid than others.

Transgender: People who do not experience congruity with the gender that their physicality presents. Rather than allowing their gender identity to be determined by simple biology, transgendered persons may need to explore their gender identity based on their internal awareness. Like homosexuals, many transgendered people have felt not only different from others from a young age but also out of synch with their bodies from their earliest memories.

Intersex: People born with ambiguous male or female sexual organs or genetic codes. An example of this would be a person who was born with both testicles and ovaries. Although this situation does not involve sexual orientation, intersex people often face the same discrimination as other sexual minorities due to the cultural demands to identify as either male or female.

Queer: Any of the above, in any combination, or simply any person who does not fit within the heterosexual norm of the dominant social construct. Whereas *queer* has often been a derogatory term, it has been more recently reclaimed by the GLBTIQ community as an expression of pride. Rather than meaning "odd and disgusting," *queer* has come to refer to someone who *uniquely contributes to the beautiful diversity of this world.* There is great power in reclaiming former words that were used with negative and hurtful intent and in reinventing one's identity as a source of pride. Throughout this book I use the terms *GLBT* or *queer* interchangeably.

Kinsey and Sexuality

In 1948, American sexologist Alfred Kinsey published his classic *Sexual Behavior in the Human Male.* In 1953, he authored its sequel, *Sexual Behavior in the Human Female.* His research led him to believe that the world of sexuality was a complex one that could not be divided into two discrete populations such as heterosexual and homosexual. He believed that "the living world is a continuum in each and every one of its aspects" and thus invented a seven-point scale to show the gradations and fluidity that exist in human sexuality. The Kinsey scale measures sexual orientation from 1 (exclusively heterosexual) to 6 (exclusively homosexual), with an additional category, X, for those with no sexual attraction to either women or men. When Kinsey analyzed individuals' behaviors and identities, he categorized most people as being somewhat attracted to either gender, even though they preferred one particular gender. However, according to Kinsey, only "10% of adult males are exclusively homosexual for a period of three years during their lives, while 4% of American men were 'exclusively homosexual' throughout their lives," (Wikholm, 1999).

Most modern scientific surveys find that the majority of people report a primarily heterosexual orientation. However, the relative percentage of the population that reports a homosexual orientation varies with differing methodologies and selection criteria. According to Wikipedia, most of these statistical findings are in the range of 2% to 7% of the American population. However it is difficult to assess who is really being included in those numbers. Savin Williams states that "any study that defines a sexual minority population as self-identified gay, lesbian, or bisexual individuals will, by design, underrepresent the overall population of individuals with same-sex attractions (Savine Williams, 2001, p. 244). Furthermore, these numbers are bound to be higher in some large cities considered to be gay friendly and much lower rural areas where being anonymous is nearly impossible.

Queer Theory

In 1994, Teresa de Lauretis wrote *The Practice of Love: Lesbian Sexuality and Perverse Desire,* which modified an old term with new meaning. The term was *queer,* which quickly became the catchphrase for gay and lesbian studies in universities during the 1990s. *Queer* acknowledges that life is a challenge for people who have come to realize that the rulebook of life was not written with them in mind.

Queer theory validates a complex view of sexuality and rejects the simplistic and often dichotomized definitions of human beings. It is informed by compassion, research, and clinical experience and is fostered by a real openness to learn things that go against socially dominant norms and ideologies that do not fit one's experiences of self or others:

> Queer theory disputes the essentialist view of sexuality and gender, and it rejects the notion that queerness is pathological. Instead, it posits that sexualities are constructed within social contexts. Labels like heterosexual, homosexual, and even queerness itself do not exist separate from the cultures and societies in which they are created. They are cultural reference points, representations of organizing principles for what is or has been allowed and disallowed. (Stone Fish & Harvey, 2005, p. 30)

Whenever we categorize a person to help ourselves organize our world, we are also limiting other possibilities. Consider how little we actually know about someone after labeling him or her as homosexual or lesbian. Such a label actually says very little about who that person really is, what he or she desires, or how he or she experiences relationships. To label oneself as heterosexual arguably says even less, because much is assumed and so little is examined under the heterosexual moniker.

Queer theorists and other social scientists are helping us move past the dichotomies of male–female, masculine–feminine, and gay–straight so that we can begin to understand that all sexualities are unique and complex. They value what Linda Stone Fish called "the border lands, where what has been elsewhere disallowed is explored and what before has been unimaginable becomes possible…. It is in these borderlands that new possibilities for love, commitment and family structure emerge" (Stone Fish & Harvey, 2005, p. 31).

Her coauthor Rebecca Harvey (Stone Fish and Harvey, 2005, p. 33) wrote:

> When you are queer you find a home on the borderlands where the ground may be eternally shifting. As Butler (1993) discussed, queerness itself is constantly defined and redefined. For queer people, who have had to question the status quo in order to know themselves, sexuality is both more freeing and more complicated. It is more freeing because, once you acknowledge that gender and sexual identity are more complex than we are taught, you are able to explore multiple ways to think, feel and act. You can have female genitalia, for example, and be male identified in some areas and female identified in others. You are less constrained then by the cultural mandates that come with gender. Yet without those constraints, life is more complicated. (p. 33)

Queer theory is but one of many such theories that reminds us of the mysterious complexity of our world. Older categories of people and behaviors continue to be redefined through new lenses of experience and scientific research. Chaos theory in quantum physics suggests the random beating of butterfly wings in South America may eventually contribute to a hurricane in Florida, underlining the reality that all of creation is linked together in seemingly random or chaotic ways. Similar complexity theories suggest that random disturbances in our lives create opportunities for growth and that humanity finds its optimum functionality somewhere between the peaceful static moments of life and the random disruptions. Could it be that gay spirituality is one of those positive disturbances that will awaken us to the beauty of diversity in the 21st century?

Changes in Spirituality and Religion

Definition of Terms

Spirituality

Spirituality is also a relational and connecting term that is a fundamental aspect of being human. It is my opinion that all humans have a spiritual core. Spirituality is often the intuitive guide that directs the choices in our lives and provides meaning to our life experiences. Given the fact that it can only be defined as a relational concept, it becomes a term of connection that extends beyond our own mind. If you don't include some experience beyond yourself, then it would be best to speak in terms of a philosophy of life, and though it has much to do with one's personal worldview, it is never limited to oneself. Harry Aponte (2004) defined spirituality as "that which goes beyond oneself, to connect with the other, and for some, the Ultimate Other." All human beings can sense a connection with something more or, at the very least, something beyond their own minds (Aponte). Rabbi Elizabeth Sarah has discovered that for many people, spirituality is what is rooted in one's experience, so it may include singing, poetry, or writing—having a deeper sense of oneself while connecting to something larger. "Spirituality," she says, "refers to our sense of being" (Sweasey, 1997, p. 12).

Consider, for instance, the following poem, which is rooted in both life experience and the connections with others, to something greater than the self.

The Moneypole

When Sibug's wife went limp, eyes rolled back,
a baby's crown
Half out of her, Sibug began to scream. He grabbled Manlangit
the priest and shook him like he was the only other man
in all the world. Outside in the dark,
cousins and neighbors circled the door, standing
helpless in the hot ropes of rain that father out
whipped the ocean of sugar cane.
Manlangit fell to his knees, in the mud that rose up
through the floor slats, and though he mouthed the Lord's Prayer
he heard the cousins outside
whispering an older magic
and he thought of planting kamote as a child,
how they hung Coke bottles from the vines
guiding their growth.

Before Manlangit finished his instruction; Sibug had swung his bolo
through the thick bamboo doorjamb. Right in half it cracked,
spilling thousands of pesos out,
coins falling like water and bills like birds,
and the cousins backed away, afraid of all that money,
and the roof caved, crashed down
pouring a falling wave of rainwater
down on Manlangit, Sibug and his wife. She bucked,
screamed and Sibug reached for his son.
The bills caught the air and flapped out
across the swaying can fields.

DAVID SNYDER

Although it would be easiest to define spirituality as feelings of inner
truth, or nuances of the spirit world, it must also be noted what spirituality
is not. It is not just human emotions or feelings, but spirituality requires
awareness of the relationships one has with oneself and with others and of
a presence of something within and outside of human bodies. Hence, one
can recognize spirituality individually or with others, but as Adam Coffey
boldly stated, "Spirituality always involves relationships" (Carlson &
Erickson, 2002, p. 32). Spirituality also cannot be measured by degrees.
No person has more or less spirituality than anyone else, because spirituality is not a quantitative construct. Granted, some people may be able to
recognize spirituality with greater frequency because of their life experiences, spiritual activities, or beliefs, but never let it be said that one person
is more spiritual than another. Finally, transformative spirituality is not
an individual's sacred journey. Spirituality always requires humans to go
beyond an individualistic experience into a collective conscience or the
sacred: "As humans move toward the Sacred, they see ostensible differences less and see spirituality more through a broadening perspective"
(Carlson & Erickson, 2002, p. 32).

Spirituality has to do with the felt truth shared by all humanity that
we are somehow connected to each other. Because spirituality is a facet
of human relationships often recognized through shared experiences of
acceptance, connection with others, and a meeting of the minds, it is
certainly an element of what happens between a psychotherapist and a
client in the therapist's office. *Lambert's (1992)* study suggested that 40%
of all positive outcomes in counseling result from factors outside of the
therapeutic experience; 30% deal with bond or relationship between client

and therapist; 15% with therapeutic techniques; and 15% with the client's expectancy (Carlson & Erickson, 2002, p. 30).

Coffey (Carlson & Erickson, 2002, pp. 30–31) believes that spirituality can affect each of these:

1. Some clients' extratherapeutic factors may be directly linked to their spirituality or religion.
2. The therapeutic relationship is a sacred trust that necessitates spirituality at its core. If a deep connection and acceptance are part of the therapeutic experience (for both client and counselor), it is a function of the spirituality present.
3. When therapists use skills that enable them to enter their clients' worldviews, a deeper connection can be made that is based on shared understandings.
4. The placebo effect, which aids positive therapeutic outcomes occurs when a client believes in the possibility of something different, such as spiritual transcendence. For instance, a client may perceive that the therapist's ability to listen and respond with hope, or any outcome that brings about well-being in the client's fractured life, stems from the transcendent power of God at work in both of their lives.

Personally, I think of God as a personable Life Force and Creator of the universe. The story of Jesus' life shows me the character and personality of God who embodies love, acceptance, forgiveness, hope, peace, patience, and joy. However, I also realize that my view is not held by everyone I meet. Some refer to God as a Higher Power (e.g., in Alcoholics Anonymous), as Energy, or as Mystery. I'm sure my list doesn't begin to contain the many ways people embody their spirituality. However, I would like to postulate that whenever we are open to the transcendent spirituality of our lives, something special enters, renewing and refreshing us by reminding us that we are not alone but deeply connected.

Spirituality for many of us includes the motivation to pursue personal morality and a relationship with the Divine, but it also invites us into a communal relationship of respect, mutuality, accountability, compassion, and love with all humanity. "Descriptions of spirituality as either objective (as is often found in extreme fundamentalist approaches to religion) or completely subjective (the idea that spirituality is wholly merely a matter of preference and individual belief) ultimately are inadequate because spirituality is a relational way of being" (Carlson & Erickson, 2002, p. 218). When spirituality is defined as either objective or subjective forces of individualism, it fails to honor spirituality as a relational way of being.

Religion
Religion often plays a specified role in people's spirituality but by no means exhausts it. Religion refers to a specific set of beliefs and enfolds them into a larger community that practices those beliefs in a certain way. For instance, the Catholic religion has beliefs and practices that differ from Baptists, and both are easily distinguishable from Islam or Buddhism. Each teaches a specific set of rituals and beliefs that is different from the other.

One of the many problems with bringing religion into therapy is that even within one type of religion there are often differences of practices, interpretations of Scripture, and beliefs, all of which can lead to difficulties. When it comes to understanding the difference between religion and spirituality, I like Bill O'Hanlon's (2006, p. 7) succinct definition: "Spirituality is a sense that there is something bigger going on in life.... Religion, on the other hand involves specific beliefs and practices."

Theology
Anselm of Canterbury defined *theology* as "faith seeking understanding" (*fides quaerens intellectum*) (Wikipedia). Although the etymology of the word began with the discussion of the gods or cosmos, Aristotle began using it to discuss the nature of the Divine. Christian scholars have followed suit by using the term to describe their studies in biblical manuscripts and subsequently have incorporated into its meaning the study of doctrines and disciplines of the Christian religion.

Theology provides people a venue to share concepts of their spirituality and to facilitate comparison among different religious traditions. It can be used to preserve or reform any particular tradition. It should be noted, however, that there is never just one way to discuss the spiritual life; even the earliest adherents of monotheism had disagreements about the impact of God in their lives. But a common language to address theology can provide the basis for ongoing discoveries in matters of faith and life. This is discussed further in Chapter 7.

Changes in Christian Religion

Because most of the opposition to gay spirituality stems from the Christian religion, it seems important to mention how Christian theology has changed to make room for other social issues over the past 200 years.

As awareness creates new opportunities for activism and change in civil law, people often realize that former perceptions were based in ignorance. New facts and social awareness have also influenced significant shifts in Christian theology. One has only to remember the work of Martin Luther, John Calvin, John Wesley, and Walter Rauschenbush to realize that in times past church leaders often led the way for civil reform. For Wesley and Rauschenbush, there was no religion that did not have social implications.

Over the past two centuries, our country has birthed nine generations of Americans (one generation = 22 years), which have led to nine significant transitions in protestant theology during the same era. The people of each generation, upon receiving new information, have attempted to find new ways to live out their faith in a changing culture. As much as some believers would like to hold onto an unchanging theology, the reality is that the Christian faith has never been static or contained; it continues to be refined and interpreted by each successive generation, as if to say, "It's a new day, a new life, a new experience of God and humankind."

Nine Generational Shifts in Theology in America

Generation 1: Revivalism
By the 1820s Charles Finney was leading a spiritual movement known as revivalism in an attempt to reconvert American's growing sense of independence from the institutional church back to traditional Christianity.

Generation 2: Benevolent Empire
The 1850s were marked by a movement known as the Benevolent Empire, where the church led the way for many social reforms aimed at bettering society's ills such as temperance, the beginning of women's rights, benevolence for the poor, and abolition. The most famous Bible teacher of this era was Chicago's Dwight L. Moody.

Generation 3: Social Gospel
After the Civil War of 1861–1865, the social justice movement came to light in response to new problems caused by industrialization and urbanization. Religious reformers noticed that it wasn't enough to save the souls of the working class without caring for temporal needs. At this time, new theological developments began to diminish the power of revivalism. Charles Darwin had published *On the Origin of Species* in 1859 and had sparked much intellectual and spiritual debate about evolution. There was also a

great influx as millions of nonprotestant immigrants in the latter part of the 19th and early 20th centuries, which continued to erode the one-size-fits-all theology of the past century. One of the notable ministers of this time was Rauschenbush, who was later called the father of the social gospel.

Generation 4: Missionary Movement

During the 1880s when the American Christian church was struggling with diminishing revivalism, passion for the foreign missionary movement was reignited to spread the Christian gospel throughout the world. Although often criticized for empire building and sublimating all cultures deemed not civilized by Western standards, these brave believers were first and foremost moved to care for the social and spiritual voids they encountered on a daily basis. They responded by building many schools, orphanages, and hospitals for native people. This era also held to a strong belief that by preaching the gospel to every nation, they might speed up the return of Christ to save God's people from the ills of modern life.

Generation 5: Fundamentalism

Those involved in the fundamentalist movement of the 1920s and 1930s believed that the social gospel movement had lost its soul. By focusing on the Scriptures that encourage believers to separate from the world, fundamentalists thought the true gospel was one devoted to piety and separatism. This movement was designed to combat the new liberal theology that accepted modern concepts such as evolution and biblical criticism and to denounce the decadent social and cultural scene that was portrayed by Hollywood celebrities.

In the 1940s, fundamentalism grew in the conviction that true Christianity was separate from all cultural decadence and apostate (i.e., liberal) churches. Holding fast to literal Scriptural interpretations and dismissing the values of higher education, this generation was marked with many prohibitions for proper conduct, such as refraining from drinking, smoking, gambling, participating in games that used face (poker) cards, attending movies and dances, engaging in extramarital sex, and adorning oneself externally (e.g., with wedding rings, ties). Some sects even forbade the use of instrumental music in worship services. Key figures associated with this era are Bob Jones Sr., founder of Bob Jones University; Cyrus Scofield, author of the *Scofield Reference Bible*; and itinerate evangelist Billy Sunday.

Generation 6: Evangelicalism
In 1942, the National Association of Evangelicals was founded in response to the heavy-handed religion of the previous generation and also in the wake of postwar optimism and confidence. The modern evangelical movement birthed many new religious institutions and organizations, such as Wheaton College, Youth for Christ, and Moody Bible Institute. Billy Graham and others helped to promote a refreshing spirituality that was not anti-intellectual, separatist, or belligerent like the fundamentalists before them. They were often known by inspiring music, great emotional fervor, and transformed lives. Due to the diversity of this group of people with many various beliefs and subcultures, there has never been one Evangelical position or theology. Throughout the 1950s, '60s, and '70s, most Evangelicals were tolerant of each other's spiritual practices when basic beliefs about salvation were shared, based on beliefs about the death, resurrection, and future return of Christ.

Generation 7: Is God Dead?
Many Christian churches were shocked and angered to see, "Is God Dead?" boldly printed across *Time Magazine*'s April 8, 1966, cover, as the publisher pointed out the growing loss of hope that many people felt for institutional religion. The article "Towards a Hidden God" stated that "the traditional citadels of 'Christendom, grey Gothic cathedrals (now) stand empty, mute with witnesses to a rejected faith" (*Time*, 1966). The main question this article posed was whether or not God was real. It was apparent that Christians no longer held to the image of God as a man who sat on the clouds of heaven occasionally intervening in the affairs of humankind: "Protestant faith now means not intellectual acceptance of an ancient confession, but open commitment—perhaps best symbolized in the US by the civil rights movement—to eradicating the evil and inequity that beset the world" (*Time*, 1966).

The loss of a meaningful church experience led many people to turn to alternative spiritual expressions such as humanism, Zen Buddhism, Paganism, New Age practices, and even hallucinatory drugs. *Time* dared to print what few had been willing to say: Americans were hungry to redefine God as someone who would touch human emotions and minds. The next few years saw the rise of the Jesus Movement, which was marked by contemporary Christian music and folk masses to speak to the question of being relevant.

Generation 8: Religious Right
During the Reagan Revolution of the 1980s, the Religious Right emerged, and the organized group Christian Coalition of America was subsequently formed. Here again is a group that began with good intentions and sincerely wanted to make a positive impact on society and culture. They were concerned over recent laws allowing abortion, changing sexual mores in society at large, and the expansion of the federal government into areas that were once the domain of state and local government. Over the next 20 years the Christian Coalition sought to align itself with the Republican Party to obtain a powerful political position to promote its causes. During this era, people like James Dobson, Jerry Falwell, and Pat Robertson took center stage. Whereas former generations believed that good Christians were to abhor worldliness and worldly entertainment such as movies, radio, and music, now mainstream evangelicals and fundamentalists were not only living it, but creating it.

Generation 9: Progressive Evangelicals
As America has made the turn into the 21st century, there has been a recent reform movement among progressive evangelicals, who are rallying together in the belief that the "Christian Right is wrong." Impassioned voices have emerged such as Brian McLaren, Tony Campolo, and Jim Wallis, who point out the need to tend to the poor and to speak up for the oppressed in an age of ultimate consumerism, promote alternatives to war, and resist the use of a political party to do religious work, as the Religious Right had done so blatantly.

Over the last decade, nearly every church, synagogue, or mosque has had to deal with the hot social topics of homosexuality and abortion. Many conservative churches have continued to condemn such ideas vehemently, whereas others are moved to refrain from judgment while stressing the need of compassion when ministering to people who are different. Even the Catholic Church has acknowledged that a person's sexual orientation is often fixed and has begun welcoming people inclined toward homosexuality while continuing its belief that sexual activity outside of heterosexual marriage is a sin. Yet the majority of Christians today do not know what to do with such information in the face of traditional religious beliefs that seem to oppose these issues.

In summary, it is obvious that the past two centuries have not only ushered in many social changes but also have reformed many religious beliefs. Where former conversations were once forbidden, new dialogues have begun. Former ideologies of absolutism and certainty that marked the age of Enlightenment have given way to the postmodern views of possibilities and mystery. Attitudes that were once harsh, condemning, and intolerant of difference are being softened by acceptance, compassion, and the position of not knowing all the answers to life's mysteries. As belief systems have transitioned with each generation, they most likely will continue to do so in the future. This gift is allowing us to more understand the beauty in all the wonderful varieties of humanity in our world, which is why I can say, "Thank God for change!"

Sexuality and Spirituality Are Intertwined

Counselors and clergy made significant progress when they realized that spirituality and psychotherapy can influence and strengthen each other. But it is also becoming more obvious that our spirituality and sexuality are also deeply intertwined. Spirituality, like sexuality, is a vulnerable topic that is not fully rational, tangible, or able to be categorized with any efficiency. Although both get people hot and bothered at times, sexuality and spirituality spring from a similar root of our being that has to do with a desire to connect outside of ourselves, to others, to God, or to the universe at large.

Because each is so intertwined with the other, it makes perfect sense that when sexuality is connected with spirituality, wholeness is nurtured in a person's life, but that when one is divorced from the other, a great deal of damage can occur in the human spirit. It is just as possible to have a stunted view of sexuality as it is to have a very limited understanding of spirituality.

Human sexuality and spirituality both have to do with intimate relationships. Both have to do with our deep desires, and our nakedness—being known for who we truly are. It is no coincidence that when we read the creation story in Genesis, God is up-front about the fact that humans are sexual beings. After God tells male and female to be fruitful and multiply, he says of their union, "It was very good" (Genesis 1:31). The great sin committed in the Garden of Eden was about greed and power rather than about sexuality. Given our relational definitions of sexuality and spirituality, one could say that the problem arose when humans failed to remember the relational aspect of their spirituality.

The book of Genesis also reveals that humans were created in the image of God, so each of us must bear *Imago Dei* at the core of our humanity. Could it be that our sexuality arises from a God-inspired desire within each of us to break out of isolation and aloneness so we can relate deeply with each other? Does our human sexuality express how intimately God wishes to relate to all of his children? Could it be that the whole universe longs for community and connection?

David Schnarch (1997, pp. 455–459) wrote that sexual intimacy offers us the greatest opportunity to know ourselves and to know and be known by another. Heightened intimacy encompasses the ability to look into a lover's eyes and soul while experiencing eroticism together. Perhaps this is why *knowing* is the term used in the King James Bible for sexual intercourse. To be known intimately and deeply is the greatest desire of both humanity and deity. In other words, if God wants to be in relationship to the whole person, then authentic sexuality is part of our intimacy with God.

Henri Nouwen, a well-respected Catholic priest and prolific author, learned from personal experience that the goal was not to repress his sexuality but to make friends with it instead, which is profoundly sound spiritual and psychological advice. Similarly, in *The Life of the Beloved*, Nouwen (1992, p. 70) wrote:

> Sexuality is the way we think and feel about ourselves. Our sexuality reveals to us our enormous yearning for communion. The desires of our body—to be touched, embraced and safely held—belong to the deepest longings of the heart, and are very concrete signs of our search for oneness.

Regardless of sexual orientation or gender identity, our calling in God is to discover that we can be naked before the Divine, revealing our truest selves, without shame. Created in the image of God, we are thus reflections of God's mysteriously diverse and wonderful creation. Perhaps one of the first steps in developing a gay spirituality is learning to reclaim one's place in the world as a person cherished by God, who celebrates human diversity.

Transitions: A Necessary Ingredient in Making Room for Difference

Although change has been our continual partner in the journey toward equal rights, it is not enough to transform social injustice. In spite of all the legislation for equal protection under the law, we are still only in the middle stages of modifying attitudes that were socially constructed to discourage difference. Civil rights laws continue to redefine the U.S. Constitution to include every person irrespective of race, gender, sexuality, class, or culture, but such external laws alone are not sufficient. What continues to be necessary is a shift in the attitudes of the human heart for true equality to be achieved.

In William Bridges' (2003) *Managing Transitions*, he explained why situational adjustments alone will not create lasting change. In his research, he found that successful corporate change can take place only when employees have modified their attitudes about a changing situation. Although his model was directed toward managers and employees of the corporate ladder, his principles can be applied on a global scale wherever human beings encounter a transforming landscape.

Bridges (2003, p. 3) began his book by stating the obvious truth, "It isn't the changes that do you in, it's the transitions." He quickly pointed out that these two terms are very different. *Change*, he said, is situational and external. In the area of civil rights, many external situations such as activism and legislation have occurred over the past 40 years that were designed to protect marginalized people. Because of such legal changes, for instance, employers and landlords have been forced to change their policies about discrimination. Sometimes changes in civil law had to force people to accept them as we saw in the issue of desegregating public schools in the South. Forced compliance is a first-order level of behavioral change but is not necessarily a secondary shift of attitude.

Transition, on the other hand, is internal and psychological. It involves "a three-phase process that people go through as they internalize and come to terms with the details of the situation that the change brings about" (Bridges, 2003, p. 3). Transition is how we respond to change, and it begins by letting go of former attitudes of the past.

Bridges' (2003) model consists of three phases:

1. Letting go of old ways and old identities: This marks the end of a former way of being and incorporates people dealing with their losses.
2. Going through an in-between time: This is when the old is gone but the new isn't fully operational. Bridges calls this the *neutral zone*. This is when the critical psychological realignments and repatterning take place.
3. Coming out of the transition and making a new beginning: This is when people develop the new identity, experience the new energy, and discover a new sense of purpose that makes change begin to work.

Successes for change and transition are also measured differently. *Change* hinges on new ideas and accomplishments, so one naturally looks for the outcome that change intended to produce. *Transition*, however, begins with leaving the old situation behind and letting go of a former reality, or the old identity that existed before change took place. This means one must be attuned to his or her feelings of loss, or former feelings of competency and privilege.

Transitions in Racial Minorities

As this concept is applied to racial minorities, it is obvious that White middle-class heterosexuals have had difficulty giving up their privileged positions in society. This was evident in 1865 when Southern plantation owners had to let go of their former entitlements that allowed them to own the slaves who worked their fields. One hundred years later, when the Civil Rights Bill was passed, White Americans had to let go of their former ideas about segregation. The facts had clearly pointed out that separate was not equal, but it took a great deal of law enforcement to change the status quo. Today, whenever we hear racial name-calling or any kind of derogatory comments about a particular minority group, we are faced with the reality that there is still much needed transition for attitudes to shift completely.

Transitions in Gender Equality

With the issue of gender equality, after 98 years of activism lawmakers declared that women should receive not only a fair wage but also one that was equal to men doing the same task, which of course has affected the bottom line of their employers. Several laws have been passed since 1963 that force employers to change their old policies. The perception was that the issue had been addressed, but the reality was the polar opposite. For instance, in 2004, the Boeing Company agreed to pay $72.5 million dollars to resolve allegations that as many as 29,000 female employees endured discrimination and gender inequities while working for the company. (Nyhan, 2004). Obviously, many male attitudes of superiority and privilege have not transitioned to the new reality that women are their equals. Perhaps as women refuse to be marginalized by banding together as a power to be recognized, men's gender bias will continue to transition as well (Nyham, 2004).

Transition in Equality for Sexual Minorities

When it comes to equality for sexual minorities, transitions in public attitudes are needed to realize this goal. According to Bridges' (2003) transitions model, something would have to be released before real attitudinal shifts will occur. It appears that the public will need to let go of many preconceptions and traditional beliefs to begin moving toward a new era where people with variant sexualities are not marginalized. We would also need to see communities ready to let go of the fear of what is different, by reexamining older stereotypes that may not be based in current realities. Fears will need to be addressed, understood, and released so hate can make room for love and acceptance and difference.

We are certainly not the first generation to do this, nor will we be the last. But as people of the present we need to make sense of our rapidly changing information and worldviews. Although at times we all tend to hold onto an old belief as the one constant thing we can depend on in a sea of changing facts, human belief systems have always been in a state of transition. They allow us to adapt to situations and events in our lives and to move on with grace.

Moving on From Victory Heights

A Victory Heights worldview has long since ruptured under the vast array of modern complexity. As scientific research continues to reveal an increased diversity in the human species, we have learned that sexuality is far too complex to support the ideas of binary opposites. As a result, we have come to value scientific scales that allow for variance in sexual orientation, gender roles, and biological differences so that there is a place for all people to find respect and understanding. Social legislation has influenced the shifting of our attitudes about race, gender, class, and equal rights for all people. Psychology has emerged from the science of pathology, which often viewed spirituality as insignificant, to a science that is increasingly interested in how relationships affect mental health and is beginning to explore the benefits of sound spiritual connections that can help to heal the wounds of the human soul.

As we continue to discover how complex and wonderfully we have been created, there are many times we are not sure how to make sense of what we know in light of traditional beliefs. Our ability to connect with people from around the world and from endless numbers of different cultures has led us to realize that one size does not fit all when it comes to matters of spirituality or sexuality.

Yet in spite of the fact that mainline denominations have experienced significant drops in weekly attendance, spirituality continues to be rebirthed in many new and creative ways. Spiritual development in the lives of sexual minorities is one of those rapidly changing areas. What we need at this time are broader theologies that will flex with our increased understandings of what it means to be fully human.

Tools for the Therapist

The fields of psychology and psychiatry, which once viewed spirituality as insignificant to the science of curing mental illness, are beginning to value spirituality as part of what promotes wellness. Therapists and clergy alike may find an inclusive spirituality to be a very useful tool for helping persons who are queer. My hope is that therapists, clergy, and all people of faith will be able to encounter *Imago Dei* in each person they meet no matter how different or variant they may seem at first glance.

Given that spirituality and psychotherapy are both inherently relational terms, therapists need to understand that spirituality can play a very key part in therapy. By making room for and honoring different spiritualities, a therapist can enter a client's worldview and find a deeper connection that is based on shared understandings.

Readers should also be informed by queer theory to appreciate how complex sexuality can be and how labeling or categorizing is often a result of the counselor's anxiety, which may not reflect the true essence of the client. Finally, since all beliefs are constructs of society and culture it would be very helpful for a therapist to understand how his or her own values have come into existence. By creating a spiritual genogram that spans three generations, therapists should note the psychological transitions that have occurred in each generation. Therapists must be open to an expanding worldview when working with GLBT clients.

2
Spiritual Connections

Let us build an American home for the 21st century where everyone has a place at the table and not a single child is left behind.

President–Elect Bill Clinton, 1993

Winter's light seems unusually beautiful today. Although the days are short and the temperatures are below freezing, the lingering glow of the low angle of the sun is outstanding as it illuminates the snow-covered ground. It is as if each crystal of ice has been made into a sparkling diamond capturing a brilliant ray of light. Most people in the greater Seattle area hate the snow, because it can turn into nightmarish driving conditions in our moist marine climate where one must compete with 3 million other people spinning up and down our steep hills. But I wonder how many people are missing the beauty of the moment? From where I sit this morning looking out on my backyard sanctuary, encased in the scenery enhanced by a post-solstice glow, my mind runs to Leonard Cohen's "Anthem," where the poet's words continue to ring true:

> There is a crack, a crack in everything
> That's how the light gets in. (Cohen, 1992)

Gay spirituality may be one of those cracks placed in our lives to enlighten America's thinking. The cracks in our lives often result from interacting with others who are different—those who disrupt our status quo mentality bring new light that illuminates our perceptions in the most unusual ways. No matter the topic, it's always different when it becomes personal. Gay spirituality has become very personal for me because of the people who have traversed my life, cracked it open, and left me forever changed. As a result of this new light, I want the world to treat the people I love with dignity, respect, and love. I want them to have an equal chance in life. I want them to be blessed by the abundance of knowing they are beloved children of God and to realize that innate sexuality does not preclude heartfelt spirituality.

Martin Luther King, Jr., 40 years ago, died in the quest for equality in America, yet his words continue to illuminate our minds as we attempt to realize a prophet's dream: "where one day my four little children, will one day live in a nation where they will not be judged by the color of their skin, but by the content of their character." (King, 1963) Since that time our collective awareness of prejudice and inequality has come a long way. Today, many people would be appalled if they knew a child had been overlooked or shunned because of her different skin color or ethnicity. Yet when that same child grows up to declare that she is a lesbian, many people find polite reasons to no longer invite her for dinner. Like Clinton's dream to continue the work of keeping issues of equality on the front burner, I want everyone to know he or she has a place at the table.

Personally, I know of six pastors' kids (PKs) who are gay or lesbian. They were all loved and treated the same in the church nursery, were taught in the same Sunday School classes as the rest of the kids, have delightful parents who do not hold extreme views, have mothers who aren't overbearing dominant types and fathers who aren't emotionally unavailable. Congregants watched them go through grade school and the awkward aspects of junior high and all the dances and proms of senior high school, and then they all went on eventually to earn college degrees. Two came out in their late teens and the other four in their mid- to late 20s. Although each one of them would claim a personal faith in God, only one person— the one who is most closeted—has made any attempt to rejoin a church community. Somehow, they know that there is no room for them to be fully accepted in the churches of their youth if they were to be authentic.

Likewise, their parents, who are lifelong church members, often feel they can't share much about their queer children with congregational friends, fearing a similar shame. Although both the parents and children believe there will be a warm reception anytime they choose to connect with the family of faith, they know their inclusion will be somewhat limiting knowing that at some point there would be a great gap of awkward silence if they introduced future partners or spoke about any part of a same-sex dating life with others in a culture whose only language for variant sexuality is sin. As one friend of mine lamented, "It's like being invited to a church potluck and told not to bring any of your favorite foods."

Sadly, due to the personal nature of these younger people's relationships, this is also the group that has the greatest chance of effecting a change of attitude in older generations, for only when sexual minority issues become personally relevant to institutions will inclusiveness become a possibility. Of course, the reality is that the queer individuals we are talking about arc just like you and me and can only take so much rejection; in our dearest places such as among family, friends, and church members the fear of being cut off is absolutely paralyzing. This is why others who do not need to fear being stigmatized must accept a larger portion of the responsibility for our brothers and sisters of faith. Isn't this what biblical verses on compassion such as Deuteronomy 15:7 encourage us to do? "If there is among you anyone in need ... do not be hardhearted or tight fisted towards your needy neighbor. You should rather open your hand, willingly lending enough to meet the need, whatever it may be."

Expanding a Worldview

Many of us have met significant people in our lives whom we would later call our mentors. I have been privileged to have known many people who have walked through my life and changed my spiritual worldview tremendously. Unfortunately, all but one have died and left me the honor of remembering portions of their stories to share. I invite you to think of those who have mentored you as well and what impact they have had on your life and belief systems.

Early Mentors

I would like to share about three men who influenced my early spiritual development, because I believe they represent the kinds of early mentors may people find in their 20s and 30s. Two were pastors who took me under their wings and allowed me to experience the world of ministry from their perspective, and one was a former missionary. Bob was a foreign missionary on furlough recovering from the depressive episode he experienced while living in a different culture a different culture. Although he was my parents' age, this wonderfully sensitive man quickly became my friend when we attended an all-city men's Bible study together. Each week, after we carpooled we often sat in the car for an additional 30 minutes, sharing personal insights of what we had learned from the Scriptures that week. It was exciting to experience such a practical faith. Through Bob's influence, the Bible became the Living Word to me, and I found myself yearning for more of its wisdom. When I first wanted to explore ministry opportunities, my path led straight to my pastor David Foster's office. David not only adopted me as a spiritual son but also took me under his wing as I explored various aspects of ministry in the church. He was truly one of the greatest advocates of my life, and later when he was a bishop ordaining me for ministry in 1991, the glances we exchanged during the ceremony were made through mutual eyes overflowing with tears of joy and love. He continued to greet me as his son in the faith until his untimely death 3 years ago in a tragic auto accident. Two years after I worked under David, we moved to an internship in Wenatchee, Washington. My new pastor opened my eyes to the world of evangelism, discipleship, and church growth. When Pastor D (as he was fondly called) invited me to become his personal assistant for a year, I learned not only many new skills but, more important the art of quieting myself enough to listen for the Spirit's gentle whispers of love and guidance. Following his example, I began to pen spiritual reflections in a daily journal, a practice that has continued for 25 years. All three of these men influenced my growing spirituality to the point I eventually knew I wanted to join them in ministry. They encouraged my spiritual development in the '70s and '80s when they chose to invest their lives in an impressionable young man. A vibrant and practical faith began to emerge in my life when religion got personal.

For 20 years traditional religious answers served me well. In a more black-and-white phase of my own development, they provided collective wisdom of a loving community that grounded and guided my life. However, as I began to interact with a larger community outside the faithful ghetto of my church, some of those tried and true answers seemed a bit lacking when it came to providing a compassionate understanding of the world at large. Since religion is based on truths that are not provable through ordinary human understanding (i.e., faith is the "conviction, [belief] of things not seen") (Hebrews 11:1), it doesn't have to learn the art of reason or compromise. It can insist on miracles and impossibilities happening through prayer or religious practices. Adherents are expected to live up to God's biblical commands, regardless of the consequences. A popular bumper sticker states this mind-set quite succinctly: "If God said it, I believe it." Though such observances may make for sublime testimonies earning followers a certain social acclaim, they may also needlessly cripple lives that cannot fit traditional ways of being or understandings of what is holy. When religious observances hinder the mysterious blossoming of an individual who was uniquely created in the image of the God, something has gone amuck.

Tom: Living With AIDS

When it came to changing my perspective about gay people, one of the most profound transformations came in the mid '80s through Tom, an amazingly talented, colorful young man who seemed to change the climate of whatever room he walked in. If Tom was there, you could count on the fact that a celebration was about to begin. He signed for deaf people in university classes by day and at church services on weekends. Tom wrote original music and sang and played the piano, all while cracking some good jokes between numbers. Toward the latter part of the '80s, he was involved with the Chicken Soup Brigade, which took food and cleaned houses for people living with AIDS. I was proud to know that a member of the church we both attended was willing to reach out to a population that most people wanted to forget. I remember thinking he was much braver than I could ever be, facing such sadness, death, and dying each week.

However, his courage made a lot more sense when, in 1990, Tom announced to his family, friends, and church that he had been diagnosed with AIDS, after having quietly lived with HIV for the previous 7 years. Everyone who knew him was in a state of disbelief. How could one of our loved ones in the church have AIDS? How could someone so vital and energetic face such a young death? Once again, the personal nature of this news began to shape our outlook. Now because of Tom, AIDS became personal —it had a face none of us could ignore. We would instead have to learn to come to terms with it in a new, more compassionate way. Although Tom contracted this killer disease before marriage in his wild and crazy gay days, no one even thought to condemn him because we all wanted to believe that his "sexual demons" had left him, as he had been happily married for 6 years and all our friends believed him to be a new creation in Christ.

Responsive Churches.   Tom and his wife, Kelley, had done a marvelous job in preparing the church for his announcement. After confiding in his pastor, Mark Abbott, about his HIV status, the two of them worked very hard with a taskforce to develop an AIDS educational program that would increase the awareness for the congregation. This led to the church board adopting a policy statement of how people with AIDS would be treated with care and respect as well as what health-related precautions would be taken in various ministries, such as the nursery where Tom often worked.

The church also provided town meetings where people could come to discuss their fears of the new AIDS epidemic. As a result, Tom and Kelley had tremendous support and love throughout their harrowing ordeal.

Sensing the need to do something similar in the church where I was a pastor, in 1992 I invited Tom to present to our congregation the human side of AIDS. Tom was the sort of fellow people quickly joined and loved. His ultrablonde shock of hair, dramatic self-effacing presentation, and sapphire blue eyes immediately caught people's attention. But then as he sat down at the baby grand to sing and play songs he had written about coping with a terminal disease, he became wedded to our souls. He performed his original song titled "My Journey Home," which included thes chorus lyrics:

> On my journey home,
> help me remember that I am not alone
> my journey home,
> I need you as family to help me
> make my journey home.

As he sang these lines, he became a guide taking everyone across the bridge of fears into a world they had never before experienced.

Tom shared with our congregation the story of a young man he met at a retreat for people living with AIDS who had not been touched or hugged by anyone for several years after his diagnosis with HIV. This fellow cried uncontrollably for nearly 2 days straight after finding a community who would love and touch him again. Tom also related some of his own horror stories of how he had been treated as a pariah by a few nurses in the hospital: They had quickly donned latex gloves and masks before touching him in any way and at times had intentionally ignored him when he desperately needed their help. Although Tom talked about how being HIV positive made him feel marginalized, I think one could say the same thing about being gay in some circles. His own words, recorded in a video of his life made by some friends, tell his story this way:

> People often become afraid and pull away. I remember when I was in the hospital, I had pneumonia and the doctors wanted to know what type because there are a whole bunch of different types of pneumonia. So they wanted me to cough up some mucous so they could do a lab culture so they could find what kind I had. I was barely able to breathe let alone cough a little up. Finally after a few days, I was able to cough a little up, and I was so excited; I had this little plastic cup, and I spit a little in there and put the lid on and I called the nurse and said, "You need to take this down to the lab." And the nurse said, "You're HIV positive," I said, "Yes, and you need to take this down to the lab," and she said, "There's some blood in there." And I said, "Yeah, I have double pneumonia and

you need to take this down to the lab." She said, "No, I don't think you understand. You're HIV positive, and there's blood in it [and] I'm not touching it." The
icing on the cake is that when you call a nurse there's a little light that comes on
over the bed, and she would not reach across me to turn the light off. She made
me crawl up the bed and turn the light off myself, because she didn't want to get
close to me…. And I did it because nurses kind of have this authority thing in
their favor and you just kind of do what they say—but after she left, I felt so dirty
and so untouchable and so unlovable.

Tom went on to say how important it was for him to be in a touchable
world, and when he thought of pastors (or in the case of this book, therapists) who try to keep the boundaries appropriate, he said:

If a young man comes in and is dealing with something and crying, and [the
pastor] gives him a hug and says, "What is the matter?" and he says, "I think I'm
gay," immediately the pastor pushes him at arms' length and gives him a Bible
verse when what he is really needing is to find some nurturing and find some
connectedness. So touch is really important.

Tom told stories like this to open the door of his life as wide as possible
to bring the face of gay people and AIDS into the church and to confront
the fears of people in society at large.

Although Tom knew he would eventually die of AIDS—as nearly everyone else did during the early '90s—he was determined to live as long and
fully as possible. One of the ways he continued to live is through the poetry
and songs he wrote so the church would learn to care for others who faced a
life-threatening illness that might have been caused by a variant sexuality.
He became the poster boy for AIDS-related ministries because he stayed
in the church and became involved in his community rather than running
away in shame. He was hired by Northwest AIDS Foundation to be one of
their speakers and began visiting high schools and corporations to educate
people about AIDS prevention—to put a face on the pandemic. By turning
his crisis into a service of hope for others, he created a welcoming door
for people living with AIDS who had become isolated and abandoned by
family, friends, and churches.

Strength for the Journey Retreat
By 1992, Tom had become seriously ill with his third encounter with pneu-
mocystis, where his lungs just refused to work on their own. His white
blood cell counts dropped dangerously low, and he had extreme sinus
headaches due to bacterial flora growing rapidly in his sinus cavities. He
was quickly losing hope and his grasp on life and thought he was ready to
die. Through an AIDS support group he learned of a free retreat hosted by
the United Methodist Church called Strength for the Journey. It was to be

a weekend of love and blessings for people living with AIDS with no proselytizing, rejection, or shame allowed. Instead, it was filled with the gifts of life, love, and encouragement for all people coping with the same health challenges. The music, laughter, talent shows, arts and crafts, homemade food, loving mothers, and professional massages had everything to do with celebrating life. It quickly became evident that all who attended that weekend were not going to be treated as people dying of a plague but with respect and dignity as they lived with AIDS. They were living with AIDS until there was no more life to live.

That weekend, as Tom was graced with total acceptance, he was encouraged to live for another 2 years. The retreat provided the needed touch and connection with other members of the GLBT tribe—a community that Tom had walked away from so he could be accepted as a person of faith. After returning from his mountaintop experience, renewed in every way, he couldn't wait to share his life-giving experience with me by insisting that I come with him the next year as a part of the support staff for this retreat. So in September 1993 I ventured into these uncharted waters. Something inside me was mysteriously urging me forward. I could clearly see the value Tom derived as a participant, but I have to admit, I was also hesitant to join him. At first I thought it was just the fear of being around a mysterious and deadly disease. So I went to my doctor to find out more about how AIDS was transmitted, wanting to make sure I was going to be medically safe in the evening hot tub socials. My doctor assured me that I would be just fine. His smile released part of my fears, but not all of them. There was a greater fear much larger than the fear of a deadly disease: It was the fear of joining a predominantly gay community. I really wasn't sure what to expect.

When the day came for me to walk with Tom through the huge, carved-oak entry doors of Rainbow Lodge Retreat Center, I felt as if I was traveling through an obscure dream. Although I was surrounded by the beauty of the forest and Mount Si looming steadily before me, I also was glad to have the comfort of a fast car if I felt the need to escape. Yet once I summoned the courage to enter this lodge of healing I was immediately transported into a strange world of wildness and beauty. We were greeted by volunteers who warmly embraced each new arrival underneath a huge, origami chandelier made from hundreds of paper cranes out of every color of the rainbow. This blessing had been created by a 4th-grade class, sent with their many wishes for hope and good health. Walking through the dining hall, I noticed the mothers who had lost their sons to AIDS dishing out homemade cookies that nurtured everyone with the taste of home. Outside, gracious wooden decks contained numerous art supplies alongside lounge chairs where people were encouraged to express their creativity or just relax in the soothing afternoon sun. This was obviously a world created intentionally to love and honor the unique life of each individual without exception.

Spiritual Connections Through Poetry Workshops
Workshops held the next day featured poetry writing, psychodrama storytelling, and music making that allowed the spiritual life of each person to emerge from the former cocoons of self-protection. Note how poetry opened one heart:

Paper Cranes

> Green, blue, orange
> Green, yellow, blue
> Above me
> Watching me
> Healing me
> I am the crane with the broken wing.

BARRY THOMA

Similarly, another poem expressed a writer's healing experience when walking alongside burbling streams with someone who knew how to really listen for an hour:

Whenever …

> Whenever there are cedar trees
> And moss covers the rocks
> And trout splash in rivers,
> Whenever spider webs glint in the autumn air,
> Whenever anyone takes the trouble to say
> No, that's not it, that's not what I meant at all,
> Whenever the distant formality,
> The bowing to the waist
> And kissing of the air beneath the ears can stop,
> Whenever sadness is held at bay for even a little while;
> Then the ice around my heart turns blue and clear
> And falls away in brittle shards
> Into the northern sea.

ROBERT GIBLETT

As the attendees read their poetry in the early evenings, spirits deepened. When crazy talent shows were performed, infectious laughter rolled through the halls, but when Seattle's Pat Wright and The Total Experience Gospel Choir sang to each person, they not only held listeners' hands but their hearts as well. Singing the words, "I don't know what the future holds/I don't know about tomorrow/but I know who holds my hand/He's never, never failed me yet," people felt like Pat had looked not just into their eyes but also into the very depth of their souls. By the close of the evening I had been elected the official hot tub pastor and officiated over more personal stories and blessed laughter until the wee hours of the morning. Various conversations of spiritual depth sprouted one after another as feet glided over each other in the warm bubbling water. Here was the pure joy of connection, and an organic spirituality I had never experienced, where sexuality and spirituality flourished side by side without shame. As unfettered spirituality began to blossom from the core of every person, regardless of religious background, I realized Tom was right in his predictions—this was something I had never before experienced.

Lasting Effects of the Retreat

After the AIDS retreat, I returned to my church hoping to share part of this weekend's discoveries with my congregation, namely, that when people have the chance to slow down and examine their lives, a spiritual core emerges. In nearly every person I met who was living with AIDS, I found a deep desire for spiritual connection. Was this the fear of death or the desire to live deeper and with greater meaning? Whatever it was, it was obvious to me that a person's innate sexual orientation certainly did not hinder a deep and personal spirituality.

This was quite different from the ideas I had been raised with, where the spiritual life had to be sought after and worked at with due diligence and where ministry was an action for others instead of a being a presence. The weekend at Strength for the Journey showed me that at the core, we all have the ability to draw great strength from our innate spirituality. We are not talking performance or new levels of enlightenment but rather being met by God in the present, here and now. The phrase "created in the image of God" began to take on an expanded meaning for me that weekend, for I began to see a reflection of the Divine nature in everyone I met. I wrote the following poem marking a reorientation in my thinking that would greatly influence my personal and professional life:

Divine Reflections

"Created in the image of God" must mean
every person reflects the Creator in some way.
Thankfully, God didn't create them as I would,
In MY image.
Otherwise, I would never have sniffed the sweet scent,
scratched my head in disbelief,
or stared in wonder at your unusual beauty.
If this reflection is true, there are shattering questions to ask.
How could we disregard someone who is different,
or judge what we do not understand?
How many of our jokes have diminished others?
Which one of God's images should we tarnish first?
Desiring to encounter Divine love
wouldn't we seek beauty in each of God's children,
forget ideas that we are normal
or more valuable than others?
What have we lost by having such a small, biased and narrow view?
Today, I will begin to reopen my soul
by marveling when I gaze into your eyes
feel flushed when I hold your hands
and shiver when you walk by,
knowing that in your presence
"A mystery of the Universe is placed before me."

A few weeks later, I decided to create a place at the table for one and all by inviting six retreat participants to speak in my church about how much the Strength for the Journey retreat had meant to them. I had hoped to demonstrate how love alone is the most powerful spiritual force we possess and how the ministry of presence can elicit a profound sense of healing. Even though a few people were still fearful of the unknown aspects of the HIV virus, the congregation in general warmly welcomed all of our guests. After church, my wife and I invited all six new friends to our home for a great dinner with our whole family. Our three children, who were quite young at the time, still remember that afternoon when their eyes were opened to a living grace as they dined with our gay, straight, bisexual, White, and African American guests. Here was a life lesson that no one could forget—for no matter how different or how stereotypical his or her appearance, every person is beautiful and is deserving of our love and respect. Every person has depth and insight worth knowing, and we can learn a lot from each other. Maybe the new discovery of that afternoon was that spirituality is not a construct but is a natural outflow of our shared humanity.

Skip, Dancing His Way In

Skip was a gay man I met at the AIDS retreat who loved to give thoughtful gifts. The first gift was an invitation to take a walk. As we walked through the woods that bordered melodic mountain streams where long green mosses sway gently from tree limbs when disturbed by the rush of human presence, we traveled at my pace, with determined footsteps, pursuing the goal of a finished task: a deep conversation, followed by a professional hug that was meant to convey personal care. Once we got back to the lodge, Skip thanked me for such a wonderful time, and then his second gift was to give me a few suggestions to improve my ministry. "First of all," he said, "next year, you and I are going to take that same walk, at *my* pace, and when we do we are going to walk slowly and notice all the things you missed today—like spider webs, and the various textures of the mosses and the changing patterns of light on the tree trunks, and …." Then smiling, yet completely serious, he said, "You also need to learn how to hug a gay man. Only straight guys hug like an "A"—where shoulders barely touch for a quick slap on the back. If you expect to minister to gay guys you had better learn to hug like an "I," where the bodies of two friends relax into the enjoyment of each other's company." Throughout that next year, I learned to relax with him and enjoy his company immensely. When the next season came for us to walk that path, he led the way, and I became his student.

Two weeks after I met him, he began coming to our church services on a regular basis. Skip, with his long ponytail, diamond studs, and tight jeans, sat in the second row of the sanctuary on the right-hand side week after week, where he consistently challenged the lives of the established church members to learn to love someone who is different. With the knowledge of a loving God and a community's acceptance, his spirituality grew by leaps and bounds. His old friends told me that during that time Skip became calmer, more centered, and more generous to others than he had been for years. His compassion for others and his ability to reach out beyond himself were the kind of things those who were around him will always remember. If someone needed cheering up in some way, Skip was the first one out of the gates. Shortly after he began coming to church, he noticed that I was acting a bit stressed due to several political and personal reasons and decided to give me the gift of an empowering verse of Scripture: Psalms 46:1, "Be still and know that I am God." He said, "Ken, if you seem to have lost your focus this week, it's only because you haven't yet learned to *be* instead of *do*. I think that verse says that God can handle it from there." It's a lesson I'm still trying to master.

As Skip endeared himself to everyone he met, he quickly became an extended member of several families and was often present at our family dining table on weekends. Another young family who also adored Skip overheard him wishing that he could witness a birth before he died. They not only invited him to be present at the birth of their son but also asked him to do the honors of cutting their baby's umbilical chord. Skip's encounter of birth, in the midst of navigating his own death, was an amazing gift that continues to bless that family today, because his countenance glowed with the ability to live fully in each present moment. A few months later, when Skip developed CMV retinitis, it was obvious he was going to need someone to drive him to church. I was interested to see who would volunteer to drive the 30-mile round trip to do this. To my amazement, Phil, a middle-aged man with little or no previous contact with gay people, became Skip's driver and faithfully transported him for the next few months. Similarly, the middle-aged mothers in the congregation greeted Skip week after week with the loving hugs reserved for children adopted by their hearts.

The Last Dance

Although people were learning to reach out in ministry to Skip, it was obvious to me that through the gift of his true self, he was actually ministering to all of us on an even deeper level. One day I asked him if he would be willing to dance his story of transformation during a worship service. In his previous career he had been a professional ballet dancer for 13 years, so interpretive movement was the most fluid language he knew. He looked forward to the challenge of using his favorite medium to communicate his personal story, which ranged from despair to hopefulness. So on a spring morning he performed to the music of a contemporary worship song, using dance to interpret the lyrics, "I am a new creation, no more in condemnation, here by the Grace of God I stand." Through his slow, precise, and painful last pirouette, we could see traces of his former rigorous ballet training and couldn't help but be moved by the sheer beauty of the moment and by the losses of his former physical strength. Needless to say, there was not a dry eye in the house.

He was absolutely exhausted after church, so we took him home so he could take a nap before going back to his apartment. The next week he wrote to me in his typical tenderness, "Good morning my dear friend," and then he told me that this opportunity to express his life story through dance not only had left him a bit dazed but had also provided a deeper understanding about himself:

It was quite some time after leaving your home that I realized just how much pain (and anger) I'd been clinging onto from my past/present; an enormous burden I've carried around so long I'd forgotten about it, considered it "normal." The exhaustion I felt was from finally laying aside what I'm pretty sure is the biggest part of that anger and pain. Without your sensitivity to my soul (center? insides? … loss for words here) I would not have had such a shattering, humbling experience. Thank you and thank God for bringing you into my life.

When he died the following summer, we all felt that God had sent him into our lives, and we came to realize that he had given us not only his most precious gifts of trust, vulnerability, and friendship but also his last dance on Earth.

Gary and Tammy: Rejected by Fear

That same year a married couple in their 30s sat in the back row in the dark, protected part of the sanctuary. It looked as if they were seeking shelter from a storm of immense proportions. Gary and Tammy had been living in a cold, leaky tent for 6 months in western Washington following the results of Gary's AIDS test. They had chosen this self-sufficiency rather than face continued rejection from family members and society at large. However, as Gary's condition worsened, the couple realized it was time to accept help from other sources. Our church helped this family find housing, jobs, and respite care. In return, Gary and Tammy became a cherished part of our community, once again enlarging our hearts as we moved beyond normal comfort zones of the status quo.

I distinctly remember baptizing Gary while sitting on a stool in front of the congregation because he was too ill to be immersed. Although he was fighting dementia, he was part of our weekly men's group and very determined to memorize a verse of Scripture to share with us. On that day, he quoted I John 5:11–12: "and this is the testimony, God has given us eternal life, and this life is in his Son…. He who has the son has life." The men's group cheered him on with wild enthusiasm. He became another testimony to the power of renewed spirituality in one who had lost hope for the most basic of human needs. When Gary died, I stayed with his emaciated body while waiting for the morticians, rereading the card he had given me previously that year: "Faithful friends are gifts from heaven; whoever finds one has found a treasure." The treasure had definitely run two ways. A few days later, together with his wife and many mourners, we buried him in a donated cemetery plot with a view of the mountains—one last attempt to restore dignity to a child of God whom some had abandoned on the journey.

John: You Were Worth It
I also met John at Strength for the Journey, and we seemed to bond right away; I believe his comment was, "I'm going to burn in hell for sure for falling in love with a priest!" Although he was married to a woman he dearly loved for the past 7 years, he had contracted AIDS in the time before marriage when his sexuality was directed more toward men. He was another man who had buried part of his sexuality and spirituality in an attempt to conform to society's standards.

When I first attempted to befriend John, he asked me what I perceived to be a rather odd question. Standing across the room as I made us some lunch, he asked, "Aren't you afraid?" I looked at him and frowned as I answered, "Of what, contracting AIDS?" He paused again, this time with an air of vulnerability—"no, of the loss." My heart melted as I responded, "Of course, but I think knowing you will be worth it." He quickly recovered with a flippant comment, "Well, I'm still not going to become a Christian!" I smiled, "Not today!" and we both laughed. What I came to find out later was that John had already been rejected by so many people that he was merely testing the waters to see if I would do the same.

Over time, John became a dear friend with whom I had so much in common that I ended up visiting him weekly before he died. As his own strength continued to decrease he allowed me to assist him with the most intimate aspects of his self-care. At times when I sat with him on his hospital bed in his home, we alternated our moments with laughter, tears, and a few prayers. Toward the end, one day we had a conversation:

John: I guess I can't spare you the pain of death, can I?
Me: No, John, none of us can do that.
John: When you do my memorial service, just tell everyone there that I never wanted to hurt anyone.
Me: OK.
John: And tell them I was a good man who loved God.
Me: Anything else?
John: Yeah. You know, I've always loved you.

All I could say in response to that was, "Ditto, my friend, ditto." As I officiated his memorial service, I began to realize the impact of his first question; the pain and loss were unbelievable, but knowing and being loved by this dear tender spirit had also been most definitely worth it all.

The Light Got In

I share these stories not only because the people depicted in them are meaningful to me but also because their sexuality and spirituality coexisted in beautiful ways that continued to grow and develop when given the chance—and as a result, so did their humanity. Perhaps the stories will still influence those who take the time to read them today. I include now a poem that Tom wrote for his wife, who could see the tender person behind all of his wounds and rapidly aging body. When Tom died, his friends gave each member of the congregation a piece of beach glass in honor of his life, illustrating again how the cracks in our lives are where light gets in when given the chance.

Beachcombing

Though not the glorious vessels
they once were,
Some fashioned for beauty,
and the aesthetic,
Others molded for service,
though broken and worn
by tumult of wind and wave,
Each piece becomes a treasure
For those who are thoughtful
And would take the time to look.

TOM UNGER (REPRINTED WITH PERMISSION)

For the next 2 years I was involved in a very intense ministry where more than 30 people whose average age was 35 died of AIDS. Many of them asked me to conduct their memorial services. On one hand, I felt honored to perform this task for them, but on the other hand, with death, I felt as if I was losing part of myself; it was the gift I had been fostering for others—an intentional community. Although most of my church responded in loving and affirming ways, there were some who just couldn't get past the gay issue, and after Skip's funeral they went on the attack. Let's just say I had an extremely difficult time coping with the results. Never having the chance to recover from my own grief, I began to crumble under the weight of clinical depression and later had to leave my ministry position.

Although I had come to greatly admire the courage of each person who had brought AIDS awareness into our lives and connected so many who lived in ivory towers to a new reality, I was also aware that Tom and others had barely begun to deal with how their sexuality meshed with their blossoming spirituality. Tom, who opened the door as wide as he dared, simply didn't have enough time left for him to do so, nor did he have a culture that could tolerate it. The worlds of sexuality and spirituality would have to be blended in a different era, but some other spiritual pioneers would have to do that work.

> One does not think one's way into a new kind of living;
> One lives one's way into a new kind of thinking.

Parker Palmer, The Promise of Paradox

During those years, I believed what the church needed to do was to step up to the plate and get over its prejudices and judgments to help people in need without asking how they got there. My agenda for over a decade had been that the church needed to become more open and affirming to gay people. I was thinking that this would provide a place for people to heal and find wholeness so they could eventually give up a "sinful lifestyle." However, as it became more personal, I began to realize that most of the gay people with AIDS I had been caring for would never "get over" their natural sexual orientation. If they were to become healthy enough to regain sexual functioning, they most certainly would do so. Compared with the issues of living or dying, it became a rather inconsequential matter. I began to stop and wonder how to deal with the sexual behavior that follows a person's natural sexual orientation. I also began to doubt if this was really a sin. Although the denomination to which I belonged at the time had reformed its book of discipline to say that it believed homosexual orientation was not a sin, it continued to label homosexual behavior "sin," which was making less sense to me all the time. How can a person's normal direction of sexual attraction be acceptable while the normal desire to fulfill it in a loving relationship is condemned? I found myself increasingly less able to believe the party line and less able to accept that an obscure verse in Romans was more defining of Christianity than the Sermon on the Mount. Like Palmer's words, I was "living my way into a new kind of thinking."

The Life of Henri Nouwen

As I searched for new insight into the essence of spirituality, I discovered the books of Father Henri Nouwen and found a wonderful resting place in his writings. It seemed as if he boiled the gospel message of Jesus down to the basics of our faith: loving God with all our hearts and loving our neighbors as ourselves. What I continue to find enlightening in reading Nouwen's works is that his writing is presented with a warm vulnerability matched by his spiritual insights. He described his bouts of depression with accuracy, while bringing his deeper emotions to the table when he described his relational and spiritual lessons. I often recommend his classic, *The Return of the Prodigal Son* (Nouwen, 1994), to clients who are struggling to find their identity in spiritual matters.

When Nouwen died in 1996, *Christianity Today* mentioned his passing by acknowledging him as "one of the world's great spiritual writers; the renowned Catholic theologian (who) left behind a wealth of insights that have brought encouragement to thousands" ("Reflections," 1996). However, the untold story of his life was that he also left behind his years of suffering as a gay celibate, who, in his last decade of life, had only begun to come to terms with his sexuality. Many clergy who have enjoyed Henri Nouwen's writings over the years have not worried too much about his same-sex orientation because they believed he was a successful celibate. But as the deeper truth comes out after his death it is obvious that much of his depression was due to his raging internal battle between his sexuality and his spirituality, which some suspect contributed to his early death at the age of 59.

Rebecca Laird and her husband were among Nouwen's longtime friends who, when interviewed, said that Nouwen spoke about the time he had grown very attached to a person who had loved him deeply in return (Laird, 1997). He recognized how that person had enormous abilities to open up a place inside him that had been closed. Nouwen in turn grew so dependent on that person that when the relationship ended, he described how he felt in this way:

> "I was totally paralyzed—I couldn't do ministry, so I left the community, and totally broke down." Nouwen's psychiatrist told him; "You got infatuated with somebody, that person dropped you and now you are depressed.... You never should have been a celibate." But Nouwen says that he eventually "knew that what I experienced was a God-given relationship, that the love was real, that I experienced something that was extremely important, and that I didn't have to leave my community." (Laird)

According to Michael Ford's (2002) biography of Henri Nouwen, there is no indication that Nouwen was anything but celibate. However, Ford says it is impossible to understand the anguish and complexity of this man without considering his homosexual orientation. This was something he was aware of from the time he was a youth but only started to come to terms with in his final years. Whereas his early years at Harvard University found him being tough on homosexual students, over time he became friends with people in the gay community who increasingly were pressuring him to go public with his own sexual orientation. Other friends, however, advised him to keep his secret, saying he would lose all credibility as a famous Catholic writer if people knew he was gay.

Before his death, Nouwen was increasingly becoming more vocal of his support for gay men and women and championed their unique place in the Christian community. Ford (2002) speculated that had he lived, Nouwen's next major book might have been a study of homosexuality. Often referred to by the title of one of his best-selling books, *The Wounded Healer*, people had little idea of the depth of his own suffering.

Here again was a man whose sexuality and spirituality had often been in conflict, and I found myself wondering how much more he would have developed had he lived another decade—when gay spirituality emerged as a buzzword in many different circles. However, even as I read Ford's (2002) biography of Nouwen, I kept most of that information in the abstract, intellectual parts of my brain. Although I often found Nouwen's writings to be a great comfort for my grief, I had also learned to put a decade of emotional distance between Nouwen's writings and the life stories of my dear friends who had died previously.

Gay Clients Helped Rewrite My Theology

I could put most of the gay spirituality debates aside until I began to have gay clients—or more to the point, gay clients who were decidedly Christian. The first time I saw a homosexual Christian couple in my office, I was excited to be able to do systemic work that combined sexuality and spirituality. It was great to help this couple process the intersection of their spirituality and sexuality while encouraging them to honor their own deepest truths. However, at the same time, deep within myself I was also judging the veracity of their faith. I remember making mental notes that would run them through all the tests of legitimate Christianity from my evangelical roots. To my surprise, I consistently found them to be right on target. Aside from having a homosexual relationship, they passed every silent spiritual test I could envision, and in fact in many ways I came to admire their exemplary faith. Moreover, it seemed that when they began to honor their sexuality as a gift from God, a path was cleared for deeper spiritual growth and self-acceptance. In short, I felt like I was in the presence of the real deal.

So, I went to work, reexamining traditional interpretations of biblical scriptures that most religious people believe are opposed to homosexuality. I also began taking a closer look at what I knew of the human experience and what scientific research had revealed, and I found a great gap between traditional religion and modern science. I noted that more than 30 years ago, the American Psychiatric Association declared that homosexuality was not a mental disorder, implying there is no need for a cure. The experts in human behavioral science were saying that homosexual orientation is as natural as heterosexual orientation, that it is determined by a combination of yet unknown pre- and postnatal influences, and that it is dangerous and inappropriate to tell a homosexual that he or she could or should attempt to change his or her sexual orientation (American Psychological Association's Help Center, http://www.alahelpcenter.org/articles.php?id=31). And like I've said before, once it became personal and I knew that we were talking about my dear friends and loved ones, it necessitated a change in my thinking. I eventually reauthored some of my theology to make room for my life experiences.

Obama's Change of Heart

I know I am not alone in this endeavor to make spirituality as meaningful and practical as possible. In reading Barack Obama's (2006) *The Audacity of Hope,* I found that he had a similar change of heart about homosexual issues after receiving a phone message from one of his strongest supporters who was a businesswoman, mother, and all-around generous person and who had been in a monogamous lesbian relationship for more than a decade. As she shared her hurts about his polarizing statements from a previous public debate, he began to understand life from her perspective. Later when he reflected on his words, he returned her call and told her that he was sorry. Christians who claim to "hate the sin but love the sinner" are often unknowingly inflicting pain and condemning very good people who are also made in the image of God. He said:

> I must admit that I may have been infected with society's prejudices and predilections and attributed them to God; that Jesus' call to love one another might demand a different conclusion; and that in years hence I may be seen as someone who was on the wrong side of history. I don't believe such doubts make me a bad Christian. I believe they make me human, limited in my understandings of God's purpose and therefore prone to sin. When I read the Bible, I do so with the belief that it is not a static text but the Living Word and that I must be

continually open to new revelations—whether they come from a lesbian friend or a doctor opposed to abortion. (Obama, 2006, pp. 223–224)

Over the past few years, I have come to believe that the wholeness necessary for the GLBT community is not a change of sexual orientation or a denial of being a sexual person. What is needed instead, is hope: hope that it is possible to connect the natural energy of one's sexual orientation to one's innate spirituality. Two themes I have heard repeated from gay clients are something like (1) "This [being gay] shouldn't be such a big deal; why can't others see that I'm a lot more than my sexuality?" and (2) "After a while being queer isn't enough, something is missing, and I need to find it; I think it is spirituality."

Transitioning Into a Better Therapist

As a result of my personal experience, much reading and reflecting, along with scriptural studies over the past decade, I have found myself in the midst of several transitions around the topic of gay spirituality. Each transition is heavily influenced by human stories. Since I have several close friends who are gay, many stories stemming from friendship have greatly modified my perspective. There are stories about the transitioning elements of my own faith and belief systems, which led me to change denominations recently so I could worship in a welcoming and affirming congregation. Then, there are the stories of how I have transitioned in my work from a pastoral counselor with the "right answer" to a licensed therapist (and minister) who becomes very curious when encountering new questions. As I mentioned in chapter 1, as a White, middle-class male who appears quite heterosexual, I have enormous privileges in life because I am seldom marginalized. One of my attitudinal shifts is to continually dismantle my cultural and social standing to be an agent of equality for all people.

Somehow, all of these transitions have helped make me a better therapist—not only for GLBT clients but also for anyone going through a life-changing event. There is definitely a parallel process between me and the GLBT clients I serve who are trying to make sense of their world. In fact, I really don't think one can do this work unless one is willing to be transformed by it.

This book really is about transformations: the personal transformations of GLBT clients and the therapists, clergy, friends, and family who are associated with them. What I am about to suggest may look something like taking a camera and rotating the viewfinder 45 degrees so that everything seems a bit off kilter. However, I invite you to look into this other view of life and not only to tolerate the anxieties that come from being a bit disoriented but also to find a place in your heart that can love the adventure. Good therapists must become not only respectful listeners but also chronic entertainers of the "why not?" We must exercise the attitude of not knowing and of ultimate curiosity to find out what ignites our clients' passions and interests as well as what brings meaning to their lives. Being curious in this way also helps to build the therapeutic bond between the client and the professional that accounts for 40% of therapy's outcome.

Letting Go of Toxic Attitudes

So, I ask you to do three things as you read this material:

1. Suspend your stereotypical ideas about GLBT people, God, and religion so that you can listen for some new rhythms in your heart chambers.
2. Open yourself up to hear the still, small voice that guides you in life so that you can hear wisdom in a new way while honoring the stories of different people that you will be reading about.
3. Learn how to bring that still, small voice into your encounters with the GLBT people whom you know so that they can also learn that their own quiet, wise mind (of God, or the universe, or ultimate energy) can speak to them as an empowering presence in their lives.

At this point, I also ask you to review the three-phase concept of *transition* found in chapter 1. When it becomes necessary to make a life transition or attitude adjustment in any form, the decision to let go of what no longer works is always difficult and often very painful. However, unless we can let go of old attitudes that cripple the soul, new perspectives can never be fully attained. The process of transitional change allows us to move forward in search of things that bring peace and blessing to our lives. Fortunately, this does not happen all at once, because there is a time when we both carry the pain of the old and the hope of the new. This, I believe, is the transition zone with the most conflict, for the old still has its hooks in our life while the new is not yet fully grasped. Here, life dangles in what seems like a limbo state of the "not yet" and the "not knowing" that can make us act in a rather schizophrenic fashion. This is where I think many

Americans find themselves when it comes to the fuller understanding that homosexuality is not an activity someone does or a depraved lifestyle that one is seduced into; instead, it is part of who a person is at his or her core. Perhaps what is needed is for people to be more curious and less condemning about something about which they know very little.

I'm sure most therapists would agree that a healthy dose of curiosity is an essential component of their work. How else would we learn of a person's worldview that is different from our own? What else would create the desire to fit together the fragmented puzzle pieces of someone's life story? Over the past decade I have witnessed many people make better sense of their lives as they learned to accept and embrace "what is" rather than hanging onto old toxic notions of what "should be," as well as learning to experience God in the present state of being rather than as a reward for excellent performance in this life.

Research That Connects the Dots

In the process of working with clients I became increasingly interested to learn how GLBT clients connected the dots between their sexuality and their spirituality while living in a culture that discouraged those connections. In fact, I became curious enough to conduct a research project that involved a series of recorded interviews with GLBT people as they talked about the things most meaningful to their lives. When I expressed my desire to do this project with my gay friends, they in turn told their friends, and so on. The response was so enthusiastic that after hearing I was doing a research project on gay spirituality, people I didn't know began calling me, saying they wanted to be part of this important work. It was as if the project took on an energy and purpose of its own that I am still discovering.

I interviewed 30 people, in 40-minute sessions, hoping to discover the experiences that made a difference in their lives. I also asked their ages, religious backgrounds, current spiritual practices, and how they would describe their gender and sexual orientation. I invited respondents to share what life was like in the closet as opposed to coming out and to tell stories of when their sexuality and spirituality were most in conflict. I also asked them to share a time when those elements felt most congruous. Finally, I asked people to describe what had been most helpful to their spiritual development and what was most hurtful. When I was done with each 40-minute interview, I felt I was standing on holy ground. I came as an outsider but quickly became the honored guest who had been taken into people's homes, offices, and the sacredness of their life stories. The depth of communication was amazing. You don't often find this kind of vulnerability in church or community events. In fact, religious people are rarely so blessed with such raw honesty. In the end, the participants and I were no longer strangers but fellow travelers on the sacred soil of life. They gave me permission to use their stories in whatever manner I chose, so I pass them on to you, the reader, in hopes that you too will be touched by these gentle conversations. A detailed summary of the kind of qualitative research I did and its major findings in included at the end of this book in Research Resources.

Survey Results

I first began the survey by creating a list of questions that I would ask each person. To keep all interviews as similar as possible I asked the same questions in the same order. Occasionally, due to my enthusiasm or the interviewees' emotional distress, I might skip over a particular question and come back to it later in the interview when I sensed it would be easier to talk about; however, that was more the exception than the rule. I knew from recording a wide variety of opinions for a previous American Association for Marriage and Family Therapy (AAMFT) seminar on Religion, Homosexuality, and Marriage that I would need to limit the duration of each interview or I would get lost in an overabundance of data, so I limited our conversations to no more than 40 minutes.

Average Age of Coming Out

After interviewing 30 individuals, I had responses from 18 men and 12 women, who ranged in age from 27 to 67. I purposefully wanted a large span of ages and human experience to get the broadest view possible. In the future, I think it would be interesting to quantify some of these questions with specific age groups, because when you are discussing coming out of the closet from 1959 to 2004, there are bound to be very different experiences that were greatly influenced by the attitudes of society in each decade. Nevertheless, in my survey the average age for coming out for both men and women was 24.5 years.

Figure 2.1 Kinsey's lab.

Orientation: Don't Make Assumptions
By the time I interviewed my second person, I realized that one of my questions was worded incorrectly. After asking a humorous man how he would describe his sex, he smiled and said, "Abundant!" By the next recording, I had changed my question to read, "How would you describe your gender?" I received some broader responses by not demanding that people categorize themselves as male or female. For instance, one man told me that although he was most definitely male with no desire to change his physicality, he felt that he was a transgendered person when it came to his spiritual identity, because at his spiritual core, rather than a warrior-like male, was a young female who guided his spirit with a Sophia-like tenderness.

Similarly, I quickly realized that it was best to ask a similar leading question when it comes to the questions about a person's sexual orientation. For several people the categories of gay or straight were much too confining, because sexuality for them was much more fluid than an either/ or statement. Even though a person may be in a committed homosexual relationship, that does not mean his sexual attraction is only reserved for members of the same sex, thus demonstrating again that one's sexual behavior is not the sum of one's sexual orientation. In fact, all but three of the persons I interviewed had had sexual relations with people of the opposite sex at some point in their lives. Many gay people had previously been married to opposite-sex partners, and others would say that for this point in time they were in a gay relationship but didn't want to close the door to other possibilities in their lifetime should this relationship come to an end. So part of my findings were that although I interviewed 18 men, only 15 claimed to be homosexual; 3 said they would prefer to think of themselves as bisexual. I found something similar when I interviewed 12 women; 9 said they were lesbian, and with 1 person, I forgot to ask this question. I find it interesting that in my results, approximately 10% of both men and women claimed to be bisexual.

This statistic points out an important issue therapists need to grapple with when it comes to human sexuality. We should not be satisfied with oversimplifications about gender, sexuality, and relationships that push people into various categories to quell our own anxieties. Instead, we need to respect the wide variety and fluidity of human sexuality in others, and perhaps in ourselves as well. As Linda Stone Fish said,

> It takes courage to take off our blinders and see the beauty of all people especially those who are very different than us. But it is this courage that will transform us as parents, therapists, pastors and individuals, and ultimately our communities. (Stone Fish & Harvey, 2005, p. 215)

Gay Clergy

Other miscellaneous results of my study worth mentioning are that five of my participants were clergy and two were seminarians; obviously, these people were connecting the dots of their sexuality and spirituality in ways not experienced by most of the general public.

Early Sexual Abuse

When I inquired about the topic of early childhood abuse, 13% said they were survivors of childhood sexual abuse, which interestingly was an equal percentage of men and women. The converse percentages, however, would mean that 87% of all these gay people had never been sexually molested. These numbers seem important to me because they point out the ignorance of the stereotype a large number of the general population holds to be true that homosexuality is caused by early childhood abuse.

Religious Backgrounds

Another surprising statistic was that 93% of all participants were from religious backgrounds. In spite of possessing a sexuality that many traditionalists would consider to be a blockage of one's spiritual life, 90% of them still participate in some sort of spiritual practice, and 56% still attend a church or synagogue. Only 10% would claim no spiritual practice at all. Perhaps the most profound discovery I have made is that most considered themselves to possess a profound spiritual outlook in life, regardless of whether they were part of a church or other religious institution.

Hurtful and Helpful

All of this leads me to the main purpose of this study: discovering what people considered to be most helpful and most hurtful in their spiritual development. To obtain this information, I went over each interview several times, listening for common threads of information and narrative until the different layers of conversations began to sort themselves out in my mind. I address these two aspects in greater detail in chapter 4 and chapter 5.

If I were to sum up a theme of what was most hurtful to people's spiritual development, it would be the result of *being beaten down from constantly dealing with oppression, judgment, and ostracism from others*. What we are talking about is simply the loss of hope of being fully accepted as a normal person. Conversely, I would say that the theme of what was most helpful was an *internal desire to be fully accepted and integrated in society*. Whenever unconditional acceptance of a person becomes a possibility, the river that leads to positive growth, peace, and self-acceptance flows freely.

The task ahead of us, then, is to find effective ways to help GLBT clients make their own bridges of transition so they embrace something that will most helpful in connecting their unique humanity to the Divine. However, before that occurs, we must all let go of hurtful stereotypes that have caused such pain and rejection. To do that, we need to understand more about the very foundations of sexual and spiritual development as it applies to homosexuals. Like all developmental models, there may be a variety of examples to choose from; however, when we speak about how to encourage sexual minorities to seek healthy spiritual connections, the process of letting go can be lengthy.

It should be obvious by now that many sexual minorities are waiting to take their place at the table—if it is indeed a table where respect and dignity are served. However, one question remains: "Who will make room for them?"

Tools for the Therapist

To get in touch with one's own potential conflicts between spirituality and sexuality, therapists need to ask themselves the same questions I asked of my survey participants:

> Tell me about a time when your sexuality and spirituality were most congruent and when they were most dissonant. What made the difference? What would you say has most helped or hindered your own spiritual growth?

However, therapists have the additional task of getting to know a queer person. It is much easier to label, categorize, or misunderstand an abstract group of people with whom there is no contact. However, whenever an issue gets personal, former stereotypes quickly lose their power. Narrative therapy is an invitation to relationship. The task, therefore, is to use a narrative approach when interviewing GLBT persons by taking a "not-knowing" stance and asking for life stories and experiences. Therapists who honor each interviewee's story as a sacred treasure will be amazed at what they find.

3

Development of Sexuality and Spirituality

For it is not difference that immobilizes us but silences
and there are so many silences to be broken.

Audre Lorde, 1934–1992

Last week, we invited our neighbors to our house for dinner. Although we'd chatted pleasantly in the middle of the gravel driveway for several years, none of us had taken the time to get to know each other on any deeper level. This year the time seemed right for a gathering. As the evening progressed from coleslaw to barbequed flank steak, we found that our dinner was opening the pages of new friendship. We share in common not only age and interests but also the fact that we've both been with our partners for more than 30 years. One of the delightful surprises of the evening was in discovering that we also share the blessing of an active and meaningful spirituality. The fact that one couple is lesbian and the other is straight soon faded into the background. What seemed more important was our mutual enjoyment of the freshly baked rhubarb pie! I found myself thinking of the statement, "The more we are different, the more we are the same."

As the topic of this book emerged, our conversations became even more dynamic, peppered with the numerous ways healthy spirituality had helped all of us overcome the crushing effects of toxic religion in our lives. For Lois, who grew up in the Catholic Church, one of the most healing aspects of her life occurred around age 50, when she entered a different religious community and experienced an inclusion that seemed for the first time in her life as integrated and complete: "It was really only after the discovery of a useful spirituality in an inclusive community that I truly began to accept myself." Today as I write these pages, I think of that rich time of mutual sharing around that large pine table as the perfect setting for this chapter.

In the past a homosexual was given a place at the table if he kept his sexual orientation hidden in silence. He could be known as the good friend, or favorite uncle, or cousin who just happened to be single as long as he could talk about sports, or fishing, or travel stories with careful editing of anything that had to do with his love interests. In fact, people might even wonder if he was gay, but as long as the topic was avoided and others at the table didn't feel discomforted, life could go on without disruption. In other words, learning to tell polite lies was always recommended if a sexual minority wanted to find a place in society.

Until the 1970s sexual minorities kept their collective silence for many reasons, such as the fear of being arrested, losing jobs or housing, or permanently losing family and friends who disowned them. However, the greatest difficulty came from their interior sense of self because they were raised to believe that homosexuality was an abomination and therefore were deplorable even in their own eyes. As a result, homosexuals often suffered from many mental disorders and high rates of alcoholism, drug addiction, and suicide. Whereas most of society tended to believe that these maladies were the consequences of offensive homosexual behavior, the real fact was that gay people suffered not from same-sex attraction or sexual liaisons but from society's ignorance and fears about sexual orientation and its resulting judgments. During the entire length of their sexual, moral, and spiritual development, most sexual minorities felt that everyone around them considered gays, lesbians, and bisexuals to be terrible, disgusting, and morally corrupt. Because of their very real fears of ostracism, rejection, and possible arrest they were forced to keep their sexual orientation a secret. With this kind of continual stress, most could not live without suffering some kind of mental breakdown; it's no wonder that the DSM II (Diagnostic Statistical Manual's, second edition, 1968, p. 44) declared homosexuality to be a psychological disorder.

Time and again, sexual minorities continue to be punished not for being different but for telling the truth about it. How many men and women serving in the military, members of the clergy, and other respected professionals still have to hide one of the essential cores of their being to avoid suffering loss of jobs and status in their communities? If they do tell the truth, they are not heralded as models of courage; instead, they are cast aside as quickly as possible. What a paradox we have created! Over the centuries, many sexual minorities have become leaders in our societies (e.g., Michelangelo, Alexander the Great, Roman Emperor Hadrian, Leonardo da Vinci, Richard the Lionhearted, William

Shakespeare, Oscar Wilde), but most likely had to learn to suppress their sexual orientation to be socially accepted. Lest we think this paradigm has shifted, we can review the headlines in 2005 about former U.S. Representative Mark Foley's indiscretions with House pages (Weisman and Babington, *The Seattle Times*, October 5, 2005, p. A1 and p. A3) (or about the downfall of Reverend Ted Haggerty, formerly the head of the National Association of Evangelicals (Gorski, 2007). While the fall from power and position is tragic to witness, the reality is that if these two men had ever revealed their sexual orientations at any time in their careers, they would never have made it out of the starting gates of their professions. This obviously has made a positive sexual identity development very challenging.

Positive sexual identity development is a challenge when one has to continually adapt the presentation of one's life to what others consider to be normal, which explains why so many sexual minorities try to appear as straight as possible, even though their interior sense of self is quite different. The poem following poem seems worth pondering at this point.

> We grow accustomed to the dark—
> When light is put away—
> As when the neighbor hold the lamp
> To witness her goodbye—
>
> A moment—we uncertain step
> For newness of the night—
> Then—fit our vision to the dark—
> And meet the road—erect—
>
> And so of larger—darkness—
> Those evenings of the brain—
> When not a moon disclose a sign—
> Or star—come out—within—
>
> The bravest—grope a little—
> And sometimes hit a tree
> Directly on the forehead—
> But as they learn to see—
>
> Either the darkness alters—
> or something in the sight—
> Adjusts itself to midnight—
> and life steps almost straight.

EMILY DICKINSON

What Causes Homosexuality?

Fortunately, our society is moving away from a model that perceives homosexuality as something someone does in bed to a broader understanding that recognizes being gay as a way of being. We are also finding that people's sexual orientation is generally formed very early in their lives from a variety of influences.

Current research shows that neither homosexuality nor heterosexuality is chiefly influenced by genetics but rather by a mixture of genetic and environmental factors. In fact, although there is genetic evidence for homosexuality, genetics may account for only 35% of men's sexual orientation whereas other environmental factors may account for 64%. For women, genetics explains about 18% of the female sexual orientation, family environments 16%, and environmental factors account for about 64% of the variations. In a recent article from *US News and World Report,* Dr. Quzi Rahman, a leading scientist on human sexual orientation, said that increasingly "… while genetic factors are important, non-shared environmental factors are dominant in determining sexual orientation" ("Genetics, Environment," 2008).

Dr. Tony Campolo, a well-known sociologist who is also a Christian, recently wrote an article calling for evangelicals to move beyond the preoccupation with homosexuality that has absorbed their discussions so that they can put their energy into living out love and justice in the 21st century: "Nobody has provided a conclusive explanation of what causes a homosexual orientation, and it develops so early in the biophysical and social development of children that it's practically impossible that it could be something that is deliberately chosen" (Campolo, 2007). Campolo went on to say that he believes there are two fairly common beliefs remaining today that are based on nonscientific misinformation: "The first is the suggestion that homosexual orientation is the result of poor socialization. This is the most common belief held by Evangelicals who sponsor ministries designed to 'deliver' homosexuals from their bondage by turning them back into heterosexuals." They usually try to pin the "problem" on a son who is overidentified with his domineering mother and a physically or emotionally absent father. This theory, of course, puts undue guilt and stress on parents who are already confused about how to deal with their gay children.

The second most common theory is that "being homosexual is somehow the result of childhood trauma that stems from the gay person being sexually molested as a child" (Campolo, 2007). Like any given population, there surely are gay people who were molested when they were children and perhaps also had domineering mothers and absent fathers. But when one reads the statistics or listens to the stories of 80% of this population, these expected pieces of information seem to be missing. Most gays were not sexually abused, nor did they have parents who were somehow more deficient than the rest of the population. (Campolo, 2007)

I continue to be amazed that so many people have such a hard time accepting the idea that homosexuality is usually not a choice. After all, it's obvious that God has created all kinds of people with various skin colors, skills, temperament; some of us are right-handed, left-handed, or ambidextrous. One of the more interesting verses of Scripture that is often overlooked in this discussion is Matthew 19:12, where Jesus states, "Some eunuchs were born that way" (see chapter 7 in this volume). Although researchers disagree on what constitutes an intersex person, Fausto-Sterling states that 1.7% of human births are born with noticeably atypical genitalia, and many more have some less noticeable form of anatomical variations that do not show up until later in life. (Wikipedia, Intersexuality 2008) How many times have we met people with exceptional brain power who lack the ability to carry on normal social intercourse? When we encounter such a person we may smile and say, "Oh, you know, that's just Joseph; he just marches to the beat of a different drum," but we would never think of demeaning his character. We seem to make allowances for all the aforementioned variants, especially if the nonnormative aspect is something we can observe with our eyes, touch with our hands, or hear with our ears. But when it comes to accepting the fact that God might have also created some unique persons possessing a different sexual orientation from our own, we still fail to accept their variation as anything good or normative. In the midst of the variety and complexities that make up human beings, innate variant sexuality continues to be pathologized—or, in extreme cases, declared to be the work of a demonic presence. Yet as you read the subsequent stories of the people in my surveys, you will discover that many gay people felt "different" from their heterosexual family members very early in life. As mature adults, they would say they knew they were gay before they could articulate what that word even meant, something that is normalized in the sexual identity models mentioned in the next few pages.

While it is true that some people have been surprised to find themselves falling in love with someone of the same gender and have therefore

chosen to be gay, others feel that their sexual orientation is just as permanently engrained in their being as being right- or left-handed or possessing
a brain that is musical instead of oriented to engineering: It just *is*. As a
result, homosexuals who are out and surrounded by accepting people have
no more problems than anyone else in society. When they are in accepting
communities, their lives are often indistinguishable from straight society
except that their affections are directed toward people of the same sex. In
fact, it seems that some of the healthiest homosexuals are those who confi-
dently reject the idea that they have a psychological disorder: "The greatest
psychological damage is suffered by those homosexuals who have allowed
themselves to be persuaded that they're suffering from a sickness" (Bawer,
1993, p. 97). Although society has not entirely freed itself from sexual prejudice, we have come a long way in the battle for equality. With much less per-
secution, sexual minorities can now live more openly and have progressively
become more psychologically and emotionally balanced than ever before.

Variations of Pride

Parade Pride

I marched in my first gay pride parade last year, accompanying our church's
banners of inclusion and support for the gay, lesbian, bisexual, and transgender (GLBT) community. Our group consisted of 20 people who were gay,
lesbian, bisexual, transgender, or straight. We ranged from 26 to 74 years
of age. As we walked alongside the shiny red Dodge pickup holding our
banners, waving to the crowds and declaring this church's 35-year history
of intentional welcoming and affirming ministry to the GLBT population,
the crowd's response was amazing. People who had been sitting on sidewalk
curbs stood up and waved; those who had been quiet shouted out blessings like, "Thank you!" and "We love you!" and the ever succinct "Hurray!"
for having been a spiritually inclusive community where everyone could be
accepted and was encouraged to find his or her place of belonging.

Of course, our group was also surrounded by more typical entries such
as the half-naked disco dancers and overly frocked drag queens and their
underdressed leather escorts, all of which made for some pretty bizarre
displays of skin and spandex. Some people actually looked like they were
from another planet, or maybe they thought their sexuality was so unique
that they really were from another planet. I found myself wondering how
many of them saw this event as an excuse to let their hair down and just

have fun. But then I also wondered how many believed they had to act freakish to be accepted by society, even if the expense meant that others made dirty little jokes about them. Although some pride participants saw this as an opportunity to educate, win over, or make friends with the heterosexual population and to promote the cause of gay equality, many people's behavior and costumes only reinforced the myths and prejudices that make for hetero-fundamentalist enemies. And, of course, the media was quick to record the most outlandish-looking people to spice up the evening news, whereas entries like ours received zero airtime.

This big party-like atmosphere was held in glorious June sunshine, complete with thousands of rainbow balloons, antique convertibles, and bands with music blasting, which set the dancing g-strings into action—all under the guise of instilling pride for sexual minorities. I wondered if this was really promoting pride and dignity for an oppressed people or if, instead, it was a subculture's defensive posturing that said, "Since we can never be like you, we will be very different; because of our uniqueness, normal rules need not apply to us." Whatever the intended meaning of the party was, I'm sure that many onlookers—instead of seeing dignity and pride from people who have mastered overcoming or who have learned to go beyond survival by learning how to thrive and contribute to society—saw a defiant subculture giving off a message that was more like, "I dare you to get close to this, honey!" Or perhaps in some subconscious way it suggested that society's rejection can be directed only at the odd behavior rather than at the core of the person wearing that g-string. While it is very easy to judge such behavior as abnormal, it might be helpful to reframe this as what it must be like to develop a secure sexual identity in the presence of a rigid subculture.

Some may categorize this as a gutsy form of gay pride, but it seems to me that real pride is something individuals tend to achieve after much hard work. Does this kind of pride instill dignity in one's core? Is this an attempt to make cross-cultural connections? Although such activities demonstrate the ability of marginalized human beings to overcome oppression, I also wonder if they reflect a particular developmental stage of sexual identity.

Bruce Bawer, who writes regularly for *The Wall Street Journal* and just happens to be gay, observed something similar in his book *A Place at the Table* (2003). He concluded:

> [Real pride] doesn't come from being gay or from belonging to *any* group. It can come, however, from dealing with the fact of your homosexuality in a responsible and mature manner, from not using it as a club to beat other people with or

as an excuse to behave irresponsibly or unseriously. The more loudly someone declares his pride, the more it should be suspected; for real pride is not shrill and insistent but quiet and strong. (p. 159)

Rallying Pride

By way of contrast, my wife and I certainly witnessed a great deal of pride last year when we attended the second rally for marriage equality on the steps of the Washington State capitol building. Here, the population was entirely different, consisting of a greater number of middle-aged faces many of whom came with their long-time partners. Curiously, there were no freak shows that day or undue attention-grabbing by outlandish individuals. There was instead a demonstration of real pride in the outstanding music sung by the Seattle Men's Chorus and Women's Chorus. Pride was demonstrated by the robed ministers of excellence, who represented many different faiths advocating equality. Pride was demonstrated by the 1,500 sober, normal-looking couples and individuals of all types, who gathered together with dignity and purpose before sitting down to talk with legislators about why equal treatment under the law was a moral necessity. Again, I must ask if this is also the result of a particular stage of identity development. Of course, the major networks didn't see this demonstration as bizarre enough to make the evening news either, but those of us who were there saw it truly as a moving experience that was helping change societal attitudes.

Legal Pride

In 2006 and 2007, the state of Washington voted two important bills into law. The first was the Murray-Anderson Anti-Discrimination Bill, (January, 2006) which, after being defeated in the Senate for nearly 30 years, made discrimination based on sexual orientation a crime so that gays and lesbians could have protection for their equal rights in housing and employment. The next year, the Domestic Partner Bill was passed (April, 2007), allowing the registration of domestic partnerships so that gay partners could make end-of-life decisions for each other and could inherit properties without a will—rights that heterosexual couples have had for decades. Although gay marriage is banned, at least gay couples can now legally care for each other.

Such legislation causes a shift in thinking in all populations. Where many gays and lesbians who have not seen the value in pursuing what was heretofore unthinkable, there seems to be new seriousness about what it means to stand up for one's rights as an equal citizen of the community. Time will tell if such changes will also make a difference in the further development of gay and lesbian relationships. Here, I can only speak from personal observations, but I was pleasantly surprised when one of my family members drove to Olympia, Washington, with her girlfriend to register as domestic partners on the second day it was legal. It seemed to me that this significant moment was a brave step forward in the coming out process and brought their relationship to a new social status that felt to them "more adult." The pictures, the framed certificate, and the story told with tears of joy for becoming a recognized entity in society certainly speak about gay pride in a way that is healthy to the core.

Identity and Gay Subculture

There is bound to be an uphill battle when we talk about developing a positive identity for sexual minorities. The "gay image" the media, and perhaps even the gay subculture, has overpromoted often reduces the lives of homosexuals into a dirty little joke. The gay subculture was birthed out of necessity, at a time when no one who was gay believed that he or she would ever be accepted by mainstream society. The subculture has produced the message, "If we can't be a part of you, then we will be as ridiculous as you think we should be, but it will be our own little joke." It has obviously been a successful message; Sarah Jessica Parker illustrated this with a flippant comment describing her character on *Sex and the City*: "basically, a homosexual man. I love clothes, I love good food, and fine fabrics. I work out. I'm concerned about my looks. I'm vain!" (Bawer, 1993, p. 163) Similarly, there was something revealed about living in the shadow of an archetype when designer William Ivey Long said, "I think being gay is like being on the spice rack: 'It's not the real food. It's just the spice,'" or when Michelangelo Signorile told *Newsday*, "I think all gay men have a bitchy queen inside them" (Bawer, 1993, p. 163).

When was the last time anyone watched a healthy role for a homosexual in a movie or a TV show? Although *Will and Grace* certainly made some breakthroughs by placing gay characters into prime time entertainment, they are really pretty pathetic, self-absorbed individuals who live up to cultural stereotypes in every possible way, with no desire or ability to do otherwise. Similarly, in movies like *To Wong Foo, Thanks for Everything, Julie Newmar* (Beeban Kidron, 1995), the general public has great laughs at the expense of gay characters in drag (complete with not-so-subtle sways and affected speech) who seem to have no meaning or existence outside their own self-imposed stereotypes. This is epitomized when Miss Chi Chi Rodriguez tells Miss Vita, "You're not a queen because you rule people or sit on a throne, baby. You're a queen because you couldn't cut it as a man."

Stereotypes

It is one thing for the general populace to ignorantly buy into prejudicial gay stereotypes, but what seems sadder to me is that many people in the gay subculture buy into those same ideas. They speak as if there is a gay décor, gay fashion, gay spirit that are universal to all homosexuals or that every gay man loves opera, owns a feather boa, and hates physical labor. Where do these overgeneralizations come from? While it is true that people do fall into those categories and that there is a subtle subcultural preference for the absurd, it is important to realize that the labeling of "all things gay" does not grow out of same-sex attraction but from the experience of being gay in a society where homosexuality continues to be marginalized and where all levels of society tend not to acknowledge its existence or take it seriously: "In such a society, a gay person cannot help being deeply aware of, and having a profound sense of himself as an exception to, the generally accepted order of things" (Bawer, 1993, p. 165). So if a person can't join the ranks of normal acceptance, he or she might find a place at the table by behaving in a way that we have all come to know as "flaming."

How intensely a person will experience these gay affinities has a lot to do with how much he feels himself to be marginalized, rejected, or invisible. Gay children who were taught by their parents to feel contempt for homosexuality and who therefore never develop much self-esteem may grow into adults who get a psychological boost from ridiculing heterosexuality. In such cases, ridicule or contempt may be a way of siding with gay stereotypes in a way that does not promote healthy psychological or moral development.

Emergence of Gay Subculture

There are plenty of historical reasons for such contempt for social standards and subcultures of separatism. Since the middle part of the last century, homosexuals received little respect from the media, their doctors, their government, or themselves. The majority of homosexuals felt a need to appear as straight as possible, keeping their sexuality a dark secret so as to avoid jail time. So they learned to keep their sexuality a secret from their families and churches and professional colleagues and to satisfy their sexual and social needs in gay bars and cruising spots, often looking down on those whose lives revolved around their sexuality and condescendingly calling them "the girls" and those who passed for heterosexuals as "the boys." Sadly, the one area both closeted homosexuals and heterosexuals agreed on was that the 100% male homosexual certainly was not a man.

After WWII, a few closeted organizations were founded to stand up for gay rights. However, the 1960s gay subculture had essentially not gathered together for political reasons; its members just wanted to have fun. When people got arrested for seeking a same-sex liaison, they assumed this was always the way things had been and that they were powerless to do anything about it. However, another deeper issue was lurking below the surface: Thanks to the ideas about sexuality with which people had been raised during this era, many believed that if someone got arrested they most likely deserved it.

As I stated in chapter 1, the gay liberation formed in 1969 began to turn things around. However, the early gay rights movement was not interested in seeking equal rights for domestic partnerships; rather, they were mostly interested in obtaining rights for sexual freedom. Whereas the majority of homosexuals were leading conservative and hidden lives that would blend into the mainstream, the more extreme elements of the gay population participated not only in demonstrations but also in building a wall around themselves instead of reaching out to educate and make friends with the wider community.

Conformity to the Subculture

As the subculture grew more powerful and visible, it began to forge ideas that gays were a completely distinct species who shared a set of assumptions about politics, society, sex, and religion that were purposefully at odds with mainstream culture. Members of the early gay subculture wanted everyone to believe that they were linked not only by their sexual orientation but also by their own version of sexual morality and philosophies, which would later be referred to as the *gay culture* or *gay lifestyle*. There was the idea that all gay people should live and think in certain ways. So when young people first begin to accept their gay identity, they would also find their way into the subculture's institutions, such as bars, community centers, or activist events. While their estrangement from families, old friends, and former religious communities was still quite fresh, they were often eager to reattach to a new community of acceptance. However in doing so, they also became extremely susceptible to the subculture's pressures to conform.

Although many GLBT people can learn to resist the subculture's demands of conformity, not every gay person is that strong, especially if he or she has been rejected by the family of origin and is living as a lost, lonely, vulnerable outed person. This helps explain some of what happened in the 1980s when the standard for gay identity meant a person who spent a great amount of time in bed with multiple anonymous partners rather than falling in love and settling down with one person. If anything allowed the AIDS epidemic to spread so rapidly, it was this widespread spiritual emptiness and out-of-control sexuality.

This is where the fundamentalist can easily judge homosexuality as a plague that needs to be eradicated. But what one must also take into account is the fact that many young homosexuals were drawn to a sexually promiscuous life because they felt so alone and confused in the years preceding any kind of societal acceptance for what they felt to be true at their core: a same-sex orientation.

> For such young people, promiscuity can be a buoyant, desperate over-response to their sudden sense of freedom and self knowledge, a swing of the pendulum away from loneliness and an attempt to shore up a sense of sexual identity and to find in the embrace of strangers a brief sense of acceptance and closeness in the wake of a family's rejection. (Bawer, 1993, p. 169)

Even today, due to the societal attitudes with which many young people are raised—namely, that being gay is an abomination or inherently decadent—many gay and lesbian young adults figure they can not sink any further and tend to run wild.

Social Oppressors

While it is true that there was no united voice crying no to all the excesses of the '70s, it would be too simplistic to lay all the blame at the feet of a subculture that tolerated and promoted such promiscuity. In the 1970s, American laws and social attitudes also made it much more difficult for homosexuals than for heterosexuals to live in monogamous relationships. Society was much more inclined to quietly accept homosexual encounters that were out of sight (and therefore out of mind) than they were to accept two mature people of the same sex setting up house in their neighborhood. To live safely and contentedly in an open, same-sex relationship requires a certain degree of understanding and acceptance of one's family, friends, neighbors, and employers. If we are to lay blame at anyone's feet for promiscuity and AIDS, we must lay it at the feet of our uneducated prejudicial society that has not attempted to understand or make room for sexual minorities.

During the AIDS crisis of the late 1980s and early 1990s there was another dramatic shift in healthier cultural attitudes. During the peak years of 1992 to 1995, hundreds of gay men were dying each day of this terrible disease, living only into their mid-30s. Caretakers were exhausted, worn out from repeated losses only to have another crisis the next day. Something needed to change. This time, however, reform began in the gay community, whose members soon realized that they needed to help themselves. So they set out to educate themselves on how AIDS is transmitted and provided free HIV testing and education on safe sexual practices and encouraged long-term sexual partners instead of frequent bed hopping. At this time there was also an increase in gays using 12-step programs and educational programs on health and wellness, and there were greater numbers seeking spiritual direction from religious houses of worship. Many homosexuals who had lived empty lives were now finding faith and inner strength to make responsible decisions to improve the quality of their lives.

William A. Henry III's observation in a 1992 *Newsweek* cover story was that AIDS "turned an often hedonistic male subculture of bar hopping, promiscuity and abundance of 'recreational' drugs—an endless party centered on the young and the restless—into a true community, rich in social services and political lobbies, in volunteerism and civic spirit" (Bawer, 1993, p. 174). Unfortunately, at the same time there was still an expectation that a young man should experience bathhouse sex as an essential rite of passage: To grow accustomed to the idea of homosexuality and to fully accept yourself as a gay person, you *needed* to sleep with lots of strangers. This has not gone away all together because even today many young homosexual men become promiscuous not because they really want to but because "they are encouraged to believe that that's what one does, what one *must* do when one is gay. In doing so, alas, they make themselves captives, in freedom's name, of a way of life to which they never aspired" (Brawer, 1993, p. 175).

As one young man once told me, "I've done the one-night stands, and even though my friends tell me I shouldn't be so particular, I know that is not what I want. What I want is a loving relationship based in a deep friendship, but I don't have a clue of how to find that."

Models of Human Development

I find myself pondering an interesting question that is based on the fact that sexual orientation often shows up very early in children's lives and may not change over a person's lifetime. Whereas the typical parent tends to react in negative ways while making every attempt to change the course of their child's variant sexuality, most current ideas of development suggest that it would be much better for the children if their parents learned to "go with the flow" of their child's latent homosexuality. If a homosexual person does not possess pathology that needs to be eradicated, then the one thing he or she needs the most is a world that promotes greater understanding of the self, wider acceptance of diverse humanity, and healthy places of connection and nurture. Surely every person wishes for a well-adjusted life, with purpose and rich, loving relationships. So the question remains: Rather than playing to the stereotype, how could we as a society promote healthy development for homosexuals and lesbians?

To help explain the many aspects of human development, researchers have suggested models to explain a wide variety of human processes. The names of many researchers have become part of our common vocabulary. For example, when speaking of childhood stages of cognitive development, Jean Piaget's name is well known among early childhood educators. In the early 1960s, Lawrence Kohlberg described various stages of moral development, and 20 years later James Fowler created a similar model for Christian faith development that ranges from the literal to universal.

Similarly, there are models of sexual identity development. Although all models listed herein differ in their specific view of human development, they all share the assumption that human beings move through life experiences within particular frameworks. Such frameworks help us to understand the process that an individual is presently experiencing or has experienced in the past as well as provide the ability to predict what stages may be encountered in the future. Such models also provide awareness for individuals to gauge their own progress in relation to others who are having similar experiences. (When reading the next section, refer to Appendices 3.1–3.4 at the end of this chapter to compare the models with one another.)

Cognitive Development: Piaget

In the early 1930s Piaget, a Swiss philosopher, natural scientist, and developmental psychologist, studied aspects of moral judgment and created a four-stage theory of children's cognitive development that rose out of his observations of the way younger children made moral decisions compared with older children and adults. As a result, he concluded that older children's cognitive abilities change considerably between 7 and 11 years of age. He stated that children between these ages operate within the framework of a *concrete operational stage* (Stage 3), where they begin to think logically about concrete events and to see rules as fixed and absolute and as handed down by adults or God in a way that cannot be changed. Here, moral judgments are made based on the consequences or fear of punishment.

Children enter *formal operations* (Stage 4) when their abstract reasoning begins to develop, around age 11 or 12. When this developmental shift occurs, the older child's worldview becomes more relativistic. Older children's ideas of moral judgment have more to do with intentions than with consequences, and they begin to realize there may be different ways of looking at a problem.

While Piaget remains the pioneer of the constructivist theory of knowing and has been a great resource for models of early childhood development, human development does not stop at this point but continues throughout a person's lifetime.

Development of Moral Reasoning: Kohlberg

Kohlberg continued to study Piaget's theories of development and began interviewing children and adolescents on moral issues while studying to become a clinical psychologist. As a result, in 1958 he began his doctoral dissertation work in a more complete theory of development, where he uncovered not two but six stages of moral development—and the first three share features with Piaget's stages.

Kohlberg interviewed 72 boys in the Chicago area who ranged in ages from 10 to 16, and he presented them with a series of dilemmas, such as the story of a poor man, named Heinz, whose wife was near death. Heinz felt he had to steal a drug for his wife from a druggist who insisted on charging top dollar. Kohlberg was not really interested in yes or no answers but in why the child thought Heinz should or should not steal the drug to understand the reasoning behind children's answers. As a result, he provided a six-stage model of moral development.

Kohlberg's Six Stages
Level 1: Preconventional Morality

> *Stage 1—Obedience and Punishment Orientation (ages 5–10):* Here a child assumes that the rules of life have been set by powerful authorities that must be unquestioningly obeyed. Kohlberg called Stage 1 thinking "preconventional" because children do not yet speak as members of society; instead they see morality as something external to themselves or as what "big people" say they must do.
>
> *Stage 2—Individualism and Exchange (ages 7–12):* In Stage 2, children are less impressed by any one single authority, because they have begun to realize that all issues have more than one side. Since everything is more relative rather than fixed, one can begin to think of making his or her own choices.

Level 2: Conventional Morality

> *Stage 3—Good Interpersonal Relationships (age 12+):* By the time children enter their teens they begin to define morality as a good person who lives up to the expectations of their respective family or community. Good behavior means having good interpersonal motives that are helpful to the family such as love, empathy, trust, and concern for others.
>
> *Stage 4—Maintaining the Social Order (age 16+):* Whereas Stage 3 reasoning works well in interpersonal relationships, Stage 4, by contrast, is more concerned with society as a whole and obeying the laws that will maintain social order. A prominent rationale might be, "What would happen if we all started breaking the laws whenever we felt we had a good reason? The result would be chaos; society couldn't function" (Crain, 1985, p. 122). An adolescent in Stage 4 would add new reasoning about the needs of law in society as a whole that far exceeds the grasp of a younger child.

As Kohlberg continued his research over the next 30 years, he became convinced that Stage 4 was the dominate level of moral reasoning in America, which can occur anywhere from age 16 to the early 30s.

Level 3: Postconventional Morality

> *Stage 5—Social Contract and Individual Rights (age 20+):* Persons in Stage 5 are more interested in principles that would make for good society

rather than in keeping unjust rules that may lack the essential ideal morality. They may begin to ask questions like, "What makes for a good society?" Stage 5 occurs when people believe that a good society is one that works to benefit one and all while recognizing that different social groups within a society will have different values. Therefore, people in this stage are concerned that all members of society have basic human rights that need to be protected and that a democratic process should be in place that would result in changing unfair laws. Although people in Stage 4 may also talk about the right to life, it will only be a right legitimized by the authority of their social or religious group (i.e., their culture's interpretation of the Bible)—so in Stage 4, whatever a person's group or culture believes is what he or she will believe. In Stage 5, however, people make a more independent effort to think about what any society ought to value. Stage 5 does not develop before people are in their mid-20s and is never very prevalent in society.

Stage 6—Universal Principles (age 30+): Although Stage 5 demonstrates a high level of morality that argues for the protection of human rights and the equality of all people through democratic process, Kohlberg believed that there must be yet a higher stage that goes beyond equal rights and democracy to a stage that defines the principles by which we achieve justice. In Stage 6, a commitment to justice trumps all laws. A good example of this is Martin Luther King Jr.'s argument that laws are only valid insofar as they are grounded in justice and that a commitment to justice carries with it an obligation to disobey unjust laws. One of King's remarkable aspects was that he was willing to accept the penalties of the law for his actions, believing that the higher principal of justice required civil disobedience.

Such levels of moral reasoning are very rare; indeed, it is interesting to note that in his later years, Kohlberg stopped scoring at Stage 6, declaring that it was so exceptional that it was more of a theoretical stage than an actual one.

Stage Transitions: One Step at a Time

It is interesting to note that although Kohlberg would say people pass through these stages in sequence, most people do not grow into the higher stages. He did not believe that these structured sequences are the product of aging or maturation. Neither would he agree that these stages are the products of socialization by parents, teachers, or mentors. Instead, he said that one progresses through these stages by struggling, thinking, and reasoning his or her way through the various moral complexities of life. While social experiences do encourage growth and development of our minds, it is only because they stimulate our mental processes. The more we discuss or debate with others, the more our former views are challenged or questioned and the more we are motivated to come up with new, more complex positions, which moves us into higher stages of development that often reflect a broader worldview.

A good example of this occurred in an after-dinner conversation among some of our closest friends. One couple was commenting on the stress they faced when their adult children began making life choices that seemed disparate with their parents' religious values. To understand their children's viewpoints, they began to read some of the books suggested by their children that explained the situation from a different spiritual perspective. By living in the tension of two solid views on the topic, the parents were forced to expand their worldviews and to make room for mystery on top of the fixed rules that had previously governed their lives. I imagine Kohlberg would have been quite pleased with this aspect of adult development.

In families learning to make room for homosexuals, we might imagine a man and woman discussing the current efforts to change legislation that currently does not allow gay marriage. Because the man desires to uphold a high moral code, he may say, "I sympathize with homosexuals to some extent, but like it or not, the Old Testament law prohibits such behavior, and our civil laws do not support immorality. Therefore, we are bound to obey the laws of our society. Homosexuals can thus either live celibate lives or risk the consequences; this isn't about equal rights—it's about right and wrong." The woman may note, however, that well-organized societies, such as Nazi Germany, are not always moral. She may also posit that from today's viewpoint it is also obvious that the pre-civil war society in America encouraging the slavery of African Americans was not moral either. Thus, the man would experience some conflict in his former ways of reasoning and would be motivated to begin thinking about this issue in a new way, thus moving a bit further toward Stage 5.

Kohlberg suggested that another way change occurs is when people have the opportunity to change roles with others by considering another person's point of view. As people discuss their problems and various viewpoints, they often develop their own ideas of what is fair and just. This process of adapting to new ideas and moral development happens best when people can formulate their ideas in an environment of openness and democracy rather than in a place where pressure is exerted to conform to an external authority.

I'm sure you can begin to see the problems that may be inherent for gays, lesbians, and bisexuals, who often do not have the supportive structures available to process the differences they feel internally. Authenticity is a great struggle when one has to swim against the powerful current of familial and social conformity. This process is similar for the parents and close friends of the GLBT community, who are also often living in the shame and confusion of secrecy. With whom will they process their struggles in making room for that which they have so little understanding? According to Kohlberg, without the stimulation of new viewpoints that challenge former views, people may not be able to reach higher levels of cognition or reasoning. Without knowing the stories of people who struggle to fit into society, they may not develop the necessary compassion that would motivate them to consider the viewpoint of another. If a person has limited most of his or her dialogues with people within a particular religious community, the potential for growing and developing in some ways may also be arrested.

Adult Faith Development: James Fowler

Although key figures in psychology such as Piaget, Karl Jung, and Kohlberg had all done some research on faith development, a solid theory of faith development did not emerge until 1981, when Fowler presented his six-stage model. Since that time, Fowler's theory of faith development has become the most widely accepted model.

Fowler believed that human beings were "potentiated," or gifted at birth with a readiness to develop faith. Some studies have suggested that therapists may not be as religiously oriented or informed as their clients (Wing, 1997, http://www.hope.edu/acedemic/psychology/335/webrep/faithdev.html):

> In one survey, 90% of the United States population believed in a divine being, and for one third of this population, their belief was a strong conviction. In many cases, these differences in religious beliefs cause a separation between the therapist and the client. Especially in these types of situations, it is beneficial for therapists to have an understanding of Fowler's theory of faith stages. Comprehending what stage a person is at in their faith development will give a therapist increased awareness and allow them to draw upon the very resources of a person's life to help them resolve problems commonly encountered in spiritual and psychological growth.

Spirituality and the Therapist

Parrott and Steele (1995) suggested that professors teaching psychology should be required to have knowledge in both fields of theology and psychotherapy. They also stated that "students of psychology should understand the implications of Fowler's theory so that they can learn effectively in classrooms full of people who may be at different stages than themselves and therefore may see things from a different perspective." (Wing, 1997)

If we apply this idea to that of a therapist's or pastor's office, the relevance is obvious. It is beneficial to assess not only a client's stage of faith development but also the therapist's level of faith development. It is possible that a client's understanding of faith may be on a higher level than his or her therapist. Young adults who are self-defined homosexuals and people of faith need to be taken seriously. A therapist who has adequately assessed a client's faith development may be more able to direct the client into new stages of moral and spiritual growth that will help the client's functioning. When persons understand Fowler's six stages of development, they may find themselves with an increased level of connection to others:

> According to Lownsdale (1997) faith has a language of its own that can easily be ignored or misunderstood if the therapist ... does not connect the meaning of a person's words to faith. Knowing what a person's faith means to him or her related to the stage they are at will allow a much deeper level of understanding between two people, and according to some psychologists is necessary for the success of psychology in a faith centered society. (Wing, 1997 pp. 1–2)

Fowler's Theory in Six Stages

Stage 1: Intuitive–Protective (ages 4–7).   At this stage a child's faith is full of fantasy and imitation that is often powerfully and permanently influenced by the examples, moods, and stories of the faith of his or her parents. Here we find the first awareness of death, sex, and the strong taboos that regulate families and their respective cultures.

Stage 2: Mythic Literal (age 7–11)

Here the community of faith is the basis for belief, and a child identifies with the rules of conduct within that community. Beliefs are literal interpretations, as are moral rules and attitudes. Symbols are one dimensional and literal in meaning. Although this is most often the faith development of a late grade school child, sometimes this stage is also dominant in the structured beliefs of adolescents and some adults. The limitations of literalness can result in overcontrolling, stilted perfectionism, or "works righteousness." It can also cause someone to overidentify with being bad because when others in authority do not think of them favorably.

Stage 3: Synthetic Conventional (age 12+)
In this stage, a person's experience of the world now extends beyond the family. People have begun to know why they believe but feel the struggle to conform to the majority, which rewards or punishes following the rules that have been laid down by the authority (e.g., church or Bible). At this stage, a person is learning to perceive hierarchy in his or her authority figures and the self is validated as seen by others. Identity is a synthesis of "my group" and others.

Stage 4: Individuating–Reflective (age 18+)
This is where young adults face the tensions between themselves and others and begin to face their commitments and beliefs seriously. At this stage, faith becomes uniquely one's own and is often accompanied by the struggle to grow and understand newfound internal beliefs.

Stage 5: Paradoxical–Consolidated (age 30+ or midlife)
Here, a person begins to realize the paradoxes of faith while learning to live with his or her faith and questioning. People at this stage begin to see other beliefs that may also be valid and then synthesize those beliefs internally to become their own.

Stage 6: Universalizing (age 40+)
The main characteristic of this stage, which is quite rare, is a singleness of purpose, where a person feels oneness with God, is at peace with oneself, and has learned to be comfortable with the mystery that surrounds us. People at this stage usually invest their lives in a cause larger than themselves and thus are unconcerned about the personal cost.

Spiritual Development of the Therapist

As a therapist today I find it quite interesting to look back on my own history through the lens of a faith development model, realizing that my belief systems have certainly undergone many significant changes even during my adult years.

As a child who was raised in conservative Christian home, I believed that Bible stories were literal interpretations of reality. Using this (Stage 2) as a template I was like many young people in their late teens, who had some religious experiences that were similar to that of my peers and formative to my adult life. As I reflect on the next stage of development (Stage 3),

I can see how those beliefs have been continually modified to understand my faith in conjunction with a variety of expanded life experiences and higher education. Looking back to my 20s and 30s, I can remember living with a rather rigid perspective of moral reasoning that was based on a very literal interpretation of the Bible (which would be right on target with Kohlberg and Fowler's Stage 4). However, as life events occurred, such as raising children and befriending a more diverse community of people than during my youth, I had to reexamine my former beliefs to find a way to live between the tensions of differing belief systems. I don't think I really began to enter Fowler's fifth stage until I was in my early 40s, when I was an Evangelical pastor ministering to people living with AIDS. My former perceptions were greatly challenged when I witnessed homosexuals embracing faith with newfound passions that gave them great strength to cope with the eventuality of their death to AIDS. Now in my 50s, I am still very aware of being a work in progress, trying to make sense of my world of faith and life experiences and writing this book as well as my own personal theologies. I can only hope to begin one day to have the courage to embrace Stage 6.

Sexual Identity Models

Some of the best-known models for sexual identity development were created by Richard Troiden, Vivienne Cass and Eli Coleman. These models were based largely on information gathered from adult men by asking about their experiences of coming out, and they highlight possible dilemmas and pathways for healthy homosexual development. Although all three models are more than 30 years old and speak about the coming out process in past decades, they can be invaluable reading for therapists who work with gay and lesbian clients.

However, when it comes to discussing any kind of coming out model, it is important to remind ourselves that developmental models can only depict general patterns in a given populace. Instead of setting up hard and fast rules of development, it is necessary to take into account that people are sure to encounter life very differently due to the makeup of their personality and the unique circumstances in which they find themselves.

Anyone who has encountered a death and dying process knows that very few people work through stages of grief in the same order or with equal time spent in each stage (i.e., the Kubler-Ross grief cycle consists of seven stages: shock, denial, anger, bargaining, depression, testing, and acceptance, (Kubler-Ross, 1969). When it comes to providing a model for the coming out process, some people will move through certain developmental stages very quickly, whereas others will take years to develop an integrated personal identity. What often makes a difference in developing a positive personal identity is to have a supportive family and societal attitudes that allow a person to become a full member of the community.

Identity Formation

The process of developing and maturing into adulthood requires children to walk a fine line between identifying solely as one of the family and individuating themselves as adults. Forming a consistent and stable identity is one of the major goals of developing and maturing into adulthood, but a large part of that depends on the congruence between how persons see themselves and how others see them. As youth learn how to form relationships with others, they are also learning how to relate their own identity. Children learn to view themselves through the lens of their family and culture, which could be ethnic or religious in nature. This process of individuating and integrating the inner self with the environment is a difficult transition for any child, but what queer children understand about themselves from the eyes of their community and family is often very confusing. On one hand, they may feel loved and treasured, but on the other they may feel shame and judgment whenever their parents and families ignore or ridicule sexual minorities. Queer children, then, are left with the task of dealing with what appears to be an unwanted and unlovable part of themselves. It seems they have only two choices: They must either learn to reject the idea that being gay is pathological or reject part of their own inner truth.

Cass's Model of Sexual Identity Development
All three of the sexual identity models mentioned previously (Cass, Coleman, and Troiden) attempted to capture the process of developmental milestones that homosexual youth move through as they develop their own sexual identity. All sexual identity models speak of the dilemmas queer youth face, such as the first inklings of coming into oneself through inner awareness, confusion, experimentation, and exploration to the acceptance stage of coming out to oneself and then to various modes of integration as they come out to the world.

Cass's model of sexual identity formation not only provides a highly developed explication of psychological process but also has six developmental stages that correlate well with Kohlberg's model of moral reasoning and Fowler's model of faith development. The sequence of developmental stages begins with identity confusion and ends with identity synthesis. Cass's basic assumption is, "There is a drive to resolve cognitive, behavioral, and affective incongruence by accepting and integrating same gender orientation within the overall concept of self. This process involves a confrontation with feelings of personal and social alienation, followed by the adoption of more positive attitudes toward same gender orientation" (Elizur & Ziv, 2001). Using Cass's model of six interconnecting stages for sexual identity as a template, I add comments from my interviews here to make personal our understanding of the identity integration process. Various stage developments represent what it may take for persons to work through their feelings of alienation in heterosexual society while increasing their sense of self-confidence in their own identity. Troiden's and Coleman's models can be found in more complete form in Table 3.1.

Stage 1: Identity Confusion
Persons in this beginning stage of a gay identity are often living with the question, "Who am I?" They have begun to feel like they are different from peers, and a sense of personal alienation is growing. Though they are conscious of some kind of same-sex feelings or behaviors, they have rarely disclosed their inner turmoil to others.

Jim spoke of this time in his life in these terms:

> At some underlying level, I'm 10 years old. Already I realize that something is different. I felt, even at that age that I was ... that there was some fundamentally important difference ... between me and the other little boys my age. I didn't really know what that difference was, entirely at that time, by any means, ... but I really think I had a sense of that going on, even in that moment.. So that was partly why, I believe, I couldn't go forward [at the altar call in his family's church] at that moment. I believe that I realized that I couldn't in all honesty say those words at that time. I think that was the emotional quandary I was in at that moment ... that salvation was available to everyone else but I knew, for a fact that it wasn't for me, from what I heard already.

There is also a conflict in the socialization process, for example, when a young woman who has felt a desire for intimacy with other women encounters the societal expectation that young girls should someday marry and have a family. Similarly, one of the young men I interviewed, the only child of a very religious family, said that before he came to terms

TABLE 3.1 Comparison of Developmental Stage Models

AGE	Piaget: Cognitive Development	Kohlberg: Moral Reasoning	Fowler: Faith Development	Cass: Sexual Identity	Troiden: Sexual Identity	Coleman: Sexual Identity
0-2	**1. Sensorimotor:** Development of movement, senses and object permanence	**1. Obedience-Punishment Orientation** (to age 10); "It is bad because I will be punished." There is only one view; same as parents				
2-7	**2. Preoperational:** Learning motor skills development	**2. Individualism Exchange** (ages 7+) Aware of different viewpoints and relativism	**1. Intuitive:** (Ages 4-7); Stories/ fantasies imitate parents' beliefs; first awareness of death and sex.			
7-11	**3. Concrete Operational Stage:** (ages 7-11) Beginning to reason concrete events **4. Formal Operational Stage** (age 11+) The beginning of abstract reasoning.	**3. Conventional Moral Reasoning** (ages 10+) Development of good interpersonal relationships. "Good" depends on one's motives.	**2. Mythic Literal** (ages 7-11) Beliefs are those of the community. Scriptures and symbols are interpreted literally.	**1. Identity Confusion** (ages 8-10) Feeling different from same-sex peers, semi-conscious of same-sex feelings or behaviors resulting in anxiety, shame, or ambivalence.	**1. Sensitization** (age: pre-puberty) child feels marginalized/ different from same sex peers.	**1. Pre-Coming Out:** Not conscious of same-sex feelings because of strong defenses that keep unwanted knowledge from reaching conscience. Feeling different from others, but not understanding why.

(Continued)

TABLE 3.1   Comparison of Developmental Stage Models (Continued)

AGE	Piaget Cognitive Development	Kohlberg: Moral Reasoning	Fowler: Faith Development	Cass: Sexual Identity	Troiden: Sexual Identity	Coleman: Sexual Identity
12 and up			*3. Synthetic Conventional* (ages 12+) Knows one's own beliefs yet attempts to conform with majority. Self is validated by others and group identity.	*2. Identity Comparison* Ambivalence continues, "I may be gay or not." Feelings of being unique, and not fitting in anywhere. Learns to pass as hetero, may understand self as gay but sees behavior as wrong. May seek professional help to change orientation.	*2. Identity Confusion* (ages 11-13) Uncertain, but knows he is not straight. May be moving to "I am gay," experience sexual arousal and use stigma management to cope with difference. May seek help to change or escape through drugs, denial, or therapy.	*2. Coming Out* Semi-conscious of same sex feelings, fantasies, and thoughts. Lots of confusion. May disclose this to a few friends while avoiding family members who may reject such ideas.

	4. Maintaining Social Order (ages 16-adult)	4. Individuating-Reflective (ages 18-up)	3. Identity Tolerance	3. Identity Assumption	3. Exploration (15+)
16+	Emphasis on civil law to support one's culture. Individual rights are subject to approved authority. (i.e. Bible)	Reflects on tensions of difference between self and others and commits to one's own beliefs. Faith becomes personal.	"I am probably gay" but only tolerating gay identity. Devalues gay culture, and attempts to inhibit gay behaviors. If positive gay contacts occur, a positive view of gay identity is possible.	"I am gay" but not socialized with other gay people. Self-hatred may be diminishing as person learns to identify with gay subculture. May learn to pass as straight to fit in with peers.	Begins to experiment with new sexual identity. Self-image begins to improve. However, if this is not afforded in own culture (or religion,) person may undergo development lag that lasts for years.

(Continued)

TABLE 3.1 Comparison of Developmental Stage Models (Continued)

AGE	Piaget Cognitive Development	Kohlberg: Moral Reasoning	Fowler: Faith Development	Cass: Sexual Identity	Troiden: Sexual Identity	Coleman: Sexual Identity
18+		**5. Social Contract** (ages 20-30) Striving to create a better society while realizing that society's rules are not always right or moral. "Good" society protects the equal rights of all people. Individual rights may take priority over social rules.		**4. Identity Acceptance** (17-19) Meets gay friends and views self more positively. May pass as straight, limit contact with gays and neg. family members. New identity disclosed selectively. **5. Identity Pride** (20+) Claims gay culture as "my people." Angry at straight society's rejections, may devalue straight institutions and turn activist.	**4. Commitment** (ages 18+) "I am gay" and committed. Realizes being gay is not what one does, but who one is. May begin to enter same-sex love realtionship and come out to significant others. Makes choices to cover, blend, or convert.	**4. First Relationships** These often do not last because the basic coming out process is not yet finished. Relationship may be too possessive, one sided, and immature. **5. Integration** (ages 20-30) Public and private identities merge into one unified self-image. Relationships are mutual and less possessive. Person now ready to cope with life.

30+

6. Universal Rights	5. Paradoxical Consolidation	6. Identity Synthesis
(30+) Living by internal principles rather than rules. Rules must be based in justice. *Universalizing* (40+ and very rare) Singleness of purpose, peace with self, one with God, and invested in causes beyond self.	age 30+) Seeing paradox in one's faith and learning to live with the questions. Also sees how others' beliefs may be valid and synthesizes them to become one's own.	(age 30+) Realizes that some straights can be trusted. Sees less dichotomy between gay and straight. Personality is fully integrated in society.

with his feelings of being different, he experienced a tremendous pressure to eventually marry a woman and produce offspring:

> There was always this growing angst in my mind, of the pressure of having to get married one day. And … I just didn't know what that would look like. Because I knew that I would not be able to perform for that woman … and you know I think, … in hindsight of course, it's clear to me that it would have been such a tragedy for both people, the gay man and the woman that he chooses to marry for him to be in that relationship, but all I could think about back then was all the expectation. But looking back, I realize that, you know, that wasn't a realistic expectation.

Stage 2: Identity Comparison
This stage could also be called the rationalization or bargaining stage, where the person thinks, "I may be a homosexual, but then again, I may be bisexual," or, "Maybe this is just temporary," or, "My feelings of attraction are simply for just one person of my own sex, and this is a special case." In this stage, there is a heightened sense of not belonging anywhere with the corresponding feeling, "I am the only one in the world like this."

According to Cass, a person has four options for reducing his or her feelings of alienation (Blumenfeld, 1994):

1. A person can learn to react positively to being "different," which is seen as something desirable, and still to pass as a heterosexual in public situations. Four ways of using the "passing" strategy may be (a) to avoid risky situations; (b) to control personal information by presenting only select aspects of one's self to others; (c) to cultivate images of heterosexuality or asexuality; or (d) to adopt a stance of detachment from anything perceived to be homosexual.
2. Some people find that they can accept the "homosexual" meaning of their behavior but discover they do not want to have anything to do with identifying with homosexual self-images.
3. Others learn to accept their inner self as "homosexual" and find meaning in their sexual orientation but view any sexual behavioral as undesirable.
4. Some see the homosexual self and behaviors as undesirable and try to find ways to change both.

Katrina tells about some of her confusion at this stage of her own development:

> Even in college I didn't think I was … gay. I remember one girl in my dorm, [when] I played a lot of sports, [was] very competitive, [and] had long blonde hair. I thought … I was going get married and have kids—just like everyone else—and she said, "Well, I'm gay," and I said, "Well I'm glad you are really happy!" [big laugh] It was like 1970, and I was very naïve! I really didn't know

about homosexuality myself at the time. That was when I was 23 and 24, and I was teaching in the late '70s. I did have some relationships with women when I was in college ... [In my] first homosexual relationship, [I was] very devoted and loyal to that person ... until she found someone else. I was devastated. I was up and down and didn't want to give her up. After that I figured I didn't want to get close to anybody, so when I was teaching I was very, very careful. I started going out with a guy who wanted to be a policeman and treated me like royalty. He spoiled me! ... I really tried ... but I finally said, "It's not you; it's me. I thought that I could break this ... 'habit' [chuckle], but this is me. I am ... you know [a lesbian]."

Stage 3: Identity Tolerance

In this "I am probably a homosexual" stage, the person begins to contact other homosexuals so as to counteract the feelings of isolation and alienation but at this point still merely tolerates rather than fully accepts a gay or lesbian identity. However, at this time the feeling of "I do not belong with heterosexuals either" grows stronger.

Katie was part of a religious culture that declared homosexual behavior to be a sin. Although she felt more attracted to women, she also wanted to remain an active member in the church:

It was pretty torturous for a lot of years. I did fall in love with a roommate my freshman year in college, and, lived with that woman for 8 years after school— well, through college and for another 4 years—and in a nonsexual relationship because that's what we felt like God had called us to. And so during that first few months or year of falling in love and kind of realizing what was going on, that was a huge time of crisis. I don't know what her sexual orientation is—we didn't really talk about it.

If the contacts with other homosexuals are unrewarding, the person most likely will devalue the gay subculture. If this is the case, personal contact with other gay and lesbian people will diminish while the person also attempts to inhibit all homosexual behaviors. Sometimes with negative contacts, identity foreclosure can occur.

However, positive contacts can have the affect of making other gay and lesbian people appear more significant and more positive to the person at this stage, which leads to a more favorable sense of self and a great commitment to a homosexual self-identity.

Coleman's model adds an aspect of this stage of development called *exploration*, where a person begins to explore interactions with other homosexuals and experiments with a new sexual identity. Whereas many people with same-sex orientations enter this period during their adolescent years, others who are not afforded this opportunity because of the

social taboos of their families, cultures, or religions may undergo a subsequent developmental lag. Therefore, some gay and lesbian people do not
enter this developmental adolescence until years (or decades) after their
chronological adolescence.

Brett, a man in his early 60's when I interviewed him, is a good example
of someone having a delayed stage of sexual identity development:

> I'd been divorced about a year, which on the surface didn't seem like it had
> anything to do with being gay, because my ex-wife wanted the divorce so it
> looked like she was leaving me. However, I did have a lot of gay friends, and
> all the gay dads I knew had to go through all this conflict of breaking up with
> their families; it was all their fault. Dad's leaving and it's because he is gay.
> Instead, my trauma was like, poor me, I've lost my kid. However, a year after
> the divorce, I began to wonder what this thing was. I wondered if I wanted to
> be gay? I decided to try that out when I went to the east coast that summer.
> So I went to Boston, and came back knowing that I was gay! That was exactly
> what I was wondering about

Figure 3.1   Mirror, Mirror.

Stage 4: Identity Acceptance

A person in this stage continues to increase his or her contact with other gay and lesbian people and begins to form friendships. This enables a person not only to evaluate other sexual minorities more positively but also to begin to accept rather than merely tolerate his or her gay self-image. The earlier questions of "Who am I?" and "Where do I belong?" have been answered by this stage.

Although some of those earlier questions have been answered, a person in this stage is left with many incongruencies with which to cope. Coping strategies may include continuing to pass as heterosexual and limiting contacts with heterosexuals who threaten their budding self-identity. This may include limiting time with antagonistic family members and friends while also selectively disclosing their homosexual identity to significant heterosexuals, such as their parents or siblings.

For some people, like Jeff, the moment of identity acceptance was a time of emancipation:

> You know, I came out just over [the age of] 20, to myself. That was a spiritual moment for me. In retrospect, the weight of the world lifted from my shoulders. I said, "I am a homosexual. I'm gay!" Could have had a V-8! You know? [big laugh] And that's the way it felt, and when I think back now on that moment, I was feeling like I was—I had a higher power's love wrapped around me at that moment, holding me up and saying, "You are all right."

Clint told of how he finally felt freed from a great burden when he came out at age 40:

> I realized that it required a great percentage of my personal energy to keep under wraps all that awareness and [to] build walls of protection—and once I no longer found it necessary to build and maintain those walls of protection, they were able to be disintegrated. Then this rush of new energy, which was my whole self, became available to me. And then I assessed a spirit inside myself that I hadn't had any idea previously existed.

For some, however, the path of coming out to oneself and the world has been a very tumultuous journey. Although Beth came out to herself at age 19, her journey toward self-acceptance took another 10 years:

> I think right when I first allowed myself to identify myself as lesbian, I stopped going to church for a couple of years. And it was [tearing up] probably one of the best things I could have done at the time; I just separated out it didn't mean I stopped praying, and doing all the normal kinds of things. I had a regular devotional during that period of time, but I absolutely stopped going

to church and tried to listen to my own feelings more. It was such a process. Probably for about 10 years in there, between [the ages of] 20 and 30, I really thought about killing myself. I thought about all kinds of stuff. I thought that I had listen to preacher types interpret the Bible for me and ignore my own feelings. That's when I felt like I would suffocate—[tears]—but once I thought from a theological point of what was going on—[that] the Bible is not a text-book of spirituality, I began to listen to my own feelings. After a couple of years I missed being in church and being around things that are very impor-tant to me, and then I was able to go back. I was more active in seeking a church that fit my current beliefs rather than the ones I grew up with and studied. I think it's emancipating, but—I don't know exactly how to describe it. It's such a thing over time. It's more like grounding, I think, because it's [like], "OK, now I feel centered; now things fit."

Stage 5: Identity Pride

This is the 'These are my people" stage, where the individual develops an awareness of the enormous incongruity that exists between the person's increasingly positive concept of self as lesbian or gay and an awareness of society's rejection of this orientation. The person feels anger at hetero-sexuals and devalues many of their institutions (e.g., marriage, gender role structures). The person discloses her or his identity to more and more peo-ple and wishes to be immersed in the gay or lesbian subculture, consum-ing its literature, art, and other forms of culture. For some at this stage, the combination of anger and pride energizes the person into action against perceived homophobia, producing an "activist."

Lucy came out in the early '70s and, during the interview, recalled her history of political activism. For her coming out, political awareness, and involvement in inclusive spirituality all happened at about the same time, when the women's movement began to take shape:

I came out in the early '70s in the context of the women's movement in a pro-gressive college town. It was very easy to come out in that situation. The early '70s were an amazing time, and all kinds of things were happening. So my spirituality—and my politics, my sexuality—I mean all kinds of things were evolving together. There's no way to separate them out. They were all hap-pening together. I was very politically active—I actually went to Mississippi one summer on an educational project. I was doing voters' rights, but we met in churches —I remember sitting there in a church when we sang, "We Shall Overcome."

Some of that activist energy today can be seen in the area of religious reform, as Katie, a young lesbian, reflected on where her passions were currently leading her:

I went to "Love Won Out." I still get [James] Dobson's mailings and updates from Metanoia Ministries, a local agency that seeks to heal homosexuality, so I can track what's going on and know what's being said about us …. One of their articles was a letter from "Justin" and how he'd written Metanoia and how he had been struggling and he was in college and was having feelings toward boys and didn't know what he was going to do. He hadn't ever slept with anybody, and he wanted help. They were saying what a blessing that Justin had written and that he was going to stay strong and encouraging him and trusting that he wasn't going to act out—and I thought, "O my Lord! You have a college-age man who is still celibate in America? What a total novelty! I'd say you have a pretty faithful guy here [who is] being told there's something wrong with him? I've got to find Justin. I have got to tell this kid that he's okay, that he's looking for love and that he's looking for the right things." I thought that maybe if I go to "Love Won Out," I can find [Justin's] equivalent and tell them that there is hope and freedom and integrity and Christlikeness and that to be gay does not mean you need to be promiscuous, drug using, [or] clubbing and participating in lots of negative behaviors that will have serious consequences in your life. And so I went, looking for conversation and relationship, and met a number of people who were willing to dialogue—and you know one of our new best friends was having a smoke in a corner, and I walked up and said, "You know I thought I was courageous being here as an 'out' lesbian. But you? Smoking on church property? That's one brave lady!" [laughter] And she said, "Well, I've got you on both counts!" We had a great conversation for an hour or so—and really—it just really felt like God was saying, "You are right where you are supposed to be; you are doing my work, loving people who are being told they are unlovable." It's a joy. So I think that my sexuality is a big piece of the spirituality God had intended for me."

Michelle found that working with other "hurting people and watching Christ transform their lives" is where her passion is strongest. However, she says:

The most inhibiting is probably my own anger toward church institutions and public institutions for the damage, whether knowingly or unknowingly, that causes so much hurt for gay people. It is definitely a challenge for me to keep that anger in check and not vent when I see those things happening. I also have to deal with my own hurt for the institutions and people who have discarded me because I have embraced who I am.

Stage 6: Identity Synthesis
Whereas in Stage 5 intense anger at heterosexuals or the "us and them" attitudes may be evident, in Stage 6 there is a softening to a reflection that some heterosexuals are supportive and can be trusted. However, those who are not supportive are further devalued. Although some anger remains at the ways gays and lesbians are treated in this society, this becomes less intense. A deep sense of gay pride continues, but persons in this stage also begin to perceive less

of a dichotomy between the heterosexual and the gay and lesbian community. This final stage marks the integral aspect of their internal identity and its integration with the complete structure of the personality.

Clint, a minister in a welcoming and affirming church in Seattle, said that he felt a greater sense of peace once he was able to be in the right environment:

> You know, frankly, I find discussions of homosexuality pretty boring. I'm not very interested in it, because that's not what my life is about. That is not what my congregation's about. You know, there are so many things right now in the world that are absolutely needing our attention that though I would never put down this issue as something that isn't important, it is not my major focus. Anyway, once I came to a place where I was nurtured and supported and could be whole and available to myself, then I realized that the strength and stamina and courage and insistence that I was able to develop in those years—where I had to build all those walls and protection actually had a value for me now. I realized when I look back: "Good heavens, I am a really strong person!" I put up with a lot—but didn't allow that distracting and negative agenda and energy to completely deplete my opportunities to serve and do good or to have a full and happy life. And now without all that distraction and [a greater] sense of my whole self, if you will, I feel I can value and maximize those courageous ways of being that I learned back in those years. So that's really an interesting "flip side" of coming out of the shame of oppression.

Patrick, a social worker in his mid-50s who has been out for more than 30 years, said that today he lives his life connecting to people and their spirituality as part of the universe:

> It's just pretty neat. [He smiles. When the interviewer asks what causes his smile:] Oh, you know, just the people who you see and the reflection they are— like another unique, beautiful piece of the universe. It's taking time to walk around and look at your garden and smell stuff and see stuff, and people are the same way—they are a neat, beautiful part of the world and the universe. Part of that poem always comes back to me—Desiderata, "Wherever you are the world is unfolding exactly as it should be, and you are doing exactly what you should be." There's part of it that really speaks to me. You don't have to be anything other than who you are, because that's what you are supposed to do, that's who you are supposed to be. A lot of life is learning more about who you are and letting yourself be. It's a mystery to me why you can't just be that way from the get go—there is a lot of internal learning and letting go of expectations and understanding who you are and unfolding of the flower somehow, but it's worth it.

Current Research

It has been suggested that although these developmental models may be helpful, they do have one major downfall: "Most profoundly, they are not true in a universal sense. Although a linear progression is intuitively appealing, extant research suggests it seldom characterizes the lives of real sexual minority youths" (Savin-Williams, 2001, p. 16).

Current researchers like Eric M. Dube, Lisa M. Diamond, and Ritch Savin-Williams interviewed youth (rather than using adults) as previous researchers did in the '70s and '80s. When they attempted to categorize them into various stages of development, these researchers found that young people desire, behave, and develop in various ways. For example, Dube found that young men often experience attraction to other men before they have sex and then label themselves gay. "Youth studied prior to 1990 were more likely to have sex first. Youth after 1990 were more likely to use other forms of experimentation like dating and Internet chatting before they had sex" (Stone Fish & Harvey, 2005, p. 55).

In Savin-Williams (2001), only 2% of the young men he interviewed followed anything close to a stage model, and none of the young women followed the stylized sexual identity models (Stone Fish & Harvey, 2005, p. 56). Many did not use sex to help them figure out their identity but knew who they were prior to gay sex. We need to remind ourselves not to give in to our natural impulses of labeling and categorizing to make sense of something that may be quite incomprehensible and to realize that sexual identity is complicated.

Stone Fish and Harvey (2005) therefore adopted a perspective of differential developmental trajectories that is based on Savin-Williams's (2001) research. Instead of looking at a person through six stages of development, they proposed that we examine queer youth to see how they are similar to heterosexual youth—as well as how the two groups may differ. Similarly, although both studies acknowledge that even queer youth will differ from each other, all will have to master some common developmental tasks on their path to adulthood. Although coming out is a lifelong process, it is often more difficult in the beginning stages.

Developmental Tasks, a New Paradigm

Dealing With Social Stigma

In a culture that promotes and protects heterosexuality, a queer person is bound to have an uphill battle to be authentic and open. Most youth keep their nonheterosexual identity to themselves for about 2 years before sharing this information with others. This means that gay and lesbian youth must deal with huge amounts of homophobia and social assumptions that heterosexism is superior. A major developmental task for queer persons is to reject society's negative view of homosexuality while creating their own positive view of themselves and appreciating their own sexuality.

When youth first begin to realize that they may not be heterosexual, they are confronted with devaluation of all kinds. They may feel devalued because everyone assumes they are straight. They may face "fag jokes" in their families and communities, or there may be an attitude of outright contempt for anyone who has gay feelings. This can be very confusing to younger children who are never given a clue that same-sex relationships are even a normal possibility. Because so many messages they hear are negative, they begin to internalize this devaluation and develop a deep sense of shame. It is my experience that many queer people conclude very early in life that their feelings are wrong and unnatural and therefore that there must be something wrong with them.

Dealing With a Toxic Environment

Youth who have not come out still have to deal with existing in an environment that is potentially toxic. Stressors such as isolation, self-doubt, loneliness, and poor self-esteem not only are experienced internally, but they may be accompanied by the very real fears of being found out, harassed, or cut off financially and kicked out of their homes:

> The majority of queer youth studied in the early 1990's reported verbal or physical threats of violence by their peers because of their sexual identity status (D'Augelli, 1995; Hetrick & Martin, 1987; Rosario, Rotheram-Borus, & Reid, 1996). Fifty percent of ethnic minority youth reported being ridiculed because of their homosexuality, 46% reported violent physical attacks, and the top stressors for these youth were coming out to their families or being found out and harassed by others (Rosario, Roterham-Borus, & Reid). Those who were least likely to fit gender role stereotypes were most likely to be abused (Hetrick & Martin). Most of the youth expected to be abused again, hid or avoided situations that might arouse suspicions about their sexuality, and did not report any abuse to authorities. (Stone Fish & Harvey, 2005, p. 59)

Figure 3.2   A-Bomb-in-Nation.

According to Stone Fish and Harvey (2005), researchers have shown that 20% to 40% of gay, lesbian, bisexual, and transgendered youth attempt suicide, and their risk factor is considerably elevated compared with heterosexual youth. Many factors contribute to teen suicide besides acting out or coming out at an early age, such as abuse, drug use, and family dysfunction. However alarming the suicide rate among queer youth is, we must also recognize that the reverse statistic reveals that 60% to 80% of gay teens do not fall into this category. The vast majority of queer youth deal with these stressors without becoming clinically depressed or addicts, and they go on to become well-adjusted members of society.

I must also emphasize that the self-discovery of being a sexual minority and coming to terms with being attracted to someone of the same gender is not the stressor that cripples people's development. Instead, the stress comes from having to deal with the pervasive belief that heterosexuality is not only superior but that it also is the one and only acceptable way to be a human.

Unfortunately, to survive, queer kids often learn to develop various coping techniques while living in an environment that does not allow their full self to emerge. As a result, many youth will live with a great deal of denial or will tell themselves that they are just going through a phase. Some try to fix their queerness by acting as straight as possible or by becoming perfect overachievers. Some may deny their feelings by getting pregnant or having many sexual partners of the opposite sex so that no one would assume the truth about their sexual orientation, and then there are others who become so hyperidentified with homosexuality that they encourage rejection, making it a challenge for anyone to get close to them.

Self-Acceptance

Self-acceptance is an essential task of adolescent development for queer individuals. Research suggests that although adolescent transitions can be very difficult for queer youth, once gays and lesbians establish an adult identity, with adult resources and coping tools, there is no functional difference between heterosexuals and homosexuals.

Many queer youth keep their sexual identities hidden, which makes validation of self by others difficult. There may be a period of time where gay youth may have great difficulty reconciling the person they believe themselves to be with the person everyone else thinks they are. What complicates this is that there are no normal dating rituals, dances, or ways to explore what it means to be a congruent sexual being, which makes developing a positive sense of self very challenging:

> "As Comedian Ellen Degeneres famously said, no one throws you a coming out party and says, "Yeah! You are out" This makes it challenging to develop an integrated, positive sense of self. "This is especially true for adolescents who are managing hormones, self-identity, and knowledge about self, all under the microscope of family, peers, and culture. How do you accept yourself when a big part of you is pathologized, ignored, and disallowed? (Stone Fish & Harvey, 2005, p. 61)

Self-differentiation is a huge developmental task for all people, but to cope with the social stigma and toxic environments queer youth must also face the task of developing a sexual minority identity, which is also known as *coming out*. Because everyone assumes they will become heterosexuals, gay, bisexual, and transgendered youth are often surprised and confused when they come out to themselves because they begin to realize for the first time that their feelings are not the norm. So a task for queer individuals that goes beyond what heterosexual kids have to deal with is to learn to value themselves in a culture that devalues their very being. This life-long process of self-acceptance begins when youth first identify differently from the norm. Once again, when one has a supportive family and affirming subculture, positive self-acceptance is more easily achieved.

Coming Out to Others

In the 21st century, queer youth are more likely to know gay and lesbian people, to be aware of the local gay community, and to have a more positive (or at least not totally negative) image of themselves due to media. It would make sense, then, that with a cultural shift toward greater openness and acceptance, the average age of youth self-identifying as gay is decreasing.

In the past, queer folk had no media images, role models, or safe community where they could come out. To say that gays felt unsafe was an understatement. Thanks to Parents, Families, and Friends of Lesbians and Gays (PFLAG), previous generations received help in coming out after self-identifying in their 20s, but there was little support for queer youth under the age of 15. In fact, queer youth were relatively unheard of even into the early 1990s. Many people waited to deal with their sexuality until well into their 20s when they had the emotional, physical, and financial resources of adults. This is borne out in my own survey, where the average age of coming out was 25.

Today, there are many ways out of the closet, and they are often complex. Now youth are more likely to self-identify earlier than in previous generations, and in many cases they identify themselves as gay before they experiment in romantic and sexual relationships. Adopting a sexual minority label is often more about having a sense of identity—that is, identifying with a community of people with whom people feel a kindred spirit—rather than focusing only on sexual behavior.

Most youth are more likely to come out to their friends before they come out to their families. They are more likely to come out to their same-age peers, and if this is successful, it becomes a catalyst for further disclosures to family and other friends. Although peers are important to all adolescents as they grow through various developmental stages, for queer youth, peers may be even more important because they often feel afraid that their parents will not understand them or reject them altogether if they found out about their sexual identity.

Coming Out to Family

A queer person often remembers choosing to come out or not to disclose or be found out by his or her family as one of the biggest milestones in his or her life. For many gays and lesbians, a particular transition in their development occurred when a parent discovered their sexuality. However, this may not occur in every queer person's life, even though many people believe that the queer person who never comes out to family will not be able to achieve the fullest aspect of emotional maturity. Sometimes it not in a person's best interest, because he or she knows that the family environment will only become more toxic. Many queer people live full and satisfying lives, are well connected in their supportive communities, and are not out to their families.

The fact is that gay or lesbian youth who do come out to their families risk a great deal, including their survival. I say this because adolescents living at home are still dependent on their families for physical and emotional support. So if they misjudge their parents, they stand to lose a lot. This shows how intense this internal conflict can be. Is it better to deceive the family so you can be assured of food and shelter or to risk being out and be on the street? Either way, there are risks and consequences that are less than ideal. Queer adolescents who are often overwhelmed by toxic social stigmas need the support and validation and protection offered by loved ones: "Unlike members of ethnic, religious or racial minorities, queer youth cannot and do not expect their families to accept or tolerate their identity, much less help them nurture it" (Stone Fish & Harvey, 2005, p. 65).

The sad fact is that some parents reject their children, kick them out of the house, cut off all ties when their child discloses something of their core nature that is unacceptable to the parents' way of thinking. This is what youth have to weigh when they are deciding to come out to their families. What a person hopes for when coming out to family is to be closer and more honest with family members and also to increase his or her self-confidence and self-esteem—and when parents respond well, this naturally is provided.

However, not all parents will act in the most appropriate ways due to their own homophobia, cultural shame, or conservative religious views.

For some reason, I am reminded of the line from the movie *A Few Good Men* (Rob Reiner, 1992) where Jack Nicholson roars at Tom Cruise, "You want the truth? You can't handle the truth!" Although it may be painful to continually hide one's true identity from the family, some adolescents will do so because they know that to come out would only add to their distress and increase conflicts in the home.

> Coming out to relatives does introduce sexual behavior as a topic, but mostly it demands the negotiation or re-negotiation of family connections. The naming of relationships, who calls whom what, and who is part of the family and who is not define how we are all connected. How an individual comes out in his or her family can also set the stage for how the family will later incorporate a partner. (Stone Fish & Harvey, 2005, p. 66)

Integration: Putting Several Models Together

Being a self-actualized human being is no small task. To move through different stages of development is often a painful process but is one that eventually rewards a person with his or her own unique version of being human. Every child must move from motor skills management to higher levels of reasoning. Most adolescents feel a need to push away from their parents to realize that they are separate individuals while finding a new way to remain connected. Young adulthood often begins with a rather black-and-white phase of reasoning that eventually blossoms into a more relativistic worldview. However, what often goes unacknowledged by society at large, is that there are times when a person is growing through several developmental stages at once, which spurs frustration as to how to integrate one's cognitive, moral, faith, and sexual development. This is difficult enough for the heterosexual population, but gays or lesbians have the additional hurdle of nondominant sexuality that often lacks the support necessary for healthy development and successful integration into society.

Integrating Development Models for 10-Year-Olds

When you put this chapter's development models together you can start to see some systemic patterns emerge (Appendices 3.1–3.4). For instance, when we look at the moral reasoning ability of a 10-year-old child, who would be in Kohlberg's preconventional stage (Crain, 1985), we realize that the child's self-knowledge basically imitates his parent's views.

When we look at that same child's developing belief system in Fowler's model (Wing, 1997), we understand that his belief system is basically the same as his parents and that his use of religious symbols and stories are understood in a one-dimensional, literal sense. However, this age is also when a gay child may first begin to experience himself as different from his same-sex peers. In the people I interviewed for this book, several of them mentioned this stage of their development as a time when they did not yet have the language or reasoning for that difference or a culture that could help them assimilate what they were experiencing. As a result many internalized their difference with feelings of anxiety or shame for not quite fitting in as they would like to.

Integrating Development Models for Adolescents

When a girl becomes an adolescent, according to Kohlberg, she is becoming aware of the differences of other viewpoints instead of the one worldview presented by her parents. Fowler's model would say that her faith systems are all about belonging to a group at the cost of one's true self, which in turn will cause much of the ambivalence Cass discussed in Stage 2 of her model of sexual development.(Blumenfeld, 1994) At this point she may be thinking, *Maybe I'm gay, and maybe I'm not.* Since adolescents will do almost anything to fit into a group, it should be no surprise that the highest levels of teen suicide begin to occur at this stage. If the child cannot fit in with others or find a group to identify with, her sense of alienation and feeling of being a misfit can often lead to toxic choices— increased isolation, substance abuse for the purposes of escape, and, for some, the tragic desire to end their lives.

If we look at a 16-year-old boy, Kohlberg's model (Crain, 1985, p. 122) states that by mid to late adolescence, group identity for him not only is all pervasive but is also a time when his rights are subjected to his culture. So, for example, if a child is raised in a strongly religious culture, the laws of society and approved external authorities must be obeyed, regardless of cost to self. If we look at the models for the 16-year-old boy's belief system, we ought to link Fowler's model (Wing, 1997) with Kohlberg's (Crain, 1985) because adolescent faith identity is also a reflection of that child's group identity. However, when we view the same 16-year-old through Cass's sexual identity model (Blumenfeld, 1994), we see that at this stage of formation a sexual identity begins to become more important, especially when a gay child begins to experiment. Because the dominant culture does not approve of or understand this, he can only begin to tolerate this growing sexual identity in a closeted manner.

The complexity of all of this can be appreciated when we take a systemic look at a 22-year-old gay male, mature enough to seek the help of a therapist to help him come out to his very traditional parents. The outcome may have very different results depending on the stage of faith and moral development of his parents. The therapist needs to keep in mind the possibility that this particular young adult may actually be becoming more differentiated from his parents, who could never imagine going against the wishes of their parents. He may register at the beginning of Stage 5 on Kohlberg's scale (Crain, 1985) and Stage 4 of Fowler's (Wing, 1997)—in both he is able to explore the tensions of one's faith and community. However, if his parents have spent their entire lives relating only to their very small religious community, they may have developed only Kohlberg's Stage 4 moral reasoning (Crain, 1985) and Fowler's Stage 3 faith development (Wing, 1997), both of which give great power to external authority figures. This combination could prove to be quite a challenge, but by assessing where each party is in the developmental process, the therapist would be better equipped to help the 22-year-old calmly state his growing reality while respecting the religious views of his parents. By modeling respect, while the focus of therapy turns toward creating a holding place for his parent's anxiety, his parents may learn to respect their son's courage and honesty. It would be beneficial to spend some time alone with the client's parents to help them process their grief and shame so that they can feel understood and valued before asking them if they would like to explore some other moral and theological perspectives on homosexuality. In such a case, sessions alone with each side of the crisis would be recommended before scheduling a joint session aimed at creating a new and more honest loving relationship.

Coming Out Is Not Age Related

What do adolescents do when their internal reality does not match their external socialization? Many begin to come out to their closest friends while avoiding the possible rejection by family. In fact, many adolescents will avoid telling family, not because family is not important to them but rather because family is so significant that they can't imagine risking alienation or loss of those people who are vital for their survival.

As the self is continually subjected to the views of the dominant cultures, gay people must learn to cope by learning how to pass as heterosexuals, avoiding any deep conversations with family, and keeping their gay and straight worlds from ever meeting. For some people who think their families or belief systems cannot make room for differing sexual orientations, this stage of closeting may last for years or even decades. However, when queer people can find a way to interact with positive models of homosexuality, they not only can improve their socials skills but also can greatly enhance their self-image without having to go through years or decades of internal turmoil.

Rather than jumping to conclusions about the lesbian affair of a 45-year-old married woman, it may also be wise to find out when her sexual identity development became arrested and how she is sexually identifying today. She may have married a person of the opposite sex to fit into their religious culture and may have never felt allowed to "come in" to herself during her child-raising years. Maybe she was just following an unexplored sexuality of her youth; maybe she is bisexual and needing some greater intimate connections with women within the confines of her marriage; or maybe it really is time to dissolve the 25-year marriage that she felt forced into, so she can live more congruently. I realize that none of these reasons will justify an extramarital affair, nor restore the damage it may have done to others; however, listening for such information may provide greater understanding for people who have found themselves in this kind of situation.

According to Stone Fish & Harvey (2005), the age for queer youth to self-identify as a sexual minority "has been decreasing at least since the onset of the gay and lesbian rights movement (p. 24). It seems that previous to this time, queer people did not feel safe to come out until they were no longer living in their parents' culture. My survey supports this, given that interviewees' average age of coming out was about 25. This age seems much older than today's demographics, which show youth coming out" to parents, on average, between the ages of 18 and 19 years, with a wide range, from 13 to "never" (Savin-Williams, 2001, p. 214). It is believed this is largely due to society's increasing stands of justice and acceptance for all minority groups.

What I have noticed in the therapy office is that many times a person's chronological age does not match his or her emotional development. Or a person may be very articulate about belief systems but may have a very difficult time with moral reasoning and thinking in terms of justice. For example, when a 20-year-old gay man has just recently come out, he can't be expected to be at the same stage of sexual identity or relational develop-ment as his heterosexual peers, who have had 5 years of dating experiences encouraged and applauded by friends, family, and greater society. Because his years of sexual identity development were largely held in the closet, he has not learned how to date or even how to be friends with people in whom he is sexually interested, which often leads to a great deal of drama and chaos that seems more like something from early heterosexual adoles-cence. In Blumenfeld's article (1994) showing the differences among dif-fering sexual identity models, Coleman (1981) is noted for stating that first relationships are often rather short because the coming out process has not yet been completed.

Society Still Hinders the Coming Out Process

Although there is currently greater acceptance of gays and lesbians than in times past, social pressures and expectations still hinder the coming out process, which makes healthy development a challenge. For instance, we have not learned how to make room for same-sex dating. Let's face it: Due to decades of ignorant teachings about sexual prejudice, the sight of an openly gay couple in public sets off people's internal alarms. While a young hetero-sexual couple makes out on a park bench or steams up the windows of Dad's Impala, most people just look past it with a smile or say to their walking companions, "Remember when?" However, if two homosexuals hold hands while viewing a spectacular sunset, people become "uncomfortable."

Is this discomfort based in encountering difference? Or is it the dis-comfort about encountering the incomprehensible—not understanding how a person could have such feelings for a person of the same gender? Or does this strong reaction have something to do with the onlooker's fear of his or her own feelings about being attracted to a person of the same gender? There may some truth to this last statement, because we are sexual beings with a wide variety of sexual thoughts and fantasies; most peo-ple have at least wondered about what a homosexual encounter might be like (and have had dreams they never reveal even to best friends). Some people are so uneasy with their own sexual feelings that they shun any kind of attachment or close friendship with a person of the same gender.

Perhaps in this stage of human development in the 21st century, most of society no longer views homosexuality as evil but rather as something that makes them uncomfortable, something they would care not to think about, something that is just best left out of sight. But when people get uncomfortable, they can find all kinds of rationalizations for prejudice and judgment.

> Prejudice is a burden that confuses the past,
> threatens the future
> and renders the present inaccessible.

Maya Angelou

Our society continues to inhibit the development of gays and lesbians with laws that do not guard against sexual discrimination in housing or the workplace while upholding laws that prohibit gay relationships from becoming mature, with the societal privileges and responsibilities of marriage. The reaction to this kind of societal oppressions explains one of the later stages of Cass's (1979) sexual identity model. With straight society, the stages of identity acceptance and pride are often accompanied by anger or distrust, for this part of the community has continually rejected and devalued what gays and lesbians feel at their core—not perversion but difference. This may also lead to an increased alliance with the gay ghetto or to activism that promotes the cause of equal rights.

I find it interesting how much of one's identity occurs in the early years:

> Current research suggests that on average, youth are about 10 yrs old when they first realize they are not heterosexual, 14 when they self label, 16 when they disclose to a friend, and 18 when they tell their parents. Newman and Muzzonigro (1993) studied ethnically and racially varied male youths and found that they reported first awareness of their "gayness" between the ages of 8 and 16, with the average being 12.5 yrs. The average first crush was 12.7 yrs. They wrote, "The age ranges reveal that a number of the respondents must have realized that they were gay even before they had a crush on another boy. This supports the view that sexual orientation is a more integral part of identity than sexual behavior alone." (Stone Fish & Harvey, 2005, p. 54)

Thus, a child may begin to perceive himself to be gay by age 10; yet, because of social prohibitions he has borne from his earliest stages of what is right and wrong, acceptable and unacceptable in his culture, he may not develop a secure sexual identity until age 50. But then maybe this is not as far behind as it first seems, because according to two of the three sexual identity models, people do not learn to integrate their public and private lives until they have reached their late 20s or 30s or, if development has been thwarted by environmental or societal stressors, even later. Cass's model (1979) pointed out that an identity synthesis does not emerge until the 30s or beyond. As people's core personality becomes increasingly integrated with society, they can begin to see lesser dichotomy between gays and straights.

Making Room for Difference: A Developmental Task for Society

How can society begin to make room for those who are different in their sexual orientation? One of the first places to begin is to enlarge our capacity for moral reasoning by providing education and engaging in dialogue. It would be a great step in the right direction, for example, to be mindful of our vocabulary when referring to homosexual issues.

Rather than speaking of sexual "choice," we must continue to speak of orientation. The one choice most gays and lesbians feel they have is to tell the truth or live the lie. When it comes to fear and prejudice, we need to realize that a person cannot be recruited to homosexuality. According to the people I interviewed, being gay is not what someone does in bed but is rather a very personal realization of his or her inner identity.

Let's also quit using the words *unnatural* and *abnormal* where they do not fit. It's just as abnormal for a heterosexual to become gay as it is for a gay person to become straight. Similarly, it is interesting to notice that society still refers to gays having a "lifestyle," whereas heterosexuals doing similar things are described as having a "life." And then there is the "gay agenda." What is the real agenda but to be treated with respect and equality and not to be thrown out of one's home or job for being different? When people speak of gay rights as special rights, they are obviously letting homophobia obscure the lens of equal rights for every person. In addition, when it comes to thinking that homosexuality threatens "family values," most conservative religions could learn a few lessons from AIDS caretakers, who have continually demonstrated what commitment to family is all about, living out "til death do us part" with the greatest of courage as seen in the stories of the loved ones who cared for Tom, John, Skip, and Gary in chapter 2.

It is interesting to learn how much of our moral reasoning and faith development occur in our mid- to later years in life. Kohlberg believed that the dominant stage of moral reasoning in American adults is Stage 4, which a person enters by age 16 and may remain in until death. He stated that it is not until the mid-20s or early 30s that rare people entertain thoughts typical of Stage 5 moral reasoning, where they begin to wrestle with the questions of justice that may supersede the norms of society (Crain, 1985, p. 128). Such a question might be "Should society be allowed to be unjust or unfair to (gay) people because they are different?" Or, by acknowledging a need for change, this thought may occur: "Maybe justice needs to make room in our society for the equal rights for another minority." Similarly, Fowler's model of faith development doesn't consider people ready to enter Stage 4 until their mid-30s (Wolski Conn, 1986).

At this time, they are developmentally able to view the paradoxes of their faith community while also learning to validate the views of others and to synthesize them into their internal beliefs (Wing, 1997). At this time of life, experiences and internal realities begin to trump external modes of authority. Perhaps it is not until members of straight society enter their fourth of fifth decade of life that they are able to make room for the full acceptance of those with same-sex orientation and their resulting partnerships and spirituality.

Tools for the Therapist

Therapists must acquaint themselves with the models of sexual identity development and spiritual formation so they will know how to nurture this aspect of human maturity. The question to ponder is not what is right or wrong in your own eyes but how would you develop a healthy hetero-sexual or homosexual? Therapists need to appreciate that questioning one's sexuality and spirituality is a sign of growth that may be developing at a much higher level than those who never challenge traditional beliefs. Is it possible that you could learn about your personal spiritual growth and development by understanding and honoring the spirituality of your queer clients?

4

Hindrances to Gay Spirituality

If an enemy were insulting me, I could endure it;
If a foe were raising himself against me, I could hide from him.
But it is you, a man like myself, my companion, my close friend
With whom I once enjoyed sweet fellowship
As we walked with the throng at the house of God.

Psalm 55:12–14

I grew up believing that no person's life could be complete without a personal relationship with God. Granted, the Evangelical Christian definition of authentic spirituality is fairly narrow, but the basic principle of being in relationship with God seems to balance the human experience. We are not only physical, mental, emotional, and sexual beings but we are also spiritual at our core. Broadening the scope and definition of what spirituality is helps us to see that all human life is improved when one's spirituality is acknowledged and developed. Karl Jung cautioned that humans needing balance and harmony would benefit from integrating spirituality into their lives (Wikipedia). However, spirituality is not exclusive to that part of the population attending weekly worship services. It is not limited to the Abrahamic siblings of Christians, Jews, or Muslims. Nor is it confined to Buddhists, Hindus, or Wiccans. Spirituality as defined in chapter 1 is that part of us that connects outside ourselves to something greater than ourselves or, as O'Hanlon (2006, p. 11) said, "a sense that there is something bigger going on in life." All human beings desire a connection with something more or, at the very least, something beyond their own minds. When spirituality can grow and develop into something meaningful, it is accompanied by a new sense of wholeness and mental health in people's lives. In fact, in a 1996 survey of marriage and family therapists, 96% "agreed with the statement that 'there is a relationship between spiritual health and mental health,'" (Carlson & Erickson, 2002, p. 111). Conversely, the opposite is also true. Whenever people are cut off from their spirituality or feel ostracized from their spiritual communities, they suffer.

I have been privileged to know many homosexuals throughout my life who possess a profound and deep spirituality. There have been times I have wondered if the painstaking process of identifying as homosexual is also a spiritual experience. There is something about having to pull back from the rest of society to do the difficult work of identifying as a sexual minority that necessitates some thoughtful spiritual reflection. My hunch is that it is much deeper than most people realize. Unfortunately, many clients feel that "their private and meaningful conversations with a personal God are not welcome in therapy conversations" (Carlson & Erickson, 2002, p. 112).

There may be a mismatch in the therapist–client relationship, because, on the whole, therapists are often not as connected to their spirituality as some of their clients:

> Gallup surveys of the general population show that "most Americans place a high value on religion and spirituality in their daily lives." Research from Princeton "found that 95% percent of people report believing in God or Universal Spirit, 85% claim to pray and 56% state that religion is very important to their lives. (Carlson & Erickson, 2002, p. 111)

This may be especially true for gay, lesbian, and bisexual clients who have felt cut·off from their religious or spiritual roots. Most therapists choose to deal with the mind, emotions, thoughts, and relational issues rather than learning how to encourage a person's spirituality. In fact, some therapists I've encountered seem to be at such a loss in spiritual matters that they seem to find it easier to try to keep spirituality out of the picture altogether. This could be linked to the fact that many therapists have not done much personal spiritual development themselves. However, it is quite probable that in holding such matters with indifference, instead of the curious position of not knowing, we may actually hinder the ability of clients to heal at their deeper levels. It would be good to note that the Greek origins of the word *psychotherapy* are two root words: *psyche*, which means soul; and *therapy*, which means something akin to healing or treating. So although psychotherapy originally referred to "soul healing" (O'Hanlon, 2006, p. 3), many therapists tend to focus too much on therapeutic methods approved by insurance companies rather than the source of our profession, which is caring for the human spirit. It is at this point where I hope this book may differ from others on what it means to help gay and lesbian clients connect with the spiritual side of their lives or the soul. I am most interested in how our society—and specifically therapists and clergy—can make the paradigm shifts that will allow soul healing to occur in the gay population when it is needed.

Similarly, when it comes to matters of religion, some will find it is too easy to trivialize the church or any other religious assembly as an impersonal, corrupt, and archaic institution. However, many gay clients were raised in religious communities, which provided their cultural foundation and served as the place they learned to connect with family and friends. It was there they encountered similar beliefs that changed people's lives for the better and where a sense of maturing was promoted to become a blessing to the world. Again, when it comes right down to the definition of *religion,* we must also remember that the Latin root is *religare,* meaning, "to reconnect" (O'Hanlon, 2006, p. 13). Finding a way to access a spirituality that connects to a client's wholeness can be one of the most effective tools of healing we have; quite often, this has happened in an affirming religious community.

Although it has always been heartbreaking to hear gays or lesbians say things like, "God doesn't want me," or "I don't think I can pray to God anymore because I'm gay," society has too often accepted those kinds of tragic mantras, perhaps believing something similar. However, my spirit was quite moved a few years ago when I began to meet out and proud gay men who also identified as being Christians. Believe me, it was a total paradigm shift! Not only did these men profess to be authentic in both identities, but they also felt that it was only when they could put those two identities together that they experienced a sense of inner peace. My curiosity was immediately hooked, and as a result I conducted a survey to find out what had helped their spiritual development. I wanted to know what happened when one's spirituality was cut out of life altogether due to its development being hindered or arrested by outside forces.

Before I began my research, the question, "What has been most hurtful to your spiritual development?" invoked a vivid scene in my mind of a gruff, old nun dressed in a black-and-white habit with ruler in hand, walking around children's desks, waiting to pounce on the first person who bucked the system. I can still remember the shocking sound of a social studies teacher's yardstick slapping the empty desktop behind me when I was in junior high school. He thought it was a clever way to keep us awake on a warm, spring afternoon, but all I remember was an inability to concentrate. Fortunately, no one shared stories of abusive nuns, but study participants did mention four main areas that they felt had discouraged their spiritual development: (1) personal reactions to others who judge them, (2) society's judgment and hate (especially hurtful was the rejection of one's own family), (3) self-destructive tendencies such as promiscuity and substance abuse that are used to mask feelings of low self-worth; and (4) the gay ghetto that may be prejudiced against people who are trying to find or reclaim their faith.

Four Discouragements in Gay Spirituality

Personal Reactions

Of the interviewees, 47% mentioned that they thought the greatest harm in their own spiritual lives was "their own reaction to church and society's judgments, misinformation, and damage to gay people." Although several of these people also cited having received inferior help from clergy and therapists, they still believed that the greatest determinant was their own reaction to the maligned treatment of others. This may be an unusually mature group of people, for such a response clearly demonstrates a great ability for personal reflection and a self-agency instead of blaming someone else for their lack of growth. It also points out how therapists and professional clergy are often the people this population may turn to when spiritual growth is desired.

Mark
Mark, who previously studied for the ministry in the Catholic Church, said that although he still prays every day, he no longer attends worship services. He recognizes that his own anger often hinders his spiritual well-being.

> I had been going to a progressive Catholic church, and I'd gone back there after having been away for a while, and then the whole sexual abuse scandal came out and I got angry and disillusioned and sad. I just thought, "You know, I think I'm done with doing organized religion for now. I was just so disheartened and pissed. I think that is the thing that has gotten in the way of my process at times. When I have felt injured by what the church has done, I kind of pull away and say, "I'll do this on my own, thank you very much! I'm not going to let you co-opt my relationship with God; I'm going to do this on my own terms." I think that at times, it's not only been painful, but I think I kind of lose some touch with my spirituality. I just kind of go away from it for awhile, and I think those incidents or those types of things get in the way.

Lucy
Lucy, a vibrant, silver-haired lesbian who has gone through several spiritual transitions reflects on her life:

I'd say what most inhibited my spiritual growth were a couple of things. One was that I reacted. As I said, I was very actively involved. I joined and went to church every Sunday. I was a member of the youth group. I was very involved in the Christian church. When I became disillusioned with that, I declared I was an atheist. So I went through this period of time being an atheist, and at some point I thought, "This doesn't make sense. It doesn't make sense that this is all there is. I think there's got to be something more." So I don't know if I want to say that inhibited my spiritual growth, as it was just part of a process. But having gone through that and then reacted against something, it was like I had to figure things out [and look] for new things.

Michelle

When this vibrant young woman with long blonde hair walks into a room, she commands people's attention. Not only does she possess a delightful confidence in her stride, but she is obviously someone who is also kind and very smart. Yet her story is all too common, having lost her leadership position in the church when she disclosed her orientation:

> I would never sign anybody up for the path of the outcast. It's a very difficult and painful place, and yet it is also an opportunity to live at a deeper level than you would have otherwise. There is an opportunity for the church and society at large to observe how discarding this group of gay people affects all of society. We miss out on so much talent, and possibilities that the gay community can bring to our world. I have known so many warm and loving people with gifts of worship and music, teaching and leadership, whose contributions have been lost when they were asked to leave. And so the body of Christ is not whole. The body of Christ is dismembered, and that is very discouraging.

Arnold

Arnold, a handsome, young Black man, remembers confessing his homosexual orientation to a pastor, who then told him he needed to be "delivered of the demon spirit of homosexuality." After going through several deliverance rituals, Arnold still believed himself to be homosexual, only now he had the additional burden of being labeled as "possessed." If that didn't do enough damage, he later discovered that the "confidential" part of pastoral care had been breached in the name of "spiritual concerns":

> While the church appeared to want to help gay people in some way, they used confidential information about my sexuality against me, which has forced me underground. Now, I just pretend that all is "fixed" because they can't hear the truth, which has led to a life where I constantly present a false self.

Jeff

Similarly, Jeff, who at age 42 has just begun to reconnect to his spirituality, said that one of the biggest hindrances to spirituality for him is living in fear:

> I have lived a life afraid to show myself, to really be myself, and to look at myself because I thought there were consequences for just being who I am. I mean, before HIV drugs became available in the mid '90s, frankly, there was a living example [of those consequences]. The far right Christians would say stuff like, "This is God's wrath." And when your friends start [dying] around you, you start thinking, "Yeah, they might be right."

Society's Judgment and Hate

> If we are around each other and this thing grabs hold of us again at the wrong place, wrong time ... we're dead.
>
> Ennis Del-Mar, *Brokeback Mountain*

Interviewees listed as the second most hurtful thing "society's prejudice and general hate for gay people, as well as the rejection of one's own family." A few also tagged onto this category that until recently, civil laws declaring aspects of homosexual behavior to be illegal also contributed to the oppression of their spirituality. A full 30% of the participants felt this had been one of the most hurtful aspects of their spiritual lives. When we are talking about what helps or hinders a person's spirituality, we must consider other important aspects such as family, civil law, and social prejudice, which highlight the reality that spirituality is never just a private affair—it is always lived out in community.

Richard

> Well, one of the things I find so disheartening is the amount of hate that is directed at what feels like me. There are completely illogical arguments—what appear to me as unchristian—being used to describe why people hate me so much. One of the most difficult things in my coming out process was in that short window of time where I was kind of trying to figure out how I could own that label. I felt that after that first night with my boyfriend I had just incurred the wrath of millions of people, because I have now discovered who I am. And that's oppressive. To see it acted out in ballot measures and laws—to say that you can vote on people's characteristics and whether they are favorable or not—is really offensive and really disheartening. I just don't understand how people can hate that much or be so fearful.

Jim

Jim said that he works at forgetting things that deter his spirituality, yet at the time of the interview he felt that his mother has always been an irritant:

> I always feel somewhat condemned, but not specifically spoken in those terms. Whatever she says, there's an underlying sense that there is some distance between us that is unbridgeable and that I, just by my nature, am some kind of immoral person. I don't accept that, so obviously I have some problems with that. It seems to be an irritant and [some]thing that runs counter to my feeling that I have a worthwhile spiritual life.

Sam

Sam, a gay man formerly married to a woman for 10 years, felt that his spiritual growth was never hindered by outside forces, but he had seen many of his friends who have been damaged this way:

> I think it's just when I come across these cases that are so tragic where gay people think they have to end their relationship with God. Or when I see the hatred that is evident in people who think God has rejected gay people: Then there is that minister who is on the East Side, who has a big church and was a former football player—he also says gays are rejected. Maybe hatred is too strong of a word for some of those folks. Maybe it's a lack of understanding, or lack of empathy, or compassion, or just understanding that homosexuals do not differ from heterosexuals in hardly any measurable way at all, and I think that is true in God's eyes as well.

Clint

Clint, a minister in his mid-50s of an open and affirming congregation, feels that a crippling ignorance is the cause of most negative messages about gays:

> The thing that has inhibited it the most is the influence of an ill-informed, insensitive, and, in my opinion, warped society and church that spends far too much of its time focusing us on distractions. We are distracted. I was distracted for many years by the bane of sexuality or the phobias of society—not just for homosexuals but for other phobias of church and society as well. It doesn't encourage a person to become spiritually mature. You can't access everything you need for maturing because you are continually distracted by that agenda and dynamic. I don't mean it is just fear that inhibits you and distracts you. But I felt I was deficient because of the ways church and society spent so much of its energy. The church isn't very good at teaching us about sexuality because we are still distracted by the influence of society and, as I said, ill-informed and ill-spirited people.

Self-Destructive Tendencies

> Ennis: If you can't fix it, Jack, you gotta stand it.
> Jack: For how long?
> Ennis: As long as you can stand it. There's no reins on this one.
>
> *Brokeback Mountain*

A total 20% of respondents identified as being hurtful "their own self-destructive tendencies to escape the pain of rejection and ostracism," which for some amounted to prolonged substance abuse that turned into serious drug addiction. As two middle-aged men shared with me, after hearing on numerous occasions that homosexuals could not be spiritually or emotionally healthy, along with experiencing familial and societal rejection, they both felt that the only way they could live was to numb the pain with drugs and promiscuous sexual escapades. Both men grew up in religious homes emphasizing that practicing homosexuals have no hope of a personal faith, so they turned instead to embrace society's archetype for a homosexual: the lost soul.

Rick

I think Rick's story is particularly relevant as he tells about how difficult it has been to undo the toxic messages that eventually led him into drug addiction:

> Part of the thing that the drug does is [to] cut you off from all that pain that's wrapped up in being gay and not having a spiritual connection with anything. The drug cuts that off. And recovery? Well, probably the lion's share of recovery is getting your sexuality and spirituality back in synch with each other, and that's been, for me, a big journey. I've always been very honest with both my therapist and my medical doctor about my drug use and going through the process with them of healing some of the damage that had been caused by family dynamics, the harshness of the Jehovah's Witnesses, and the ultraconservative family dynamics, but all of it was tied together. I'm actually a fairly strong individual, which I never knew before. [Previously] I always ran and hid behind the drugs. It has helped a lot, being able to integrate the spiritual and the sexual. I'm not there yet. I have a long way to go. I have a lot of issues around sex, and part of that is still some old programming. Part of it is the bind that happens with sex and drugs. It's like they become married the same way that religion and spirituality were married.

Gordon

Gordon has a similar story about his drug and sex addiction, for which he is currently in recovery:

> I've had substitutes for spirituality over the years. Sex itself became a spiritual substitution. I still think it is, but it was out of balance. I like having a spiritual life, which for me these days means some quiet times for reflection and prayer and a community that cares. But at the time, when I first came out, sex was a spiritual experience. I was like, "Wow!" I mean, it was like a drug—a little bit addictive. [It was] like it had been denied me, and all of a sudden it was there and I was 20 years old and wore 29-inch jeans and felt good about that! (laughter) Coming out is a process. There's coming out, and there's coming in, and I think I'm definitely on

this inward journey. I've got a wonderful partner who I adore and love and who I am absolutely sexually attracted to, but we both are working through addiction issues with methamphetamines, and the correlation with sex is incredibly strong. (Interviewer: Because they were used together?) Yes, those were spiritual experiences! I mean, of a kind—you know, higher than God. It's not necessarily that you are with God. You are clearly not. But you are feeling things that you could not; you are escaping your body and what felt like a prison, and that was freedom. In a way, the drugs are still in the way. I think it's going to take some time. We are actually seeing a sex therapist, who especially understands these addictions. We haven't seen him for awhile, but one of the things we got from him was that it's just going to take time to pull [apart] those thoughts that you spent years tying together. And those chemical changes in the brain are going to go away. So it requires action. I've just never lived a life before where I couldn't run away or have a mechanism to run away from things that were daunting or emotionally challenging. Now we don't, and life is the best it's been.

Monty

What's most inhibited my spirituality? Probably my sexuality! (laughter) I don't find sex to be that spiritual; I find it to be a pretty physical thing. There have been times when it's been close to spiritual, but sex is just an odd duck all by itself. That might be when I am most disconnected from God or the universe. I always feel like we all have an invisible-like string connection to God. But when I am using substances or alcohol or having sex in an unhealthy way, I find the disconnect and absence of my spirituality. The void essentially gets me into trouble. I feel out of balance then.

The Gay Ghetto

Finally, from listening to my transcripts, I was surprised to hear that 7% of the people in my study felt there was a spiritual hinderance in "the unhealthiness of living in a gay ghetto where there was a prejudice against gays who profess to be Christians." My surprise obviously comes from my own stereotypes, because I had never heard a gay or lesbian refer to the GLBT community as an unhealthy ghetto, nor did I realize how difficult it might be for a person to identify as a gay Christian in a subculture that has experienced so much rejection from religious institutions. Although it could be very easy for most straight people to believe it would be better for sexual minorities to be with their own kind, this particular study does not report this as an optimum situation. Many times people are glad to have "difference" out of their sight so as not to rock the status quo. But what kind of society would we have if people are banished to live in cultural ghettos where one's "own kind" has a predominant characteristic of being wounded and marginalized? America discovered through the desegregation years of the 1960s that separate is never equal. What this statistic tells me is that society has not fully learned this lesson. Most of the GLBT people who I know prefer not to be cast into a special club but would rather blend in with the rest of society. For them, visiting the gay community is like a bimonthly night on the town but not the place they have any desire to develop their roots. The fact that many devout Christians have exiled their own has most definitely influenced the gay community's distaste for Christians, even if the believer is a sexual minority. For many people who have faced extreme rejection time and time again by the church, getting close to Christianity may feel too toxic.

Douglas

When I asked Douglas what most inhibits his spiritual growth as a gay man, he responded in a way I wouldn't have expected:

> As a gay man? I mean, if I want to think about times in my life about being gay, I do sort of think that there are aspects of gay communities that can be very discouraging. I'm not even talking about the bar culture or the promiscuity. What I'm really talking about is that sort of immersing one's self in a community and then everything I do is gay, and it's gay this and gay that. [There is] all the segregation that goes along with that. And I would say the heterophobia. I think that while some people—and maybe even for myself at one point—have retreated into that, it is certainly an understandable phase of development. But unless we grow beyond that, I think it's a dead end. It gets in the way of connecting more. I was a member of the Seattle Men's Chorus for many years, and I think it's a wonderful organization. I'm totally in line with the mission, and I've met some wonderful people there. But sometimes there is the sense of being there and being disconnected from the rest of society. It really takes over your life. It's a huge commitment. It's not that everything you do there is gay, but there's an element of that to it. Yet they are trying to build bridges to other people. There's a certain tension there. So it's not like I'm down on gay life. I think it does have potential to lead us to great spirituality. I think these radical fairy gatherings—I've never been to one, but I've had friends who have, and for them it has been an incredibly liberating experience. Hopefully it is something they carry back into other parts of their lives. But my spiritual framework wants to deal with [banding together] and then let's go beyond that. Sort of understanding that we need to be okay with ourselves as gay people or whatever kind of people we are, but once we deal with that, then the spiritual questions are just much larger—about how humans interact with each other and help each other to build something greater.

Two other people spoke about how narrow life would be if we were all the same and were resisting the pull to be with only like kind. One person said that with the overly available sexual encounters in the gay ghetto, it has hindered not only his spiritual life but also his ability to be committed to his family. But it was the answer of another minister that perhaps best summarizes the effect of others being too focused on ghettoizing his sexual identity.

Thomas

Well, I think some of it is just the daily frustration with that part of the Christian tradition that is way more preoccupied with my sexual orientation than I am. I try to do my best to stay focused on what I feel I'm called to do and what the Christian message is. As far as sexual orientation in the church, it's one of those battles that I just can't walk away from. Sometimes I feel like I'm dragged into it when I don't even feel like I want that. So I'd say that's a relatively huge hindrance to my spirituality. I used to tell people that the thing that is most unfair about being an openly gay minister was giving someone that information. It was like giving them a cup and they pour into it everything they believe that to be—and I don't get any choice. Once I hand them that cup, they fill it with their stuff. For them to have a relationship with me, they have to dump that out so they can get what I have to give to them. That's a hard thing that people don't want to do. It is easier to just assume. In terms of frustration around my own spirituality and the issue of sexual orientation, I'd not just say that is true of conservative people; it's also true of liberal people. When I came here, it was clear to me that the game plan—while no one said it—was for me to be the poster boy for gay Baptist ministers, and the vision was that there would be all these people who would flock to this church because I am gay. Yet, here I was, and (a) had they said that to me out loud, I would have said, "I'm not interested"; and (b) I don't think that does anyone any good to be the poster child of some cause because, again, it goes back to authenticity. I am a human being of which sexual orientation is a part. I'm a Baptist minister who also happens to be gay. That doesn't mean I want to run away from the realities of being a gay man or the difficulties of my sexual orientation or the way it impacts the world, but I am fundamentally a human being. I think liberals sometimes want to prove their credentials on my back, and I have no interest in doing that for them.

Something Is Missing!

As I went over the responses to my qualitative study listening for themes, one of the most often repeated themes sounded something like this: "After a while, being queer isn't enough; something spiritual is missing, and I need to find a way to connect with it."

Many people in the GLBT community are seeking to incorporate new spiritual ways of being that are not toxic to their soul. However, in spite of this quest, many barriers continue to clog the path of spirituality for gay people to access that fundamental spiritual element that comes with being human. Some of those barriers are so large that they have forced homosexuals out of the mainstream. And we are the poorer for it. The church and greater society are missing out on a lot of wonderful, talented, deep people who will not darken the doors of institutions that do not accept and affirm who they know themselves to be. What keeps them out? It is others' stereotypes and prejudices and their own seeking after healthier places to connect.

Stereotypes That Become Spiritual Toxins

Gays Can't Be Spiritual

A common theme I heard in my interviews was the toxic stereotype that if an individual was gay or lesbian, he or she could not be a spiritual person—or at least not Christian, Jewish, or Muslim. Even if gays and lesbians claimed a spirituality, it had to be something considered substandard. Accompanying such judgment was the belief that the consequence of being gay was to live an unhealthy life marked by great unhappiness.

In recent years, James Dobson's Focus on the Family held seminars called "Love Won Out" to help people leave the homosexual lifestyle. Although the title of these seminars sounds very caring, one of my interviewees felt that it completely missed the mark of anything that she considered healing:

Katie

I think the misinformation promulgated by the corporate church really creates a self-hatred and fear that there's something wrong at the core of you—and that is just petrifying. Our people group was categorized as unhealthy and neurotic, without knowing the people, and stereotyping as a class. I just can't fathom a gay or lesbian person attending that seminar and feeling God's love. It was a pretty scary dissemination of misinformation.

Bob

When I asked Bob to tell me of a time when his sexuality and spirituality were most in conflict he responded by saying:

I would say in my early 20s when I was really fully realizing that my sexuality was not going to change and in the church situation where I grew up—the two were not compatible. So there was a great deal of conflict because there was very much a sense that [people thought] I wasn't a good enough Christian, I didn't pray hard enough, God didn't love me enough. What could I do to change this? It was a very miserable time. Through most of my 20s I felt very conflicted. I would have sexual experiences, and then I would feel dirty and ashamed. But it didn't stop, and it didn't change. In the church world I came from, there was a message that the two were incompatible, and I was so ingrained in that culture—in that conservative "red state" (laughter)—that there was just no counter message to that anywhere until I came to Seattle. [Previously] I had a conversion experience where I regained God, but I never thought I was going to regain the church. So a lot of my 20s and 30s were pretty miserable.

Because of these kinds of stereotypes, about 30% of my respondents said they had left the church knowing they could never fit in; 10% were forced out of leadership positions, and two respondents lost their jobs due to their sexual orientation.

Beth

> I attended Baylor University—a pretty traditionally Southern Baptist school—and was a really strong Christian. But I had my first sexual experiences with women within that framework. I had no one who could support that those ideas could exist. (Interviewer: You mean being a lesbian and Christian?) Yes, that those could coexist. I talked with a woman, I talked with my pastor, I talked with professors, I talked to someone at the Baptist Student Union, and no one was any help. It seemed as if—basically it was sin and you needed to "straighten up," so to speak. (smiles) So I tried.

Figure 4.1   Things that hinder.

These same prejudicial stereotypes can also be seen in therapists—even those who are good clinicians who really care about their clients. Beth went on to tell how she later went to a Baptist seminary, partially to make sense of these areas where her faith and sexuality intersected. At that time she met with a female therapist who also happened to be a sincere Christian:

> She was really caring, very good, but underlying there was always the pressure to [change]. I could sense it. If you're a sensitive person, you can sense that really she didn't want me to be lesbian. I could tell by where she directed the conversation, what we focused on. I came out of that experience understanding my previous sexual experiences with women as anomalies and got myself engaged to a good seminary doctoral candidate. But thank God, before that went any further, we called it quits because it just was not meshing. During that time I think I was most conflicted. I just couldn't reconcile all those difficult pieces.

Shortly afterward, Beth began entertaining thoughts of suicide. Although she never made the attempt to end her life, today she looks back on that decade between her 20s and early 30s with tears, knowing how close she came to the edge of extinction.

I Can't Be Gay

Stereotypes about homosexuals, however, go beyond deciding who is in and who is out of the church. These stereotypes extend into the very core of society's idea of who a person can or cannot be. For instance, in my survey several people said that there was a time when they didn't believe they could be gay because they didn't fit the stereotype of "queer." This idea emerged repeatedly. Consider the stereotype suggesting that all gay men are effeminate, flamboyant, promiscuous, and rebellious: If a young man has only sexual dreams and secret attractions to men and otherwise doesn't fit this description, he must not really be gay. Again, what are the normal stereotypes? The screaming queen and the diesel dyke. And what kind of stereotype comes to mind when someone says he or she is bisexual? Although the term is only meant to describe a person's orientation rather than behavior, the stereotype suggests that "bi" must mean a person who has sex with both men and women concurrently. Such stereotypes keep people from connecting with their truer sense of themselves.

Richard

> It was just a few months before my 30th birthday, and I was pretty much ignorant of my sexual orientation and had suppressed all of my thoughts and urges up until I met this guy who was clearly gay and hitting on me. I had gay

friends in college and hung out with them, so it was no big deal. But it never dawned on me that I might be gay because my stereotype of being gay was so foreign to what I was or what I perceived myself to be that I just didn't think that that was something that I could be. So it wasn't until my first boyfriend that I realized this. When we first got together, I was completely dumbfounded at how wonderful I felt and realized that I was gay. I was very involved in my Episcopal church, and I remember just really struggling at the time about how I could be gay when I'm not the things that I thought being gay meant—like being really flamboyant and sexually promiscuous and being a sexual predator and all of those kinds of stereotypes. It was very incongruous for me to think of myself as being gay when I was none of those things I had associated with being gay.

Sam

Sam was married for 10 years before he identified as being a gay man. After a painful divorce he has now been living happily with a male partner for several years. He recalled the struggle of understanding his sexual identity:

> There was sort of a transition time when I started to think, "Wait a minute; am I really gay?" to a realization of, "You know? I really am!" For a long time—the first 35 to 37 years of my life—I did not identify myself as being gay; I identified myself as being straight. I had homosexual leanings and homosexual tendencies, but, naively, I thought straight people had the same thing, the same yearnings, the same feelings and that they dealt with it and that was just part of being a straight man. So I never really saw myself as being gay. I didn't really understand what it meant to be gay. I didn't know anyone who was gay. When I conceptualized what a gay person was like, it was never someone like me, so I just thought I was a straight guy. It wasn't until this process of learning what homosexuality was and accepting that that was part of who I was that kind of accelerated the coming out process.

I Can't Be Whole

What alarms me the most about the perceptions of gay spirituality is finding people who believe that being gay precludes any spiritual connection, for without that added ingredient it may be nearly impossible for wholeness to emerge. Human beings are fundamentally spiritual in nature. Everyone has what I would call a soul, a deep core part of our humanity that longs to connect with something greater than ourselves. If that part of us is stolen or damaged by being made out to be evil or pestilent, then people suffer greatly.

A good example of this was in a *Seattle Times* article about the now infamous U.S. Representative Mark Foley, who, though being a semi-closeted gay Republican since 1994, ambitiously supported the social conservatives who elected him in Florida. When he voted in favor of the Defense of Marriage Act, which would prevent gays from marrying, he was challenged by a gay activist as to why he voted against his own self-interests. Foley responded, "I could never compare any relationship I have ever had with the nature of my mother and father's relationship" (*Seattle Times*, 2006, October 5, p. A3). This illustrates my point: Mark Foley's world must have been full of secrets and pseudo-relationships. Somewhere along the line, he internalized the sad message of a stereotype that he could never be as good or as whole as his "normal" heterosexual parents—which apparently became a self-fulfilling prophecy.

Thomas

There was no way I could be authentic. Either I had to pretend I was somebody I wasn't or I had to put what I knew to be the truth about my life in the sin category. This meant that the only way to deal with it was that this part of me had to be cut away. So, obviously, a sort of internal separation was the only way to deal with it. The downside of that was the way it forced me to deal with my sexuality as a category of sin that was held against me. On the other hand, I could never really feel saved either, which was the ultimate thing, right? I could never truly feel that there was any sense that God could save me from this. (Interviewer: So sin was always hanging over you?) Exactly! As I've said to other people afterward, because the sin category was filled with my sexuality, there wasn't room for anything else. So any other way of being in the world, perhaps being at odds for what God would want for me, didn't matter because the point was the sin category was filled by my sexual orientation. So there was no wholeness about it. I could not think of my life in good terms—in ways that were holistic—neither could I think of ways my life was destructive, because everything centered on sexual orientation. I have since come to learn that this is not the case. I could be broken in all kinds of ways that have nothing to do with my sexual orientation! (laughter) They may be exacerbated by that sexual orientation, but they have nothing to do with it. So wholeness could never come while I was in that mode.

Rick

When I was 14, my parents divorced, and I moved in with my paternal grandparents, who were very devout Jehovah's Witnesses. I was expected to fall into step, and I did. We went to church three times a week and had Bible studies. Besides that, we were to proselytize anyone who would listen, and that happened all the way through high school. During that period of time—during my sexual awakening as it were—I was told over and over again how being gay was the worst possible thing that you could do. The way I was brought up, I could have taken a bloody ax and walked down the main street of town chopping people's heads off, and they would have somehow dealt with that—but not being gay. That was like the ultimate sin. I came out my freshman year at college. I was 19, and I kind of decided that I was going to put all of that [religion] behind me. I think subconsciously that is what I was doing. But you can't just shut it down. For years, I thought I was doing what every gay man was supposed to do—be sexually promiscuous and self-destructive. Basically what happened was I went into a self-destructive downward spiral, which basically lasted 20 years. I rejected religion. I rejected spirituality. I rejected all of that stuff, because it was so tainted. I decided that it didn't apply to me. Did I believe in God? You know, I never really pondered that question for a long time. Like I said, it didn't apply to me.

From these responses about people dealing with constant oppression, judgment, ostracism, and the prejudices of others, the overall theme that surfaces of what is most harmful to spiritual development is loss of hope. Over the past few years, I have come to believe that the wholeness needed in the GLBT community is not going to be found by attempting to change a person's sexual orientation or by demanding that he or she give up being sexual. What is needed instead is the hope of being a complete human being that finds meaning in being both sexual and spiritual: hope for fuller understanding and acceptance; hope that encourages maturity and well-being; and hope that the world will make room for true dignity and equality when people find themselves attracted to a partner of the same sex.

Stereotypes About the Closet

Coming Out Is Always Traumatic

Another item that may be toxic to one's spiritual growth is society's stereotype about coming out of the closet. It was interesting to find that 30% of my interviewees said they were never in the closet or that they had passed through the closet in a very short time. Once they were able to identify themselves as being gay or lesbian, these people just began telling those closest to them about their new discovery and living authentically. This appears to be a rather recent phenomenon of the last decade as cultural attitudes toward homosexuality have relaxed. What is also interesting to note is that most of those who had the least difficulty coming out were from nonreligious or semireligious homes that were very supportive of their children's sense of identity. Two people told me that they were actually very grateful they had not been raised in religious homes because they didn't have the baggage of most of their gay friends who had grown up in a religious community.

Douglas

When I asked Douglas if there was a time when his sexuality and spirituality were most in conflict, he paused to think, and then replied:

> I think I'm an oddball in that sense, particularly in this culture. I never felt that my ideas about spirituality helped me deal with what a sense of being gay is or the consequences of that and how that fits into our culture. I know that is true for other people, but it's not for me. I don't have the emotional and other baggage in being trained in one particular faith. Most traditional denominations in this country teach that homosexuality is a sin. But I didn't really grow up in all that. Certainly there is a message in society at large that is like that, but I never felt there was any personal message like, "This is bad," directed at me. Clearly, I was not comfortable with my sexuality as a younger person because I just didn't understand what it was, and I certainly didn't have any models. But I also didn't have any extra layer that I think most people do—"I'm doing something that is sinful or bad, and I need to overcome it," or "How do I fit this into my faith of what is moral and ethical, and does God love me?" So I really didn't have that [baggage] a lot of my friends certainly talk about.

Although nonreligious families may make it easier for a child to self-identify as gay or lesbian, one should not equate this with how much parents love their children. If one child can come out at an early age and find familial support in that discovery yet another feels he or she has to wait in the closet until he or she moves away from home to declare his or her sexual identity, it does not mean that one family had tighter bonds or more love than the other. Most likely both kinds of families love their children equally. But in families who identify as more fundamentally religious, one has to recognize that there is also a dual allegiance to God and the family. The stricter rules of conduct, the insistence of church attendance and Bible study, or even the repression of variant sexuality often stems from a great desire of the parents to protect their children from what they believe would be a cosmic disaster—a life without God's protection or blessing.

The Closet Is Always Unhealthy

There is a great misconception that if a person is in the closet, he or she must get out of it as soon as possible to be healthy. The truth is that there may be many reasons to avoid rushing the process of coming out. When one considers the many aspects of development that may be going on at the same time, declaring one's sexual identity to the world may not be the most prudent thing to do. Clients have a strong sense of knowing which family members will react very strongly. Some reactions may even jeopardize one's support or safety. There may be varying degrees of being closeted that are more in line with a client's best interests or comfort levels for that stage of life. Though it is true that living a closeted life will result in a great deal of unhealthy isolation, persons may also consider a nondisclosing option as a healthy place for a season while they address the deeper needs of their core self (or soul).

Of the people I surveyed, 25% said that being in the closet for a while provided them a place to pull back and think deeply. Some used that time to do research or to study various theologies that helped them to new truths they could live by. For many adolescents, this was a place to ponder the questions of life at a deeper level than most of their peers. For others, it was a place where their faith was forced to see the bigger picture or to grow deeper. Or, as one young man said, "Knowing I was gay, I had nowhere to run but to God."

The Closet Can Never Be Helpful

Mark

When I asked Mark what effect being in the closet had on his spiritual development, he paused to reflect:

> I think it forced me to develop an adult sense of spirituality. I knew I couldn't swallow whole and incorporate what was being presented by the institutional church because I wasn't experiencing it. It forced me to think and to ask questions: How could it be that a God who I had experienced as mostly a very loving, powerful guide be connected with something that was so clearly judging and critical—telling me that what I felt was right was wrong? So it forced me to think for myself, which was really a beneficial thing. When I got to college, it spurred me on to do what I've continued to do the rest of my life which is to study things. I think this was partly why I double-majored in psychology and theology. I found that I was much more emotionally engaged in my studies of theology than with psychology because I was working all of this stuff out. I was using other people's thoughts and writings and reflections to come to my own conclusions. I had such a strong sense of a relation with God all through my childhood and adolescence that, when I was struggling, I always found guidance and support. It always felt like I was never alone when I was facing things that were very difficult and confusing. Having a personal relationship with God ... helped me navigate some of this and also to look for people in ministry whom I respected as guides and for sources of support.

For many people, being closeted was a healthy, temporary resting place where they could begin to think for themselves and how they might begin to integrate their sexuality and spirituality. This can also be a great time to seek the help of a therapist. Several of my clients have told me stories of when they first began to identify as a sexual minority and sought the help of a therapist to change their sexual orientation back to "normal." How various therapists and counselors responded to such a client-based request made a huge difference in their developmental process.

Reflections on the Closet

But for everyone who has a nonreactive experience or a positive association with the times of their lives that were lived in the closet, about 50% of my respondents had horror stories to tell. Several people felt betrayed by God. Others felt angry with God for making them this way or feared that they were so damaged that they would never be good enough to be loved. One man said, "For a while, I wondered if I'd lose my soul. It was all very confusing."

During this time, many interviewees shared that they left the church or began living highly compartmentalized lives. Bob recalled this type of compartmentalization exhausting: "I was a church worker by day while being a patron of South Dakota's only gay bar by night. It takes a lot of energy to hide your true self." Almost everyone's story agreed with that principle. Others would tell how dishonest it felt, how secretive they had to be to survive, and how isolating it was. Some find the whole idea very traumatizing and cannot seem to get past it because of their fears of rejection. They still feel that they must choose survival over disclosure.

For instance, some people described how defensive they had become when they were first in the closet and how spiritually damaging that time was for them.

Michelle

> Being in the closet and struggling with that … makes you feel like you are crazy because your experiences are so vastly different from what the world tells you they should be, and there is so much fear in divulging the tiniest part of what you are struggling with. I was very much aware of what the church's position was on homosexuality, and I was very aware of what the world's position was about discrimination. I had been convinced that homosexuality was something that was not compatible with the teachings of the Bible or what God wanted for people's lives. And so to find yourself against all of your known experiences and

all of your known places of safety and security is very daunting. You wonder if you've just finally lost it. How could I be the only person in the world who feels like this—who goes against all these institutions that have been supposedly the stronghold of truth for centuries? And so a real crisis of faith occurs because you have no sense of validity for your own experiences. When you finally take this step to start working through those issues you are having to learn things about Scripture and church institutions that you didn't know before, or that you now view in a different light, because it's in a different interpretation or you are learning things about biblical history that you were never taught before. That tends to make you wonder what else you were taught wasn't true? Then there's this certain sense of being upset with God and wondering if maybe he's not real either! It's a real test of faith to find out- what you really believe.

This time of life can also be damaging to people like Douglas, who connects with nontraditional spirituality.

Douglas

There were definitely times I was more in the closet, and, yes, it did have an impact in some sense. I guess I conceive of my spiritual development as my sense that we are all connected to each other. My standards and values are about honesty and truth, caring, and compassion for other people. I think being in the closet certainly presents a dilemma, because it means that you are not being honest with everyone in your life about who you are, and that's troubling. It's troubling on a spiritual level to be in the closet about anything. So in that sense, I think there was certainly an isolation that cut me off from certain experiences that I might have had with people if I would have felt more comfortable in my own skin. I guess it's in conflict with some of my values. I think my spirituality is very much grounded in the sense of having loving, caring relationships with other people. I look at those as some expression of the greater good and a higher power. On the other hand, I would say that my spirituality and having those values probably helped me come out of the closet.

Limitations of the Partial Closet

It is also good to realize that being in the closet is a relative term. Rather than saying one is in or out of the closet, it depends greatly on the situation one is placed in and who the audience is. It would probably be more accurate for most people to pick a number on a scale from 1 to 10 to describe how much closeted living they encounter. There are continual variations of how much disclosure people is needed or wanted in a person's life. Although others may think that being out of the closet would bring great personal relief and emotional integrity, it is also appropriate to learn to honor the lives of people who are only partially out.

Sarah

I would say that I'm only partially out. I come out to people that I trust and in situations where I know that I'm not going to be ridiculed or pushed aside because of my orientation. So I still have that protection, but after people get to know me and I'm more comfortable around them, I will let them know. I think a lot of people are rather surprised, and I kind of look at them and think, "If you only knew—I bet you have a lot more friends you don't know about who are [gay], than you even care to venture." So in some ways it's freeing, yet in other ways, if you're still working through that trepidation, it can be nerve-racking. It's very stressful. But when you are finally able to tell someone, it is a huge release. Yet you have to have good judgment in who you tell, because there are people out there who will use it against you. I'm still someone who is very cautious and very skeptical when it comes to dealing with a lot of people. I shouldn't have to be that way, but I am. We have gay friends who aren't. They are out and like (slaps hands together), "if you don't like it, too bad!" Well, that's good. I'm glad it works for you, but it doesn't work for me. I don't have that kind of mind-set.

Still Choosing the Closet

We must also realize that some people may choose to live in the closet for the duration of their lives. This is more apt to occur in older populations who came out in the 1950s and early 1960s when there was no acceptable place to disclose the affections of their hearts except with an extremely limited number of people. My oldest interviewee was a 68-year-old woman who is still in the closet 47 years after identifying herself as a lesbian. During this interview even the thought of coming out seemed traumatic. Just talking about this topic created moments where it was difficult to keep from disassociating.

Julie

(Interviewer: You said you are still in the closet. What impact does being in the closet have on your faith or your person?) Well, a lot of times I think I'm a hypocrite because I tolerate derogatory comments about gays, because no one knows that I am gay. And, um, tell me the question again? (Interviewer: You said no one knows at work) Well, no one knows. No one knows other than the circle of friends I had when I had a partner. No one knows. Nobody in my family knows; nobody knows at all. You know? Uh. (Interviewer: So, the question was, what impact does that have on you?) Well, it's very subterranean in my mind and in my heart when I'm with 99.9% of the people. You know, I'm just this person doing their job. I have off-and-on lived with another female. I had two long-term relationships—one for 13 years and one for 20 years, monogamous—and it never occurred to me that any straight people or anybody would think I was in a gay relationship. It was never brought up; it was never mentioned unless

I was with gay friends who knew. But for the outside world, if they thought about it or wondered about it, nothing was ever said. The first time that it was ever an issue, I was selling real estate and a new person from the East coast came and sat at the desk next to me. We became fast friends, and the first time I had her stop by for lunch while we discussed a listing, apparently I was talking quite a bit about my partner unknowingly. So she said, "Julie, are you in a gay relationship with so and so?" And I looked right at her and said, "Why on Earth would you say that?" (big laughter) And (pause with tears), I said, "No!" Now, homosexuality is not a forbidden topic. I mean, it's all over the media; it's everywhere. And I hear celebrities that come out, like Melissa Etheridge who was on Oprah the other day and talking about her breast cancer, or people that I know that have come out. They always talk about what a sense of freedom that they have and what an empowerment. I would like to feel that. I think I would feel the same way. I am just tired of hiding. I am tired of being in the workplace and hearing all the comments about gays. They are not as derogatory as they were in years past, because I think there's more education and more acceptance out there now, but that doesn't stop the comments. However, I have a very good job now, which was difficult to get at my age. I need to work for another year and half before I retire so I put up with it. But I would so like to say, "Hey, you've got one working for you. How does that make you feel?" But I'm not there yet, and I need this job, so I will not, (Interviewer: Take the risk?) No, uh-uh. And I don't know that I ever, ever will.

Developmental Tasks of Getting Past the Hurtful

Living in an environment that is hostile to your inner sense of self is like negotiating a toxic minefield—never quite sure where the next life-altering step is going to explode. Although GLBT adults have formed an identity with resources and coping tools that GLBT youth do not yet possess, there remain huge obstacles to overcome on the way to being spiritually and psychologically healthy. Thus, many toxic hindrances to gay spirituality can also be viewed as developmental tasks that one must master to regain some sense of mental, emotional, and spiritual health. As identified in this chapter, those seven tasks might be as follows:

1. Challenging one's personal reactions to other's judgments. Always go with the number one rule of life: Do not work against your best interests.
2. Learning how it may be possible to identify as a sexual minority by challenging the socially dominant discourses of gay stereotypes.
3. Finding ways to connect spiritually with something that works as opposed to believing that it is impossible to be a person with spiritual connections to the bigger picture, beyond the self.

4. Looking at oneself holistically. Our identity should be as a complete human being. We are more than gay, straight, or bisexual. We are also mental, physical, emotional, and spiritual beings. Learn to focus on identifying equally in all five areas.
5. Learning how to use closeted times of life in productive ways before disclosing such a vulnerable part of one's self to others.
6. Finding support resources before coming out publicly. Seek networks of gay friends, associations, and welcoming churches and synagogues.
7. Challenging stereotypes of gender roles, sexuality, and spirituality. Focus instead on what it would be like to be true to your most authentic core.

Tools for the Therapist

Due to the reluctance of therapists to bring up the topic of spirituality in therapy in general, we may unwittingly contribute to the oppression and constraint of the religious and spiritual stories of our gay clients: "Thus, both therapist and client alike may be waiting for cues from the other about the appropriateness of addressing religious and spiritual beliefs and issues. Perhaps the onus is on family therapists to take the first step to integrate religious and spiritual issues in therapy" (Carlson & Erickson, 2002, p. 112).

I want to challenge every therapist or clergyperson reading this chapter to examine your own personal biases and assumptions that may impede the therapeutic process with queer clients. Do not assume that because someone has not disclosed his or her sexual orientation that you do not have any gay, lesbian, bisexual, transgender, intersex, or queer clients.

When therapists are listening to the difficulties in a queer life, they are to be empathetic while challenging a client's internal stereotyping. Cognitive behavioral therapy can challenge negative self-talk. Questions should be asked that will challenge a client's personal toxicity such as the following:

- Is it true that you have no spirituality?
- Has this always been true?
- Is that completely true right now?
- What would happen if not being spiritual was a false statement?
- What would it be like for you to let part of that idea go?

Once a client desires a different outcome for his or her spiritual life, narrative theory can be employed by asking clients how they might want to change the outcome of their story if they were free of toxic beliefs. One of the best gifts a therapist can give a GLBT client is hope for a whole life that includes the possibility for spiritual connection.

5

Embracing the Possibility of Gay Spirituality

O Karma, Dharma, pudding and pie,
gimme a break before I die,
grant me wisdom, will and grit,
purity, probity, pluck and grit.
Trustworthy, loyal, helpful, kind,
gimme great abs & a steel trap mind,
and forgive, Ye Gods, some humble advice—
these little blessings would suffice
to begat an earthly paradise:
Make the bad people good—
and the good people nice;
and before our world goes over the brink
teach the believers how to think.

PHILLIP APPLEMAN (WITH PERMISSION OF THE AUTHOR)[*]

Teaching believers how to think is never an easy task, because our human nature prefers to believe in simple, concrete ideologies and repetitive patterns. It's just more comfortable that way. The theory of cognitive dissonance tells us that this is part of being human. Because our brain wants so much for things to be resonant, it will override new ideas that challenge former ways of thinking, which explains why it is so difficult to change our minds once we have taken a position. Smokers don't want to die of lung cancer, and overeaters do not want to be obese. When new information challenges ourlives, we tend to reduce the dissonance by taking a position of self-justification so that we can preserve our beliefs that we are good and righteous people who want to encourage only the best in this world.

---

[*] Appleman, P. (2009). Karma, dharma, pudding and pie. New York: W.W. Norton.

The problem is that in our brain's desire to keep the status quo, we develop cognitive blind spots that distort the facts and confuse our stories.

So what do you do with the fact that there are as many acceptable ideas of being spiritual as there are ways of being human? If all peoples of this planet are not only emotional, mental, and physical beings but also spiritual beings, then to mature we are going to have to come to some resolution about spirituality. How are we going to make the existential connection beyond the self? How will we answer the age-old questions of why we are here and what or who else is available to us in our lives? If we already have a spirituality or religion that works for us, then how will we be able to assimilate new ideas and challenges that push the boundaries of traditional belief?

Spiritual development does not lead to a static place of arrival but to a process of growth and awareness that unfolds over time with new thoughts and life experiences. This development is for some aided by church catechisms and family values, whereas others may have found traditional ways of understanding God or "The Other" that are crippling to their spirit. For people who do not fit in with the dominant paradigms, spiritual development becomes something of a creative and frustrating endeavor. Some people find it too taxing and just shut the door on this embroiled topic, because their brains yearn for resonance rather than toxic dissonance. If they haven't found a good way to connect the most congruent part of their lives with the spiritual, they find some other way to make meaning in their lives. I find it fascinating that although spirituality is as old as humanity, each generation seems to find new ways to think about God and humanity so as to serve the needs of contemporary culture. Quite often a new movement is founded by someone who felt the need to minister to people who do not fit in with the mainstream.

The life of Reverend Gwen Hall is a prime example of this. She couldn't find a church where she felt welcomed as a lesbian and an African American, so she started her own. I met her at a retreat for people living with AIDS in 1993, when she was a pastoral counselor and educator who felt moved to do something about disenfranchised gays and lesbians in the Black community. In her desire to minister to African American families dealing with AIDS in the early '90s, she found herself alone. Unable to find fellow clergy to take on the social justice issues she felt called to, she founded Sojourner Truth Ministries in 1995 as a welcoming place for African American gays and people living with AIDS whom she believed had been abandoned by their community. Her longtime friend Trina Banks described her as a woman of action: "Gwen always said she didn't have the luxury of standing on the sidelines and watching things happen" (Turnbull, 2007). As a result, she not only founded a very unique ministry but also took a stand on many issues other clergy were not willing to face, and she never backed down from the hardest challenges. Unfortunately, Gwen died at age 56 from complications related to heart failure.

Over the past 3 decades, the number of gays and lesbians who have wanted to join mainstream American churches has increased. Many stayed within their own ranks to rebuild the infrastructure so that there would be a welcoming presence to the members who were sexual minorities. Others left their former churches where they felt excluded to find new communities of worship that would welcome and affirm their sexual identity, because they felt that staying in their former culture would not allow them to be authentic in either their humanity or their spirituality. As a result, more than 3,500 welcoming and affirming churches in America have become linked by the common desire to provide a place for gays and lesbians where they can be reconciled to the church (http://www.welcomingresources.org; this site is also a great resource for Bible studies, gay, lesbian, bisexual, and transgender [GLBT] information, and ways to help congregations move toward inclusion).

This shift is a wonderful illustration of cognitive dissonance. Since the 1950s, scientists have continued to provide new facts about the wide variety of human sexual orientations and behaviors that were unknown when the Bible was written. Some denominations have been able to gain new understanding when fresh discoveries about humanity occur whereas others have not been able to find a way to reconcile this kind of new information with their traditional belief systems. The congregations who allowed the science of human sexuality to influence their understandings of Scriptural principles often constructed new theologies that were designed to be eradicate their institution's oppression of sexual minorities. After congregations voted to become inclusive of GLBT believers, many houses of worship reported a new breath of life in their sanctuaries. As former walls of entrenchment that divided rather than united people were ripped down in ways unthinkable in the 1960s, new congregational energy and hope emerged. As the following interviews demonstrate, this renewal has also been one of the greatest encouragements for gay Christians who grew up in the church and longed for the day they could bring their whole selves into community for the purposes of spiritual development.

However, as today's cultural norms are rapidly changing, church attendance continues to wane, which makes it very obvious that many no longer feel a need to be aligned with the institutional church. Yet, according to a recent Gallup poll (Gallup, 1998), "almost 90%of the people who come to see therapists have a sense that religion is significant in their lives

(O'Hanlon, 2006, p. 3). It is my opinion that the desire to connect spiritually to something beyond themselves remains one of the fundamental aspects of being human. In seeking a place where deeper parts of the human heart can connect to something beyond the self, some people have found a growing spirituality in the wonder of the earth and the mystical seasons of nature. Others may have found their spiritual connection of tapping into mystery through higher learning or scientific exploration. Some people have found a spirituality developing when they connect with others who share a desire to minister to the human needs of others.

O'Hanlon (2006, pp. 14–22) suggested seven possible pathways to spirituality, all having to do with our desire to connect:

1. Connection with the soul.
2. Connection through the body.
3. Connecting to another being.
4. Connecting to community.
5. Connecting through nature.
6. Connecting by participation in creating or appreciating art or music.
7. Connecting to the universe, higher power, God, or cosmic consciousness.

However it happens, it seems that each generation continues to create new spiritual ways of being to satisfy the human need to connect beyond the self looking for strength; to find a place to express gratitude, or for wisdom to see the bigger picture of their lives.

Things That Help Spiritual Growth for Sexual Minorities

Places of Acceptance

In my survey, 60% reported community acceptance—including loving support of family, friends, sympathetic clergy, or an enlightened therapist—as the most helpful in aiding their spiritual growth. Sometimes this support came from a family of choice instead of from biological parents, who sometimes reacted adversely after learning they had a gay son or lesbian daughter. Although it is a well-known fact that a minister is often the first person people turn to when facing adversity, not enough clergy have been properly educated to truly be of help (Lombardi, 2000): Tony Campolo suggests that there are no easy answers that clergy can offer to gays and lesbians who ask about changing their orientation, and that it is very rare for a person's sexual orientation to change (Campolo, 2007).

This leaves many pastors wondering about how to care for the homosexuals in their congregations. Many give a standard solution for what they believe to be a spiritual dilemma: If a person isn't a married heterosexual, the only other acceptable answer is celibacy. It may be suggested that this might be achieved by putting one's sexual energy into some other spiritual passion. However, this highlights one of the greatest problems about the myth of homosexuality. When thoughts of being gay are mostly constructed in terms of what one does in bed as opposed to a way of being, there emerges a preoccupation with sex that completely misses the deeper aspects of self-acceptance or seeing oneself as a whole person.

Such traditional ideas fall short of addressing deep concerns of gays and lesbians who are seeking a new way to integrate faith into their personal journeys. "The community that seeks to be welcoming does not push people on these journeys but gives them permission to be where they are. A community can honor different journeys and at the same time be a place where LGBT people are fully affirmed." (Hobbs, 2008) (For an excellent article on pastoral ministry to gays and lesbians, see *Climate of Care*, by John Hobbs, *Christian Century*, 2008, March 11.)

Early in my ministerial career, I was sympathetic toward homosexuals, but my seminary education provided only minimum training in counseling and nothing when it came to areas of sexuality. Apparently, most people at that time would have preferred that the topic remain quiet and out of sight. However, I was hearing many embattled stories of people wrestling with their sexuality, like the young man who confided his homosexual desires to his hometown pastor. His minister responded by telling him in a kindly voice that if he acted on his sexual impulses he would be shunned by the church until he repented of his sin. He then told him that he was acting out of love! The only help I knew to give was traditional interpretations of the Bible that mandated chastity outside of marriage. The thought was that if people loved God and knew the rules of our faith, they would be given the spiritual resources to change their behaviors. However, as I began to realize that many faithful people would never be able to change their sexual orientation, the traditional answers ceased to be congruent with my own spirit. The problem was that the only education on this topic I had was my religious culture's literal interpretations of Scripture that discouraged further thinking on this topic. A good example of this mentality occurred when one of my former parishioners felt I wasn't interpreting the biblical ideas on homosexuality as literally as he would like and shared his opinion with me in a voice filled with paternal overtones that declared his displeasure: "It's not about what you think, Ken; it's about what God says!" Sigh.

Although my gut was saying there had to be a different way to look at homosexuality, I felt stuck having to advise people who had homosexual tendencies in the traditional manner for fear of losing my job. If they couldn't change their orientation, the only option left was to be celibate. Talk about cognitive dissonance! I knew that if someone had given me that advice, I would have failed miserably and would probably be plagued by chronic guilt for the rest of my life. I look back now and wonder what the outcome was for some of the people I once advised in this manner. (So to anyone whom I advised in the past, I apologize. How I wish I could have provided you better care and counsel than you received. I hope you will forgive my former ignorance and any unnecessary heartache I caused in your life.)

Accepting Communities

One of the most helpful things for GLBTs in spiritual development is to find a supportive community where people can feel complete acceptance without having to hide any important aspects of their lives from others. Human beings long to be fully accepted and loved for who they are. This can happen only when the shame of being different or being seen as less than is removed. This is akin to a person finding his or her tribe or a place of belonging where others have similar values and beliefs—a place where one can be fully developed. Notice in the following interviews how often straight allies are mentioned, which says a lot about how healthy it is to be assimilated into a diverse congregation rather than being relegated to a gay or straight ghetto.

Victor

> I grew up in my faith just assuming that God loved me and that I was perfectly all right the way I was. When I was in a mode of thinking that I had to be someone else to be acceptable to God, I realized that was my issue and not God's. That was when I really came out. But I have to say that in 59 years, I've always been active in the church. I grew up in the church. I've never felt alienated from God. I never felt I was separated out. Even when I was asked to leave the church, I just assumed that it was that group of people and not necessarily God who didn't like me and that there were other people who probably would. There are many congregations that are caring and supportive. They may not understand who you are or what you are doing. But if you, as an individual, come in as a seeker and you are willing to go along the journey with them, they'd like the company. Generally speaking, some do, anyway.

Mark

I think probably that there have been nongay people within the church who have been allies—thoughtful, attentive, and committed to deviating from the institutional church. That made a huge difference to me because my parents had difficulties with my being gay. To have some heterosexual people that were, clearly, good Catholics who were embracing, affirming, and supportive of me made a huge difference. They didn't tell me that I needed to make a choice but that I needed to explore both of these important areas of myself. I was ready to do that, but I just needed somebody I respected to encourage me and say, "Go for it!"

Evelyn

When I was living in Oakland, there was an organized lesbian spiritual group that met Sunday mornings and sang, and people would speak on various topics of interest—socially, ecologically, politically. And that was very spiritually encouraging. I still miss it.

Thomas

I think being part of my church community, where folks just expect me to be a human being and let me live my life and relationship in a way that is up front, has been the biggest benefit to being part of this congregation. It has certainly helped me grow. And having the connection of [the church conference] has been incredible. I will be at events with my partner, and if I'm not there with him, people who I know disagree with me theologically will still say, "Where's Keith? Is he okay?" And that creates an opportunity for a spiritual life in community that I think is pretty rare and wonderful. I realize as I'm talking about this that a lot of what I've had to say has a lot to do with institutional life, which I know is problematic for a lot of gay and lesbian folks, but it works for me.

Richard

I think having a supportive faith community and family are probably the two hugest positives in coming out and feeling secure, because I know that those really paved the way for me. I've seen how the lack of those has affected Bob (his partner) and other people as well who have had to completely reform the way they were raised—either in their religious community or their parents' political background. I think overcoming those is a huge obstacle that I didn't have to surmount. I always thought my parents were kind of conservative, but in hindsight I have found that all of those fears were unfounded, because when I came out to my parents, both of them were immediately supportive—and that's not the case for many people.

Brett

I'm thinking of three things in church that have hit me about how this is good and right and that have made me glad that I'm Brett and that I'm gay and part of my church. One example is when I would look around the church and see two guys sitting with their arms around each other in church and in front of me would be two women sitting there with their arms around each other. I would think, "Wow! This hardly ever happens anywhere else I have been." That was really pretty neat. The second [way] sexuality and spirituality came together was when we had this cute, young gay couple who became youth leaders of the middle school group when my daughter was there. All these kids would get together, and all these programs, service opportunities, and Bible studies were happening up and down the hall where Matt and Tom were. It had gone so well. We'd seen all these pictures of kids piling up on top of Tom and Matt in the snow. Later they told us they never thought they'd have a chance to work with kids and be so accepted like that. It meant so much to them. So that was a great thing. I thought that if spirituality, in part, is to see how people treat each other and what the future can hold, those are moments I look around and see the grace and think we've got a future together as human beings—and to me that is spirituality. Then, when Pat and I had our wedding in the church, the two Methodist ministers didn't even change the wording. She just said, "This is a wedding!"—right in the service. We had [about] 80 friends there; it gave me a chance to come out at work; and then invite my coworkers to a Methodist wedding? I'd never heard of such a thing! To have a wedding, I think, means the exact same thing to gay people as to nongay people, but we knew it was significant—to have all these friends come out for us. Pat had some friends from work, I had some friends from work, and our kids were ring bearers. We even had dancing in the reception downstairs in the church. That was a really spiritual moment! So those are some examples [of] how people treated us. They were a "God in our midst" kind of thing. These three very real examples told me that there's hope for the future: God among people, loving us.

Beth

I'd probably say that my sexuality and spirituality are more in sync right now—closer than they ever have been. I think that's occurred having a small community outside of the church, family that supports me and my partner, and a church to attend [where I can be myself] rather than a "don't ask, don't tell" congregation. So I feel more valued. And in that context it's just a lot easier to worship—just to let my boundaries down. As far as what has most helped my spiritual development—seeing women in ministry who shared their interpretations of the Bible from a feminine perspective probably helped me sort it out the most. It's also been very helpful to hear heterosexual men who are supportive of gays and lesbian issues and don't treat them as if they were dirty or something. It communicates more of a value. Like, if you are going to have a couples' retreat and it could actually include same-sex couples, that would be so validating! In the Southern Baptist church, where I grew up, that would never happen. The only valid couples would be heterosexual. Even if they are cheating on each other, they would still be more valid than gay couples.

Clint

It was being in an environment like I am now, where I was nurtured and supported, whole, and available to myself, that I realized the strength and stamina and the courage and insistence that I was able to develop—character building, if you will. Those years when I had to build walls and protection actually had a value for me now. When I look back, I realize that, good heavens, I am a really strong person! I put up with a lot and didn't allow that distracting, negative agenda and energy to completely deplete my opportunities to serve, do good, and have a full and happy life.

Accepting Families

When it comes to finding a place of belonging, nothing can really be as healing as one's family. Conversely, nothing can hurt so much as to be rejected by your own people. However I think it is good to recognize that *household, kin,* and *family* are not always identical terms. *Household* may refer to anyone living under the same roof, such as roommates, whereas *kin* usually is reserved for blood relatives. However, *family* in this sense can really be all these things, since people often refer to their closest friends as their family of choice. *Family of choice* can be equally important when discussing GLBT relationships. Several interviewees mentioned that their partners or families were by far the most significant part of their spiritual development and growth. After dealing with life's stresses all day, there is nothing like coming home to a place of love and acceptance, which several people described as part of the spirituality that sustains them.

Jeff
After 20 years of floundering in escapism and inconsequential relationships, Jeff has had the pleasure of making a home with his partner, Rick, and others:

> My family has widened with Rick and his mom, aunt, and family—and [by] getting a cat! That's our son! (laughter) People may think that's weird, but it allows us to learn to love. Previously, I kept trying to destroy myself. My self-esteem was not high enough at all. Now, it's beginning to grow. I have acted out of fear my entire life. We began this conversation about faith and fear. We learned in AA [Alcoholics Anonymous] that faith is the opposite of fear. I'm sure it's been said in many other places, but this is where I've been able to hear it.

Bob

> I think [my partner] Richard has been a huge part of my spirituality because I tend to be an isolationist. He's brought that out. We actually met online, and the title of my personal ad was "Gay Christian is not an oxymoron!" (laughter) And [so I found] this other Christian person whose faith was very important

to him—[he was] looking for the same thing. I think our journey together has helped me be more spiritual. He has been very supportive of me [when I was] going to seminary, [by] walking through this second [bout of] cancer with me, and [when] my parents treated me poorly. His family has been very warm, accepting, and loving, and all of those things have really helped mirror God's love for me and helped me be comfortable with who I am. Now, I have no hesitancy speaking about my sexuality and spirituality. Some people still have some issues, but they are not my issues. I talk about Richard just like other people talk about their spouses, and I think that's part of my call. I'm just going to be who I am; we're just going to be who we are and have people to dinner at our table to see the reality. Here's the "gay lifestyle": We're in bed by 9:00! (laughter). Once I got God back, came out of the closet, and found Richard, it's been more normal. The more normal my life became, then my spirituality could assume its perfect circle in my life. It's all just part of who I am rather than what I do. It's taken me a long time to get there. Now, other people see it and comment on it. (Interviewer: It must be nice to have that additional confirmation.) Yes. Definitely.

Finding Resilience

You light up the soul O God, and make the eyes sparkle. You give health and life and blessing.

Ecclesiastes 34:20

When we use the word *resilience* in everyday conversations, we are usually referring to how tough a person is or how it's possible for them to tolerate much more adversity than anyone imagined. People who have learned to accept themselves as sexual minorities are indeed resilient. Most of us would also agree that the life path for homosexuals is bound to be more difficult at times than the lives of those who are straight. A person who learns to bounce back after the rejections and judgments of others (who often say they have good intentions) is bound to develop a great deal of resilience.

But when we speak about the therapeutic concept of resilience, we are talking about something quite different. Therapeutic resilience is something people can carry with themselves that keeps hope alive. O'Connell-Higgens (1994) conducted a study about resiliency in adults who been able to demonstrate "loving well" and "working well" (p. 349) in spite of the fact that they had absolutely horrific childhoods. The data for her research was gleaned from clinical interviews with 40 resilient people who had been "facing [extreme] stress for most of their childhood and adolescent years"(p. 349). The areas of stress were financial, illness, chronic fighting in the family, substance abuse, parental mental disorders, absent parents and repeated sexual or physical abuse (p. 350). These remarkable people were able to carry something inside their core self that helped them face the unthinkable situations of life and go on to live fairly normal lives, when others in the same kind of situations were permanently damaged. Most trauma theories would expect many recurrent episodes of posttraumatic stress disorder (PTSD) in the life of a person who, for example, was repeatedly kicked across the room by a raging, alcoholic father. It would be expected that this kind of trauma would severely hinder a person's ability to form decent relationships and functionality. Yet out of a group of people who have faced severe trauma, a handful of them seem to be able to create well-adjusted, productive lives and to have loving relationships. What made for some of the difference is that with the resilient subjects, someone outside the family system checked in on them at times, asked how they were doing, and posited in them the hope of something better. Many times it was only one specific person who made all the difference: someone who could bear the pain and losses without shrinking from the trauma, someone who continually reminded the storytellers that they were not crazy and there was indeed hope for a better future and a meaningful life. "You do not have to pull a dove out of your sleeve to make a difference. Many of the resilient emphasized that their hope was continually buttressed by the sudden kindness of strangers, integrated into the broader fabric of resilient faith over time" (O'Connell-Higgins, 1994, p. 325).

The role an enlightened therapist plays in the lives of troubled clients is paramount. Sympathetic therapists who can help a person sort out healthy life-giving options for their clients can mean the difference between life and death for some clients. The trusted relationship between therapist and client is often where the seeds of resilience are planted. To be educated and empathic so that true support can be provided for the gay son or daughter who has faced so much rejection already is no small thing. When a family therapist is able to help family members come together to discuss what they have been avoiding at home, resilience can become a systemic implant that may bless a family for generations.

> Hope is the thing with feathers
>   That perches in the soul,
>   And sings the tune—without the words,
>   And never stops.

Emily Dickinson

The Accepting Therapist

During my survey, although I did not ask questions about what kind of therapy people had received, quite often the conversation turned in that direction when we began talking about what or who had been most help-ful in their spiritual growth. The following interview is one woman's quest to find a competent therapist. In the process, she encountered therapists who helped a great deal and those who did just the opposite. Former cli-ents often continue to carry resilient messages in their minds for many years by remembering those exact words of hope that were first implanted in their lives during their course of therapy. This is a gift that keeps pro-viding internal healing for many years.

Debra

After two failed heterosexual marriages, at age 35, Debra fell in love with a woman, feeling that she had finally settled the question about her sexual identity. However, when this fairly closeted relationship began to dissolve, Debra was faced with a new dilemma of how to integrate her sexuality and spirituality. When I asked her to describe a time when her sexuality and spirituality were most in synch, she responded profoundly:

> It's a different question. If they weren't in sync, then the question for me is sui-cide, because I can't live without being who I am. Either that person or persons who stand in the way of me being who I am have to go away or I have to go away. I knew that suicide is not a solution and that I needed help, so I began to seek therapy. My spirituality got me through that crisis by sustaining me through the breakup of the best relationship I ever had—which doesn't say much for the other relationships I had, which were pretty out of sync. But that deepened my spirituality, and I never questioned my sexuality after 35. I knew that I needed to express being myself and feel I had nothing to hide.
>
> I had some counseling, but I wouldn't even dignify it by calling it therapy. He was a pastoral counselor—a friend of a friend. It was in the early '70s, which was in the breakup of one of those marriages, and he came on to me, so I prob-ably didn't get any good therapy out of that. But I didn't even call him on it, because I didn't even know what a professional therapist was.
>
> I wrote a paper about this once: The people around me at turning points in my life, particularly clergy, who could have done something to help my per-sonal awareness and growth didn't do anything. I think clergy have to be a lot spiffier than the ones I had those dealings with. So I tried another therapist when this was all breaking up in my late 40s and early 50s, and that didn't work very well either. She didn't exploit me, but she didn't know very much. I actu-ally looked for a lesbian so I wouldn't have to hide anything at all. Then I saw a male psychiatrist for a while, but I just didn't trust him because I had a hard time trusting men.
>
> Then I [found] an excellent therapist in my early 50s who said, "Where'd you go?" and I said, "What?" She said, "You're not here anymore." I said, "I'm not?" [And she answered] "No." We did that a few times, and then she said, "We need to start meeting two times a week." Well, at this point I had a master's in counseling, and I knew I was in big trouble! (laughter)

So I went to work, and learned how to connect my emotions with my life experiences. I could talk all around every issue: backwards, forwards, and from all sides, but I couldn't name a feeling to save my soul. There were times I worked hard with my therapist and other times when I just sat there. Then she would say, "Well, just sit with it for a while," and (laugh) I'd just sit there in silence—but finally I began to catch on.

The thing that hindered [therapy] the most was that I was not connected to my feelings—I was not a whole person. So I would never come at something both with feelings and thinking at the same time; therefore, I could make one decision one minute and the opposite the next minute, and I didn't know how to sort it out. I didn't really know what I thought on a personal level. I knew how to give the right answer, and I knew how to sound like I knew the right answer, but I didn't know the right answer until I got hooked up. It's very embarrassing for me.

I went to seminary shortly after that, or after I'd been with [that same therapist] a couple of years, and [then things] really began to [come] together for me. I started rewriting my theology, which was the thing that helped the most—that's when I really began to feel connected and whole.

Self-Acceptance

Happy are those whose hearts do not condemn them, and who have not given up hope.

Ecclesiastes 14:2

In the survey, 33% of interviewees cited "self-acceptance, learning to live my own life, rather than pleasing others" as second most helpful in aiding spiritual growth in their lives. Although this sounds like a normal developmental process straight out of Murray Bowen's *Theory of Self Differentiation* (http://psychology.wikia.com/wiki/Murray_Bowen), it is especially poignant for queer people, who find the process of declaring their true self to be an even greater challenge. Self-differentiation is hard enough for socially dominant privileged groups; imagine how much more difficult it is for a cultural minority that is even more dependent on those natural togetherness forces to ensure basic survival.

Consider, for instance, this story told from one of my interviews. Aaron had an immense challenge presented to him as the only child of a family with not only a very conservative religious faith but also with ties to a very tight racial and ethnic minority of American immigrants. As a young boy he was very bright and compliant—the apple of his parent's eye. As a polite, quiet adolescent, he was rewarded for properly honoring his parents' wishes as his ethnic culture expected, yet inwardly he was growing more confused about why he was never interested in dating someone of the opposite sex. Like his parents, he was rather relieved that he was not facing the problems with lust that his other friends did. He was relatively content to think that his maturity had not yet peaked. Although he had thoughts and dreams about same-sex attractions, he quickly discounted them and tried to stifle his deeper feelings as quickly as possible, knowing they were culturally and religiously unacceptable. Up to this time his self-acceptance was based on doing the right thing, which pleased his parents. Shortly after college, however, he met a man that not only enlarged his life but also hastened the unraveling of the whole platform of his former idea of self. The first time he acted on his natural gay sexuality he experienced both relief and horror. The relief was to finally acknowledge that he was a mature sexual being, capable of great depths of emotional connections that he previously thought were impossible; the horror was the fear of how his community's reactions could cost him everything he held close to his heart.

Self-acceptance for this young man was therefore much more difficult than it would have been for a heterosexual child. Before he "came in" to himself, he wondered what was wrong or deficient with his sexuality. Afterward, he feared that as a gay man he would not be able to remain close to his parents and the culture that believed homosexuality was a grievous sin. He was also worried that he would have to renounce his faith, which was very precious to him. He had a choice to make: He could either choose a complete emotional cutoff by his family and God or a cutoff from his deepest self. He chose to remain with his family by repressing his sexuality for another 5 years. On the occasions he would have a sexual encounter, he would always feel terribly anxious and shamed afterward. As he continued to please his parents by excluding his truest self, his self-acceptance lessened. One day, another gay man sensing his ambivalence invited him to a Bible study sponsored by Evangelicals Concerned, whose motto is "Creating Safe Places for GLBT Christians." (Their Web site, http://www.Ecrw.org/, has many personal stories of how people have integrated queer sexuality and spirituality and also provides alternative pro-gay interpretations of Scriptures that have long been used to condemn homosexuals.)

At the Bible study, this young man found a group that encouraged members of the GLBT community to embrace their God-given sexuality and the Christian faith at the same time. They had found a way to connect the dots of spirituality and sexuality. As the evening went on, the young man, now 26, sat in stunned silence, continually wiping his brimming eyes unashamedly. When someone asked him what was wrong, he responded softly with amazement, "I never knew this was possible."

Aaron

> In summer 2000, I looked at myself in the mirror and said, "Okay, you're gay. What are you going to do about it?" That was the first time I really acknowledged myself for who I am. And shortly after, when I met a gentleman who identified as both gay and Christian, I began a spiritual journey. That was the first time I heard that concept, and I just started to consider the possibility that one could be both gay and Christian. So I started to open my heart to the Spirit's leading. I met a bunch of gay Christians and heard their testimonies, and I saw that it is possible for one to live as both—being true to yourself and true to God. I read a lot of books, and I began to see that I was supposed to take the Bible in context and not just the most literal interpretation that I had grown up with. So after I reconciled to myself, coming out was the most natural thing to do. It [was] good news: "Hey, I'm okay as I am!" Now, I can't help but tell other people about it.

Figure 5.1   Leap of faith.

Not all interviewees reported self-acceptance in the context of others. For many people like Aaron, the first step in their own personal healing was to look in the mirror and accept who they knew themselves to be in spite of what others might think.

Katrina

The thing that most helped my spirituality to develop was accepting myself, finding my power, and feeling comfortable. The more comfortable I am with myself, [when] I find others who don't agree with my lifestyle, I know that is their problem and not mine. I'm comfortable with that now. When I was 21 or 22, I'd crawl on coals to be accepted because that's just the way I was. In the Catholic Church we were brought up to be submissive, but I think that self-acceptance has helped me to be closer to God. I also think self-acceptance is most important in being comfortable with yourself because if you are uncomfortable, then you're fighting yourself. That negative energy doesn't help spirituality at all; in fact, that really negates anything you can think of in a positive light.

Gordon

Feeling at peace with my sexuality has definitely enhanced my ability to feel spiritual and at one with myself. It's all been one empowering thing after another, really. When I think of my sexuality, I think of the peace that I feel with God, with others, within myself, and my family. It's been an extremely long road, with innumerable tiny steps that have brought me to this point. But I can honestly say this is the happiest and most peaceful I've felt in my life.

Developing One's Own Spiritual Practices

Heed the counsel of your own heart, and above all pray to the Most High that you may be guided in the way of truth.

Ecclesiastes 37:13, 15

The third most helpful practice for spiritual growth in the lives of those interviewed (33%) was "to develop their own spiritual practices" (e.g., prayer, singing, meditation, quiet times of reflection, learning to serve others, and for some rewriting their own theology). These are things that any person would find to be spiritually helpful. When one's faith is practiced on a daily basis, it becomes a natural strength engrained into the fabric of one's being and of great help in times of distress. Again, for a heterosexual, middle-class, White person, this normal developmental task can be very demanding. However, since many GLBT people have felt the need—or in many cases been told—to leave the established religion of their youth, this can become a nearly impossible task due to the lack of welcoming places and an inadequate number of available role models. Without traditional community input to encourage, share, or teach spiritual disciplines that have proven effective for generations, queer people are often left to their own thinking and creativity. Though this may eventually become something very meaningful and centering for a person, it may also be a daunting challenge.

Patrick

After his divorce, Patrick started experimenting with different kinds of churches other than the Catholic faith in which he was raised. As we discussed during the interview what had been most helpful in his spiritual development, he talked about how his spirituality has evolved over time:

> The guy I got involved with after my divorce and during my coming out was Buddhist, and that really didn't connect a lot for me. I tried the MCC [Metropolitan Community Church], but that was more fundamental than I was used to, and it just had a different flavor. I hung out there for a while, but it just didn't seem like it fit. And so I didn't do much with that the church] until I moved to Seattle and got involved with the Methodist church for a number of years. It was accepting, and we could take our kids there when they were young, and we could all participate in the parish life on all levels. It didn't feel like there were any second-class levels in the local church. But when you got beyond the doors of that church to participating at the conference level, it sort of felt like you're somehow not acceptable. You could be a parishioner, and you could be involved in that church—I was even involved in the process of searching for a pastor for our church. But if you are openly gay, you couldn't be a minister. You could never be ordained. I think that point is when I just decided I had had enough. I decided I wasn't going to be involved in a formalized church ever again. If gay, lesbian, bi, and transsexual people couldn't be fully accepted and affirmed throughout the whole system, I was done with it. On the other hand, it also made me think for myself and be more clear that belief in God and having a spiritual life didn't always have to be connected with having a formal relationship with an organization. I think that part was helpful and powerful. As you know, taking time every day to meditate is really important to me—and to feel in touch with that spiritual part of myself and not discount it or throw it away. Just to be at peace with it is powerful. To be aware of it as I live my life and connect with other people and their spirituality [and] to share their part of the universe is just pretty neat.

Sarah

(Interviewer: When would you say your spirituality and sexuality are most in sync? Let's take religion out of it.) I can't wrap myself around that question. Taking religion out of it—I guess for a long time I did equate religion and spirituality. I know spirituality goes beyond religion. I think I believe in God or whatever is in your heart, but it is also [about] believing in yourself—I don't know. (Interviewer: I'm just curious; is this because if you're gay you can't be religious?) No, it's not because I'm gay and can't be spiritual. I don't think that's it. I think it may be because I just haven't found what I find to be truly spiritual for me. I think that probably the closest thing I can find is being out in nature. The sheer grandeur and power of nature is where I feel most spiritual. It's where I feel in awe at what's out there and how it intertwines. Even though we as human beings don't sometimes think it does, it does connect with all that's going on. So, for me, being out in the middle of nowhere is a spiritual experience, and the feeling of calmness and letting your mind go and be in touch with everything in that environment is very spiritual.

Rachel

In the last 10 to 12 years, I [have] started reading some Buddhist things—Tik Naht Hann and accessible kinds of stuff. It was very attractive and helpful to me for day-to-day living. I went to a couple of retreats, and it didn't seem like it mattered what your sexuality was or even what your religion was. It was very open and inclusive, and I liked that. As time went on and I went to some different groups or retreats, I felt like I was different in a way because I was lesbian, and I wanted to find some other lesbian women who were on a similar path. I ended up at this retreat about 4 years ago that was taught by a lesbian and all participants were women. I loved it! It made so much sense. Everything came together, because that teacher definitely brought a gay perspective; some of her experiences were things I could relate to. It made my interest and acceptance of a lot of Buddhist ideas a lot easier.

Julie

I've never worried about my spirituality. Never. I've always felt very close to God. In my times of trouble, I don't say, "Why did this happen?" I just say, "Please walk with me; help me find the way." Sometimes I think, "Well, what lesson am I supposed to be learning here? I can't quite see it yet." (laughter) But I don't know where I'd be if I didn't have my daily talks with God. I remember being in college in Minneapolis, when four of us shared an apartment in this big old converted mansion, where a couple of wonderful guys had an apartment above us. We invited them down for a spaghetti dinner because that's all we could afford. Since we lived across the street from this big beautiful park with magnificent gardens, two of us went out as soon as it got dark to cut flowers for our table. Even back then I was talking to God, asking him if he could understand why we were doing this. (laughter) Anyway, it's been a daily thing.

Cora

I do a meditative practice. In Toaist tradition, there was a female immortal named Swin Bu Ar, who was the only female immortal. There are only eight immortals in Taoism, and then seven of what are called real people, who were sort of like junior immortals—[They] didn't quite attain the level of status the eight immortals did. Swin Bu Ar developed Taoist practices specifically for female cultivation of spiritual growth and refinement of the physical body, so I practice her foundations. I was taught those techniques by the man in Beijing I studied with. So I meditate along specific lines with a Chinese medicine application that is making alchemical changes in my body. I'd also say my Chi-Gong practice is a big part of that too because it sends healing energy throughout my body.

Lucy

What encouraged my spiritual growth has been other people, but basically I think it's been my own spiritual experiences. One of the things my mother taught me was that help is available if you ask for it. I've had the experience of asking for help and receiving it from the universe. Part of my belief is that there is something greater, which some people call God. But I don't see it as a person but [as] an energy. Maybe we are all part of this energy that some people call God—and there are what I think of as helpers who hear me pray. I [haven't always] used the word *pray*; I used the word *energy* or something—but I'm feeling more comfortable in using those words when I pray. I often don't know who I'm praying to, but it feels like I'm praying to one of these helpers. I personally feel like I have a fairy godmother, who some people might call an angel or a saint. But I have prayed and sent energy to these individuals, and they have helped. They help spiritually, psychologically, in real life. When I was an atheist, I would have thought that was deluded, but I don't really care now. As far as I'm concerned, it's having a spiritual practice that helps. It works. That's what keeps me real.

If I were to summarize the common theme of these three helpful things, I would say it is the desire to be a fully accepted and integrated member of society. Whenever unconditional acceptance of a person becomes a possibility, the river that leads to positive growth, peace, and self-acceptance will flow freely.

The Still, Small Voice: The Birth of Human Spirituality

Let me hear what you will speak when I turn to you in my heart.

Psalm 85:8

One of the things most helpful in allowing people to begin believing in the possibility of a connected spirituality is a concept I call the *still, small voice,* which comes from an ancient story in the Hebrew Scriptures.

Although Elijah was considered to be the greatest and most powerful of all prophets in history, there is a peculiar story told about a time when he was running for his life. After Elijah's all-powerful God had defeated Queen Jezebel's prophets of Baal in a spectacular showdown greater than any Fourth of July fireworks in modern history, Elijah became terrified of this spiteful woman. Apparently forgetting that God demonstrated a power that far exceeded any human ability, Elijah panicked and ran off into the desert to Mt. Horeb, where he was sure he was going to die. As I read the story, it certainly sounds like he was suffering from intense anxiety and clinical depression! As he ran to this mountain, he fully expected to find safety in the shelter of El Shadai, The High and Mighty One. Once he arrived, he was met by an angelic ministering presence who not only fed him but also directed him to the entrance of a cave high on the mountain, where he would most certainly hear the voice of God.

Standing on this mountain, Elijah most likely expected God to show up in spectacular fashion like he had previously done. But the Scriptures tell a different outcome:

> Then a great and powerful wind tore the mountains apart and shattered the rocks before the Lord, but the Lord was not in the wind. After the wind, there was an earthquake, but the Lord was not in the earthquake. After the earthquake came a fire, but the Lord was not in the fire. And after the fire came a gentle whisper. When Elijah heard it, he pulled his cloak over his face and went out and stood at the mouth of the cave. Then a voice [softly] said to him , "What are you doing here, Elijah?"
>
> I Kings 19:11-13

Not only did God show up in the most unexpected fashion, but the question put to Elijah is also a surprise. The still, small voice said, "What are you doing here, Elijah?" This could be interpreted as, "Why did you need to come to a mountaintop; did you think this is where I live? Don't you know God is everywhere?" Or perhaps God was asking Elijah, "Why did you run in fear? Didn't you believe I would be with you at all times?" It is really a great existential question for someone who has lost faith. "Why run away? Why come here? Why seek me only in the spectacular?" In asking these questions the answer implied is that God is everywhere; God is present and loving and as close as the slightest whisper of your conscience.

Beloved

I remember one such moment in my own life, about 10 years ago, when I felt much like Elijah must have felt. I was not only depressed but also full of an internal shame for some grievous mistakes I had made and angry at those who refused to understand or give me a break. In other words, I was a mess. So I decided to get out of town and go to my family's cabin and build a deck to try to accomplish something constructive and to divert myself from excessive negative thinking. At first I began driving the nails with an exceptional passion that was fueled by anger. I think I actually named a few enemies as I bashed the heads of the nails into the soft cedar planks. (No, I didn't have any issues, thank you for asking!)

But after my anger was expressed, I remembered something I had read that morning about the love of God from one of Henri Nouwen's books (2000). As my mood softened, I became aware of other things besides my personal toxins: Birds sang as they flew overhead, and the wind made a refreshing sound as it passed through the tall evergreens that surrounded me. Then I began to internally experience the surge of the waves lapping on the beach below our home; they seemed to measure out a cadence, and a Zen-like moment illuminated me as I imagined those waves as the soothing nature of God's voice. That was when I heard the word *beloved* with each wave that caressed the shore: "Beloved! Beloved! You are my beloved son!" At that moment, I knew beyond a shadow of a doubt that somehow, in some way yet to be explained, I was loved beyond words and that I would be all right. In my recent interpretation of this event, I would call this the spirit of God or the Cosmic Christ, who transcends every molecule on the earth, wooing me back into relationship. Others may call this the voice of God, an angel, or a saint; the universe; energy; or the sound of my own wishes, but it definitely was a profound moment in my spirituality when I knew I was loved and accepted in a way that was rock solid.

When I have given seminars on this topic, I have encouraged participants to think of a time when they experienced something like this in their own lives—a time when they felt guidance or a presence or some kind of certainty that was one of the most profound truths of their lives. If we were going to go back to James Fowler's model of spiritual development, this would be "the logic of conviction"(Hanford, 1993, p. 95), when one has an experience of his or her inner voice that trumps all external authority.

Whenever I have asked attendees to tell the stranger next to them of a similar story in their lives, I have always been amazed at the outcome.

The first time I did this, I wasn't sure what to expect. Would people who didn't grow up in the church or were not exposed to a specific kind of religion be able to access spirituality in this way? Apparently, the answer is an overwhelming yes! Because each time I have tried this, the energy level in the room raises several bars. Sometimes it is almost tangible, and it takes a bit of finesse to bring attention back to the presenter. The look on people's faces at that moment is also something very special. They look peaceful, energized, affirmed, and connected—all of which illustrate my point that we all have the spiritual capacity and resources of connecting to something greater than ourselves and when we do, our lives take a turn for the better.

This, in essence, is the birthplace of human spirituality: people connecting the still, small voice to their core self. This voice is not parental or given to societal norms and prejudice. It goes beyond the language of feelings and nuance. It is the voice of inner awareness that grows whenever spiritual development is encouraged.

This mystical approach may sound much like Eastern religion's concept of the wise mind or of mindfulness, which is often used to bring tranquility and acceptance of "what is" into the clinical setting. However, the still, small voice urges the person to go deeper into the present moment, to connect with his or her spiritual heritage. This enables past wisdom a place to bring full acceptance into the present, which is often accompanied by an assurance of further connectedness and well-being in the future. This can be a very useful tool for many people to make spiritual connections in ways that are currently relevant.

I realize that for many religious conservatives this may stretch their concepts of traditional spirituality. Others may declare it to be a "less than" concept. After a recent exercise like this, a pastoral counselor remarked, "All this mystical stuff kind of really throws me. I'm much more used to a teleological approach to spirituality." I fully understood where he was coming from, having been raised in the tradition of passing the truth on to the next generation. Although this concept has been the mainstay of many religions, it has also left many people feeling excluded for reasons beyond their control. Many gay people have experienced such exclusion and toxicity from institutional churches that they cannot or will not touch traditional spirituality with a 10-foot pole. What is needed is the deposit of resilient hope in their lives: hope for accessing their personal spiritual nature; hope for connecting beyond their petty, little, lonely selves. Tapping into mysticism is one way that makes that possible.

People's Experiences With the Still, Small Voice

You love all things that exist, and hate nothing that you have made.

Wisdom 11:24

Brett, You Are Okay!

Talk about internal awareness! I remember now [about a time] when I first was going to spend a night with this cute guy I met in a gay bar. We talked and negotiated for a while and decided that we'd get together the next Saturday, have dinner, and spend the night together. I remember at some point wandering around thinking, "I wonder if I'm going to lose my soul and become a different person or something?" But it was never like that. I remember that next morning when I was leaving his apartment to catch the [subway for work]. It was going to be a hot, muggy day, and the [subway] in Boston is noisy and sooty, and already my clothes were getting kind of sticky and the people standing around were all hot. But it was just one of those grace moments—not a beautiful day but a grimy, gray day—and it was just like God was talking to me saying, "Brett, you are just okay." I was being held in His hands again. It was that voice I've only heard maybe three times in my life, I think—those moments where God has talked to me. God told me, "Brett, you are mine; I made you." So, it was pretty neat, on the sooty [subway] on a hot sweaty day to have God tell me that life is good and I'm still His!

Jeff: A Higher Power's Love Was Holding Me

I was running away from having any kind of inner peace, running from spirituality and homosexuality But I don't think I had a clue as to what spirituality was. I came out to myself around 20. That was a spiritual moment for me. In retrospect, the weight of the world lifted from my shoulders. I said, "I am a homosexual. I'm gay! Could have had a V-8!" (big laugh) When I think back now on that moment. I was feeling like I had a higher power's love wrapped around me at that moment, holding me up and saying, "You are all right." That was powerful, because that was the catalyst to begin telling my family and friends, "I'm gay."

Bob: The Rest Is Grace

My kind of conversion moment or watershed moment happened when I was going to Michigan in October 1994. I was driving, and the trees were stunning. [The highway] follows right along Lake Michigan, and I was once again praying, "This isn't going away; what am I doing wrong?" And it's like I almost heard this voice, and it was God saying, "What do you believe?" It was the traditional thing: "I believe Jesus Christ is and was who he was and that he died for me" and that whole thing. Then there was this message: "All else is grace." And it was like, "Whoa!" But from that moment on I had God back, and I always knew that. Even though there were many years of struggle from being in the closet and from being a two-time cancer survivor—times when I didn't know if I was still going to be here—there was a new sense of freedom.

Beth: I Began to Listen

You know, probably for about 10 years between 20 and 30, I really thought about killing myself. I thought about all kinds of stuff (tears) when people told me to listen to the preacher and let him interpret the Bible for me. That's when I thought I would just suffocate. (chokes up) But once I realized that the Bible is not a textbook of spirituality, and I began to listen to my own feelings rather than thinking, "I ought not to listen to my own feelings," it was emancipating. But I don't know exactly how to describe it. It's such a thing over time. It's more like grounding, I think. Because it's like, "Okay, now I feel centered; now things fit," rather than a "Yahoo! Here I am. Hurray!"

Do these kinds of stories sound uncomfortably familiar to you? They might if you have never considered that gays and lesbians can be spiritually aware. Using mysticism probably seems fine to most of us as long as people back up our traditional belief systems. As I said in the chapter on development, it may be possible that the person who hears a different message that contradicts society's traditional understandings may be operating at a higher level of spiritual development than those who have never had to question.

Could it be that a young lesbian who has spent 3 years in the closet doing Bible studies and reading every book on spirituality she can get her hands on is growing into a higher level of spiritual development than her "good" sister who spent every week in church?

I've heard some pretty wild statements in Christian circles that went unchecked because they were aligned with popular notions of that religious culture but that would sound preposterous to outsiders. For instance, someone may say, "I think God is calling me to Africa to become a missionary." No one questions the sanity of such an extreme statement if it fits into traditional understandings of a particular religious culture. If Matthew 28:20, "Go ye, into all the world and preach the gospel," is interpreted literally, people may hear this as an imperative statement that is direct from God. Or how about a little old lady who is convinced she needs to send an excessively large check to a televangelist promising to take Christ's message to Mexico? Most people outside a fundamentalist culture would think this unwise without doing some background checks. (Is this "mission" a resort in Cabo San Lucas?) However, if she believes it was something God told her to do, some will most likely admire her for being so sensitive to God's leading. Some people seek to spiritualize everything they do to feel closer to God, as in the case of a friend of mine who was praying for a sign to help her decide if she should marry the young man courting her at that time. When the log in the fireplace immediately dropped off the grate, she believed she had received her answer and divine guidance. As she told this story with utter spiritual conviction, no one challenged her logic or her belief system because her Pentecostal religious culture placed great emphasis on miraculous signs and wonders.

Predecessors Who Bucked the System

Awake! Awake! Put on your strength!

Isaiah 52:1

Spiritual and community leaders have long prized the inner voice of their convictions over the voices of traditional norms. Many progressive Christians have come to believe that the majority is not always right or necessarily moral, which has fueled their motivation to focus ministries towards social justice issues that could lessen the suffering of those who are oppressed by others. Even before the time of Jesus (who certainly challenged the religious systems of his day), people had been reinterpreting the Scriptures and traditions to improve the human experience for all people as moved by God's spirit. For example, in Acts 10:9–16, the Apostle Peter had a vision that declared all things clean, which not only freed Christians from ancient purity codes but was also interpreted to mean that Gentiles were no longer to be considered unclean and outside the care of God. As a result, this revelation drastically changed the course of two religions.

In the 16th century, Martin Luther was convicted by his understanding of grace, which led to a revolt against the exploitation of the poor by papal power and to the rise of Protestantism. John Wesley, in the 1700s, said he "felt his heart strangely warmed" when he learned that God was personal (Wesley, http://www.ccel.org/ccel/wesley/journal.vi.ii.xvi.html). This eventually led to the rise of Methodism, a movement that was intended to reform the Church of England, and later became the Methodist Church. Through Wesley's influence, the hearts of his fellow countrymen were united by hope, which helped England avoid a bloody revolution similar to what had previously occurred in France. Abraham Lincoln certainly went against many religious convictions when he signed the Emancipation Proclamation at a time when the majority of Americans believed that slavery was sanctioned in the New Testament. In the last century, Martin Luther

King, Jr., marched against oppression because of his dream of equality: "I have a dream that one day my children will not be judged by the color of their skin but by the content of their character"—at a time when White Americans did not fully grasp the gross inequities of segregation.

So should it be considered heretical if a gay Christian has heard the still, small voice and says, "God told me I was all right. He assured me that my sexual orientation and commitment to my life partner is not a sin. I belong in this church. I would like equal respect." Could this be another revelation from God? Acceptance of such a statement hinges on our differing views of reality. I recently attended a seminar led by Dr. Ken Hardy (2007), who said:

> I believe the notion of reality is often at the core of most conflicts in human relationships. Whether it's conflict between intimate partners, cultural groups, small communities or nations, clashes regarding reality are usually central. Reality-laced conflicts are often compounded and magnified by the unexamined belief that reality is a fixed universal phenomenon. In this regard, it becomes rather easy for warring sides to stand firmly in the righteousness of their rightness. Both the impetus for and the perceived solutions to these types of conflicts evolve around the issue of "right" and "wrong." The assumption of course is that "the solution" to "the problem" is to determine who/what is right/ wrong.

The point of this chapter is not to begin urging homosexuals to hear voices but to make room for people to experience the possibility of connecting with their spirituality in a meaningful way. Granted, this may result in possibilities different from traditional thinking, but if we make room for others' truths and respect the reality that no two people are going to see the world exactly the same, we can begin to realize that although different we can still remain connected. John F. Kennedy said, "The great enemy of truth is very often not the lie, deliberate, contrived and dishonest, but the myth, [which is] persistent, pervasive, and unrealistic" (http:// www.quotationspage.com/quote/27085.html). Mythical statements surrounding homosexuality that label gays and lesbians as abnormal, evil, shameful, pathological, or perverted are much more dangerous than civil laws that do not promote equality, because they fuel prejudicial stereotypes that cripple the soul.

To promote connections that heal, we have to cease activities and thinking that encourage us to see those who are different as "Other." To only see other is to be trapped into seeing people in a subjugated position. It supports an insidious oppression that fails to reveal how much we are all alike and how connected we can become. When we learn to see ourselves as complex rather than simple, we can begin to view others just as complex as we know ourselves to be. We have all arrived on the scene of life with differing amounts of baggage with various cultural and experiential backgrounds. To view others as complex is to make room for the idea that we are not static beings but are all growing at differing rates of spiritual, emotional, and mental development. When we refuse to see other but instead see our other selves, we will release profound healing in this world.

Being able to fit into the dominant social group and easily living within accepted social norms is a privilege that is not shared equally. To encourage sexual minorities to make room for their own spiritual development, it is going to take some movement from those who are privileged to be in the socially dominant positions of society. When it comes to healing racial tensions, we have learned that equal power or privilege is rarely shared. When one group is dominant, the other becomes subjugated, or as Hardy often reminds his students, "Those with the most privilege must bear the greater share of responsibility."

If we apply this principle to gays, lesbians, and bisexuals, then there needs to be a much greater portion of straight allies who are willing to step up to speak out against gay bashing, sexual oppression, and spiritual ignorance. At the beginning of this chapter I mentioned that 60% of my survey participants identified human support systems as the greatest help for spiritual development in the lives of GLBT individuals. What is most needed is the kind of community and familial support that says, "We get it. We will not judge you because your sexual orientation is different from ours. Learn to realize that your God-given sexuality does not need to hinder your innate desire to connect spiritually." What a great thought!

When will we begin to make room for this to happen? Perhaps a day much like today:

> In the gift of this new day,
> In the gift of this present moment,
> In the gift of time and eternity intertwined
> Let me be thankful
> Let me be attentive
> Let me be open to what has never happened before,
> In the gift of this new day,
> In the gift of this present moment,
> In the gift of time and eternity intertwined.

Newell (2002)

Tools for the Therapist

One of the chief skills therapists gain in this chapter is to walk with clients while they search for their own inner voice of truth. If a client has spent a lifetime listening to the directions of others, hearing a personal internal voice may come very slowly. Using poems and stories, or even verses of Scripture, that value one's unique place in this world can start the ball of possibility rolling. A personal truth may suggest a latent sexuality or a spirituality that does not coincide with organized religion. Keeping queer theory in mind, therapists can honor the possible complexity of a client's worldview. It is also important for therapists to realize the important role they have in their clients' lives. Family therapists are trained to be relationship experts and thus "should play a vital role wherever relationships exist, which is essentially everywhere" (Hardy, 2007). It is our calling to promote hope and healing in our world. A therapist may represent the one place of safety and support, the one voice of hope, the one person who posits a healthy outcome for gays and lesbians that will encourage inner strength and resiliency.

6

Coming Out Is a Spiritual Experience

Confluent Streams

Two halves do not make a whole
unless you are speaking of dollars;
But when a life is segmented in two the pull
towards authenticity is scary as hell,
for wholeness embraces all deeply hidden fragments.
Years of subterranean rage
shamed one half of the man to recess into dark, smoky corners;
but the pain of isolation is beginning to demand a change.
Truth, insists on coming out, accepting nothing less than full
   recognition
and continues to produce a rift.
Secrets that suffer alone,
can attract indifference and self hate
that turns weeping hearts to stone.
Yet, there is water in this rock that cannot be contained.
A fissure is seeping-
The dam is leaking! Relentless forces are
streaming, cascading, rushing,
to the parched desert of the soul,
pooling into an aqua colored genesis
where adversaries desiring confluence can make amends.

KENNETH BURR, 2008

Many questions in life can be avoided for a time, but the one question that cannot go unanswered is, "Who am I?" As people consider what makes the intellectual, emotional, physical, sexual, sensual, and spiritual areas of their lives come alive, certain identities seem more congruent than others. What

167

systems theory terms *self-differentiation* (i.e., http://www.thebowencenter. org/theory.html), queer people identify as the process we have come to know as *coming out*. To differentiate, to be authentic, to grow into your own—these are the questions that everyone must answer at some point in his or her identity development.

I once had a friend who liked to ask people, "So what is your flavor?" which means what kind of person are you attracted to? As we increase our understanding about what we are attracted to in life, certain feelings are more alive than others, thus revealing our life preferences. This includes the gender and kind of person we are attracted to as well as certain beliefs that resonate more congruently than others at the deepest core of our being. In all the things that make up our uniqueness in this world, we can really be sure of only one thing: No one is a carbon copy of another. No two people will see life in exactly the same way or believe everything that their friends do. We all have to savor the individuality of our own lives even if our preferential flavors cause others to flinch. So whether a person sees himself or herself as a White heterosexual husband and father, a bisexual middle-class Christian with a passion for ecology, a lipstick les-bian Buddhist who loves sports, a straight Democrat who loves art films, or a transgendered Republican who still loves women, every person has to come to terms with understanding and validating his or her own ways of being on this planet. We all have to find what is most authentic in our lives and live the most congruent life possible. Coming out, or differentiation, is about being one's most authentic self in society.

Moving from a socially accepted identity to a nonheterosexual one that is often scorned can cause a great deal of emotional distress. As a result it is not uncommon for mental health problems such as depression, panic attacks, somatic concerns, eating disorders, chronic stress, suicide, and substance abuse to develop in association with coming out. The source of these stress-related illnesses is usually not about feelings of disconnect from one's self but rather is about the fear of the judgments and reactions of others. These issues may become magnified for gay, lesbian, bisexual, and transgender (GLBT) adolescents, who may still be dependent on their parents for nurture and protection and may have no idea how to cope with adversity or hostility from those who are supposed to care for them.

In addition, queer people often expend a great deal more energy just being themselves than heterosexuals expend being "straight." In every new setting there is a decision for a GLBT person of how much to dis-close about themselves. Some researchers have referred to this as *triple consciousness* (Trujillo, 1997)—that is, "what society thinks of them, what they think of themselves, and the dissonance between the two" (Perez, DeBord, & Bieschke, 2000, p. 165).

Although plenty of horror stories are associated with coming out, more than 30% of the people I surveyed reported little or no distress when they declared their sexual identity in their closest relationships. Another 35% reported short-term distress that they were able to get through, and the final 30% said it was traumatic. However, almost without exception each person spoke of the process of discovering his or her sexual identity and sharing that with others to be a very emancipating and empowering experience.

Although most people have not had the coming out experiences that gays, lesbians, and bisexuals have had, we have all had opportunities to reveal personal vulnerabilities to others in ways we never imagined. Sometimes sharing is carefully planned, and at other times words just spontaneously move past our lips. As much as people think others will reject them for perceived weaknesses, people generally draw closer when vulnerabilities are shared more so than when conversations stress individual strengths and victories. Although most of those experiences can usher us into greater adventures of intimacy, there may be situations beyond our control when the people with whom we have been vulnerable will use the secrets of our hearts against us. The consequences of some betrayals may alter the course of our lives forever. Whether this change will be for the better or worse will largely depend on how much we are willing to allow our old wounds to be transformed into agents of healing and blessing in our lives. Survivors learn to adapt to life's messy situations. Those who thrive in a new life have learned to become masters at it. Although much of life is uncertain, one thing seems to remain constant: Learning to live with authenticity is always a spiritually deepening experience.

Considering the fact that sexuality and spirituality are the parts of our lives that connect us to ourselves, to others, or to God, coming out should be viewed through the lens of spirituality as well as the lens of development. When listening for spiritual themes as people reveal their stories about coming out, it is nearly impossible to deny the developmental component.

Some life stories seem to follow developmental models quite well. For instance, when Aaron first shared his story with me, I could easily categorize it into Cass's six stages: (1) identity confusion; (2) comparison; (3) tolerance; (4) self-acceptance; (5) group pride; and (6) the arrival of a congruent identity (Blumenfeld, 1994). However, as I listened again for spiritual themes, it was obvious that in each of the six stages, significant spiritual growth occurred as he increasingly came to terms with his personal identity.

Aaron: A Sense of Liberation

When Aaron was asked how coming out affected his life, he remembered being so conflicted and secretive that he had nowhere else to turn except to God. He would pray daily, often with great angst, asking God to take this affliction away from him and just make him "normal."

Many people growing up in faith communities have similar stories of not being able to reconcile with the expectations of others in their churches or families. They turn to God for a miracle because they are exhausted from not being able to be true to themselves. In an attempt to be true to their faith, they want to believe that God will hear and answer the most sincere prayers of their hearts, but they often become deeply disillusioned when nothing changes. As a result, they either feel that God is powerless and indifferent to them, or they sink deeper into shame believing that somehow they are not faithful or worthy enough for God to love them. In place of what should be a life-enhancing relationship with the Divine, they find themselves caught in a high-drama roller-coaster ride of attraction and repulsion. New life begins when they can finally be authentic.

Aaron came out to his parents immediately. Even though he knew they believed homosexuality was a sin and would be very disappointed in him, he just couldn't imagine withholding this kind of important information from them:

> It's one of the most difficult things you ever have to do in your life, at least for people of my generation. But it's also one of the most freeing things you will ever do. I work in the volatile dot-com industry where I coined the expression, "After you come out, losing your job is nothing." Truly that was the case. It seems like the amount of preparation that you need to get ready to come out makes you such a mature person. It takes years; it's difficult but gratifying. But I feel like I literally got a second chance in life, because before this nothing made sense. [I took] things for granted—like listening to that stupid love song over and over again on the radio when people get all teary eyed and happy at the same time because of the lyrics. I literally had no concept of what that meant. It's almost like someone who was blind at birth suddenly receiving sight. It's like you have been given a brand-new sense that you didn't know you had, and suddenly you have it and you get to experience life differently.

Coming Out: Like Being Born Again

Because being in the closet is a kind of living death or a life-denying restriction, it is not uncommon for people to say that coming out is like being born again. A new life can begin when one learns to be genuine.

Many of the words and phrases queer people in my study used to describe the first time they shared the news of their sexual identity with someone close to them were *liberation; a new start; experiencing a resurrection; finding one's spirit reborn; feeling grounded, whole, at peace;* or *finding a rush of new energy.* These terms sound very similar to how people describe spiritual experiences. Perhaps this is because these expressions are full of spiritual meanings that mark a reorientation in life. Like a religious conversion, these terms describe a time when one's life was turned around for the better.

Conversion experiences are spoken of not only by Christians; Buddhists will also speak of times when they were spiritually enlightened. The joys of discovering mindful, centering meditation can lead to new self-discovery. In Judaism, the theme of liberation is often repeated as people recall how the Hebrew nation was called by God out of slavery in Egypt. Rabbi Sheila Shulman says, "That fundamental image of liberation is at the core of Judaism. It is the first of the commandments. It is how Jews understand our relation to God … a God who is passionate about people's particularity, their uniqueness, and is engaged with them in their struggle for the freedom to realize their liberation." (Sweasey, 1997, p. 33) Consequently, Passover—the festival that commemorates this coming out, and one of the holiest occasions in the Jewish calendar—has an added significance for lesbian and gay Jews. Another gay rabbi, Mark Solomon, has adapted lines from the Passover liturgy for the text that is used in regular worship by London's Jewish Gay and Lesbian Group: "We have come out from darkness to light, from slavery to freedom, from anguish to great joy, from the closet to the world" (Sweasey, 1997, p. 33).

Coming out is a way of declaring truth about an inner spiritual revelation: "I am who I am; and I am gay." It invokes a similar statement of the self that we see in the Old Testament when God introduces himself. In Exodus 3:14, Moses asks the voice in the burning bush to be identified. The answer is, "I am who I am." It is a label without limits and is the essence of authenticity. Similarly, people's authenticity—to know how they connect with others, who they are at the core of their beings—is also represented by the words, "I am who I am; and I am gay." Although not every gay or lesbian who has uttered these words would claim a moment of spiritual insight, all would agree that such self-declaration is certainly a moment of personal growth. Could it be that personal growth always has a spiritual element to it?

In this sense, coming to accept one's sexual orientation could become a pathway into a deeper spirituality, even if it puts a person in direct conflict with the beliefs of his or her religious community, because to come out is a commitment to live the truth. "Telling the truth is a spiritual quality and crucial to spirituality. It would be difficult to make spiritual progress if something was being hidden" (Sweasey, 1997, p. 35).

Living the Truth

More than one person I interviewed talked about how depleting it was to try living a spiritual life with an essential kernel of truth missing. Secrets rob people of vital energy. Rather than seeing the value in "passing" as a heterosexual in society or in conforming to the expectation of others, most people felt like being closeted infected their lives with toxic shame. After years of expending so much energy trying not to be gay—or at least hoping not to appear gay—there was an amazing liberation unleashed when people could finally find the courage to share their authentic selves with others in a nonprovocative manner.

Katie

Katie recalled several years of internal chaos before she accepted her sexual identity as lesbian. She fell in love with her freshman roommate and continued to live with her for another 8 years following college. During the interview she described this as a nonsexual lesbian relationship, but for years she just felt confused about that "relationship that did not have a name." She eventually moved out and began dating again, only to find a few months later that she was very attracted to a female coworker, and she immediately experienced an inner crisis of identity and faith:

> That was probably the first time I fell madly, crazy in love. It was a pretty yucky relationship on a lot of fronts, but it was the first time I really got bubblies. I dated men, but it was never passionate. This whole "let's be celibate" thing wasn't really all that difficult for me because I had never experienced that "throw caution to the wind, gotta have ya" stuff yet. So this [falling in love with a woman] was pretty radical for me!

Not knowing what to do, she left the church and her softball team and pulled back into a closeted time to process her feelings so she could understand her attractions. She decided to seek help from a biblically based counseling service specializing in helping people with same-sex attractions to lead straight lives. After several months of Bible studies and group processing, she found some stability after coming to understand many lesbian relationships were unhealthily codependent and that, at the core, this really was a spiritual problem.

To keep working on her spiritual problem, she joined a women's Bible study, fully determined to have only platonic, non-codependent, healthy, balanced relationships with women and to be held accountable for her "weakness in the flesh." There, she met Michelle and fell in love for the third time while continuing to ask, "Why is this happening to me?"

After 15 years of crisis points in her sexuality and spirituality, she decided to accept that she was a lesbian and needed to seek God's guidance on what to do about it. Finding a great deal of encouragement from Web sites such as Anita the Christian Lesbian (http://www.sisterfriends-together. org/category/anita/) and Evangelicals Concerned (http://www.ecwr.org/) she eventually came out in a supportive group of GLBT Christians. Since that time she has noticed a renewed sense of life and hope, the biggest change being the following:

> I was able to focus on all the other areas that God wanted to work in my life as opposed to the rue that was before me, namely, that I needed to focus my energy in trying not to be gay. But as long as I was doing that I wasn't really giving a lot of energy to ideas such as, "How kind am I being? How gentle, how compassionate, how transparent or how Christ-like am I being?" When I stopped worrying about whether or not I was gay, I was able to come to a new place where I was able to be a vulnerable, kind, and gentle person.

The Liberation of Authentic Community

Clint

After fully coming out, Clint realized that being closeted required a great deal of personal energy to maintain walls of defense to keep people from knowing his personal life and using it against him:

> Once I no longer found it necessary to build and maintain those walls of protec-tion, they were able to be disintegrated, and then this rush of new energy, which was my whole self, became available to me. And I assessed a spirit inside myself that I hadn't any idea existed previously.

Interestingly, Clint is a minister who had been out for several years to those closest to him, including the leaders of his local church, but he remained closeted in many situations to spare his family and his church unnecessary grief:

> I did not want them negatively impacted by ignorant people who were not well informed of mind or heart. So I spent a lot of energy in those years, protecting my children, myself, and my ministry.

Unfortunately, when he was absent from a church conference, he was outed by a fellow clergyperson who called for his credentials to be revoked, his agency to be removed from church mission roles, and his church to be disfellowshipped for promoting homosexuality. Although his attacker's motion died for lack of a second motion, the damage had been done, and Clint's secret had been broadcast in places he had worked hard to avoid. As a result, people whose relationships he had cherished over the years turned their backs on him, leaving him with additional pain and suffering.

For the next several years, Clint created newer and thicker walls to protect his emotions. It wasn't until he came to an open and affirming church in Seattle that really understood what it meant to be inclusive that he could drop his defenses:

> It took a few months to believe these people. Although I believed their message intellectually, I wasn't fully able to trust anyone due to my previous experience.

Clint's watershed moment came when he was about 40 years old. One Sunday after church as he greeted people at the door, he was suddenly confronted by a 97-year-old woman leaning on cane, who said:

> "Are you that fellow we brought here from Chicago?" and I said, "Yes." "And is it true what I hear about you?" I thought immediately to myself, "Oh, here we go!" but replied, "Well I don't know; what is it that you have heard about me?" "I heard that your wife was still back in Chicago." I didn't know what she heard. So I just quickly said, "Well, I don't have a wife, but I do have a partner." And she looked up at me and said, "Oh? What's his name?" And I immediately thought, "If a 97-year-old woman knows my partner is a man, she's pretty enlightened!" So I smiled and said, "His name is Mike." She retorted, "Well, is it true? Is he still back in Chicago?" and I said, "Yes, he is." At that point she jammed her cane on the ground and said, "Damn this church! I'm going to go talk to the president of the congregation. We shouldn't be bringing people here to work for us if we can't find jobs for their partners and spouses!"

He laughed for joy as he remembered this story, because that was the time he let all his emotional barriers down and decided to quit spending his energy building walls to keep people out. A few months later he began to realize that there was a new spirit inside him—one much grander than he had experienced before, something that allowed him to access all of his energy for the first time in his adult life:

> When one doesn't siphon off a third or a half of his energy to maintain those walls, you suddenly have all your energy to do your ministry. So my professional abilities just skyrocketed. I found myself with much more refined skills than I'd had before. I was more energetic, thoughtful, creative, and articulate. I was more at ease, more kindhearted, and more available to other people. So spiritually, my person was really reborn at that point.

Living in a Truth-Avoidant Society

Because those who have come out have had to do some very courageous truth telling in their lives, they are often drawn to truth tellers, especially where sexuality and spirituality intersect. One of the problems they often encounter, however, is living in a truth-avoidant society. We really don't want to hear what makes us uncomfortable or what requires us to change how we approach life. Unfortunately, because many religious groups are especially scared of the alternative truths, they put pressure on their members to suppress personal ideas that may rock the boat to maintain the appearances of niceness and conformity. Whenever we use "niceness" as a badge of membership we are going to "produce hypocrites, because it will limit the ability of its followers to admit the truth about themselves" (Sweasey, 1997, p. 35).

Father Bernard Lynch, who has worked with many people living with AIDS, says that the virus taught us that it is better to be whole than good:

> "Being good is the stuff of religion—which is about control. Whereas being whole is the work of spirituality—which is about integrity freedom and joy." He also said that the conversion of coming out "may involve an exodus as personal and political as Moses and the people of Israel from Egypt [faced]— "leave your family, your country, and your father's house, for the land that I will show you."—here the soul grows by a process of subtraction. For all spirituality is based on truth; the truth of our experience." (Sweasey, 1997, pp. 35–36)

Truth is a relative construct that has caused disagreement among people for centuries. Even during the most famous trial in history, we see Pilate asking Jesus, "What is truth?" Because truth is always based on experience, it is bound to vary from culture to culture and person to person. Although many of our truths intersect, no person's truth is exactly like another's. One of the reasons we are so afraid of truth in today's society is not that we can't find it but that there are so many versions and interpretations of it. It is so varied that our traditional ways of knowing and cataloging truth are overwhelmed. Exceptions keep popping up whenever we think we've got the lock on something. And again, this isn't just a modern-day problem, for it also seems to be the point of Jesus' parable about the "Good" Samaritan. To Jesus' initial audience, those two words "good Samaritan" were mutually exclusive. That surprising element of mystery keeps us searching for the essence of our true spirituality.

Coming Out: Exploring Alternative Spiritualities

Life experiences that take us beyond common understandings often drive us deeper into the meanings and languages of religion, as people look for a spirituality that is viable. However, if people find only condemning answers that declare their God-given sexuality to be evil and are told that their experiences are aberrant, people will doubt the relevance of anything that religion has to offer and will seek answers elsewhere. However, when this happens, a person's spiritual life may be limited by not continuing the struggle to be in a community where others can provide deeper insight into the human–Divine encounter. Sometimes the best a spiritual community can do is to honor people's questions, and learn to live with the tension of dichotomy while seeking fresh insight together.

Coming from very conservative religious families that could not make room for homosexuality, interviewees Jim and Rick also used their coming out declarations to sever their ties with anything religious or spiritual. To survive, they felt they had to value their internal experience over the external authorities that refused to understand. If the choice was going to be God or an authentic self, they felt they had to choose self. They found no use for a god or for God's people who would not accept them. Where there is no hope for true inclusion in a former community, taking a new spiritual path that is more congruent may lead people to greater peace. Years later, both these men found a way to feel very connected and nurtured by authentic spiritualities that continue to lie outside the traditional forms of religion.

Monty

Monty says that although he came out just shy of 19, he continued to be a practicing Catholic until he was 23. During those years, his sexuality was in constant conflict with his religious upbringing. He was never able to reconcile what he had been taught with who he knew himself to be as a person, so he decided to leave the church:

> It was not just being gay that caused me to leave the Catholic Church, but it was kind of the topper. It was like, "Okay, I can't do this anymore." I found myself at mass, [self-] editing all the time. In fact, I edited more than I would take in so that pretty much told me, "This is not for me." That was when I said, "Sayonara! Enough!"

Because he had a strong desire for God, Monty's declaration created the challenge for him to think much deeper than most kids his age. During college, he took many religious classes to develop a broader view of the world's religions. His mother told him that his exploration of other religions would only strengthen his own faith. Monty laughs, "But I think it kind of backfired on her!" Eventually he came into contact with people on similar spiritual quests and ended up subscribing to many New Age philosophies that continue to nurture his spirit today.

Douglas: Feeling Blessed

Although not subscribing to any particular religion, Douglas also understood himself to be a person whose spirituality was enhanced by coming out:

> People in the closet tend to carry the world on their shoulders in a lot of ways. I definitely cut myself off from the support of other people in my life that could have been there. I'm fortunate that in my process I've never had an out and out rejection by anybody that really matters to me. [Instead, I have] the experience of feeling in touch with myself and grounded in who I am and [connected in my] relationships, which are about trusting and loving and caring. And then there's that process I came to appreciate that I would call grace, or the sense of the universe being an abundant place. What was it Mother Theresa said? "Love is a fruit in season at all times, and within the reach of every hand." That's so much a piece of my spirituality! I definitely encountered that sometime around that time; I even wrote it down somewhere. It felt like, "I'm very blessed!" So I think that also strengthened another aspect of my spirituality.

Coming Out: A Lifelong Process

Coming out is a gutsy, life-affirming response that is, at the minimum, a three-stage process. What begins with a heightened sense of *self-awareness* (i.e., coming into oneself) helps people fit missing puzzle pieces into their lives so they can begin living with greater authenticity. *Acceptance of the self* follows when plans for creating internal peace with this knowledge lead to adaptation to a new life. What finally emerges is the *ongoing process of connecting with others while sharing this news of self-discovery* (i.e., coming out). Sharing such intimate information with one's closest friends and family is not only courageous and empowering but is also quite spiritually liberating as well. If one of the definitions of spirituality is connecting one's life to others, this certainly fits the bill.

However, coming out is also a lifelong process, occurring on many levels and in numerous ways. It always involves a person telling his or her closest friends. It usually includes family members, and there is a great desire to disclose such personal information to one's parents. But that is not where coming out ends. There is also the decision whether to come out at work, in communities of worship, and to the neighbors. Some people seem to need to do this with an edgy attitude. Not long ago, in what my wife calls our "Martha Stewart suburban neighborhood," one of our neighbors had a young housemate who suddenly began flying the queer nation banner from their flagpole but never made any personal connections with the people next door. In a different neighborhood, some middle-aged friends of mine are much more content to be known as the guys next door who have to deal with all the normal aspects of home ownership. They would also be the first to show up at a block party. Both of these examples demonstrate ways of declaring personal truth, but only one is mindful of connecting with others. Most likely these differences are more about people being at different stages of development, but the latter couple appears to reflect a more congruent and connected spirituality.

Some aspect of coming out happens every time two people apply for a loan, buy a car together, or book passage on a cruise line. Sometimes coming out happens without a word ever being uttered. Coming out to the new postal worker and the dry cleaner occurs when it is obvious that two people of the same sex are cohabitating or when someone continues to show up with the same "friend" at social functions and family gatherings. Unfortunately, the early gay community made coming out sound like a one-time event not unlike a cosmic birthday party filled with blessing and feelings of great emancipation—it was billed as the freedom to finally be true to oneself. But many times it has also been the ticket to increased ostracism and violence in a queer person's life. We have to look no further than the shortened life of Matthew Shepherd to know how terrifying homophobia can become. (http://www.matthewshepard.org/site/PageServer?pagename=mat_Matthews_Life)

There is much more to this new awareness than just declaring one's unique view of the world with others. On a deeper level, it has to do with an ever-expanding set of integrating circles where one connects all of oneself to the various communities of which he or she is a part. In his interview with me, Thomas said this lifelong process is multifaceted:

> One of the things the early gay movement didn't do well—and therefore ended up doing a disservice to a lot of people coming out—was that it framed coming out in terms of telling the truth about your life to as many as people as possible rather than seeing it as the process of integrating a whole self. And because it did that, people would get to the end of their truth-telling phase and say, "Why is my life still a wreck?" Or they would get to some point in their life and would be disappointed because coming out didn't do what they thought it would do, which was to be this great liberating moment. Well, of course! Just telling the truth about yourself is only part of the process.

Figure 6.1 Coming out…it never ends.

Although the sexual identity model presented in chapter 3 explains this through six stages of development, the reality is that coming out is far too complex and varied a process to reduce to six easy steps. Although it might be fairly simple to write a chapter that would articulate six easy steps for coming out, people rarely follow the suggestions completely and always seem to find the exception to the rule. As anyone in the midst of upheaval knows, following such a list is nearly impossible, and it often produces low self-esteem for not being able to accomplish tasks that sound so straightforward. Since no one needs more guilt around this topic, the remainder of this chapter offers 10 helpful tips for making this life event a bit less chaotic as seen through the eyes of people in my survey.

Ten Helpful Tips for Coming Out

- Tip 1: Be aware of your best self and honor what you find.
- Tip 2: Radically accept your new identity and life difficulties.
- Tip 3: Learn to adapt in new ways that engage life.
- Tip 4: Make a plan to avoid crisis events.
- Tip 5: Find social support and use it.
- Tip 6: Avoid reacting to the reactions of others.
- Tip 7: Make a plan but be flexible with the results.
- Tip 8: Take your time with Mom and others.
- Tip 9: Make room for differing amounts of being out.
- Tip 10: Integrate spirituality into all parts of your life.

Tip 1: Be Aware of Your Best Self and Honor What You Find

As I mentioned in chapter 3, many homosexuals have known they were different from their peers from a very early age but lacked the language to describe it. Although the first awareness of difference can occur before age 8, the acceptance of sexual identity usually does not occur before the ages of 18–19, and for some this identity may not come about until midlife. As stated in chapter 3, many times there is an early and concurrent awakening of both spirituality and homosexuality. Both are profound realizations that may be followed by an immediate sense of dread and panic. Thus, many youth live a great deal of their lives with conflicting thoughts and emotions about their sexuality asking questions like:

- Am I gay or not?
- Do I fit the stereotype?

- If not, then what is this I sense about myself?
- Why am I not able to have the emotional feelings my peers speak of with the opposite sex?
- Why do I want to be so close to my same-sex friends?
- Is there something wrong with me?
- Is this my curse in life?
- Could this be a blessing?
- If I come out, will my parents continue to love me?
- Will God love me?
- Will I burn in hell?

These kinds of questions can be bouncing around like ping-pong balls in the mind and heart for years, until one day the desire to be truly known begins to move forward as self-awareness increases.

Some People Have Known They Were Gay or Lesbian for Years but
Couldn't Find the Courage or Internal Security to Declare It to Others
Many people talk about this experience as a moment of profound insight. When Jeff first discovered what was going on with him, at age 19, he said it was the most liberating news he could imagine because he now had a category for his feelings. As he told the story he laughed with delight remembering the first time he realized he was gay. Like a lightning bolt of clarity, he exclaimed, "I am a homosexual!" Before that time he was a very confused adolescent who couldn't figure out what was going on in his inner life. Aaron, who understood himself to be gay from an early age, remembers the time he finally realized he could be both gay and Christian. He felt like he had a second chance at life, knowing that he was finally capable of deep emotional connections that previously were not available to him. He cried, "This really was my resurrection!"

When people are retelling their experiences of coming out, it is difficult for them to separate coming in from coming out or to separate how their sexuality informed their spirituality because it is often blended into the same package. Coming in empowers people to own their self-awareness. As more people become more conscious of self, perhaps they are also influencing our society to become more conscious in a global sense. For these reasons, the first stages of coming in can often feel similar to the spiritual enlightenment the Apostle Paul experienced in his conversion while traveling on the road to Damascus, (Acts 9:1–30) when he was blinded by a divine encounter. Such experiences change the direction of a life forever.

Some People's Self-Awareness Came Later

Although the previous stories demonstrate a relatively short process of coming in, some people's coming in processes took several years. Several people would say it took about a decade before they could accept their own gay identity. Catrina spent several years after college trying to date men and eventually became engaged to a wonderful man who treated her like a princess. As she grew more aware that her attraction to women was not lessening, she broke off her engagement, knowing that it would not be fair to her or her fiancé until she could name what was happening to herself internally. Beth also said that during the entire decade of her 20s she wrestled with this sexual tension, dating men while continually being attracted to women. When she finally accepted her lesbian sexuality, she felt grounded and whole for the first time in her life.

Although Gordon's current partner is a male and he identifies as a gay man at work to avoid confusion, he felt that declaring himself to be gay for this survey was too restrictive. He has preferred to be known as bisexual. His self-awareness, which began in his adolescence, is not unusual. He began experiencing the inklings of his bisexual orientation in junior high; however, he wasn't prepared in his own mind to accept it within himself until he was nearly 17, and he simultaneously began sharing his convictions with others. He had the good fortune of attending a high school where there were openly gay and lesbian students who were popular. Although he claims to have had "a pretty good heterosexual track record" up to that point, he gradually started sharing his thoughts about being bisexual with his friends. By the time he left for college, he had told his parents as well and from that point on was completely candid with everyone he met, which freed him to begin actively dating men as well as women.

Bisexuals usually come out later than gays or lesbians due to the overwhelming belief that sexual orientation has only two expressions, straight or gay: "Bisexuals are marginalized in both the gay-lesbian and the heterosexual communities and therefore, are likely to have internalized negative messages from both communities" (Perez et al., 2000, p. 169). Gays often believe bisexuals are not accepting of their homosexuality, and heterosexuals are usually unable to accept the fact that a bisexual may be attracted to same-sex partners. One middle-aged man even said that his former therapist kept pushing him to come out as a homosexual because he believed that most bisexuals were just closeted gays.

In addition, many bisexuals have stretched traditional norms in the gay community by experimenting with different types of relationships.

Coming out as bisexual has different challenges from coming out gay or lesbian:

> For some bisexuals, sexual identity depends on the gender of the person with whom they are in a relationship. If a bisexual woman is in a relationship with a woman, she may identity as lesbian. If she is in a relationship with a man, she may identify as heterosexual. For other bisexual persons, self-identification may also depend on situational contexts. (Perez et al., 2000, p. 166)

For example, a bisexual male might identify as a homosexual in a gay bar and as a straight man at work. However, many bisexuals' identity is stable no matter what the context.

For Others Awareness Came as a Surprise

Julie.   All through high school and college, Julie dated and enjoyed having sex with men. Although she did have a crush on a young woman in her dorm, she wrote it off as just wanting someone to think she was special and never considered that she might be a lesbian:

> However, when I was 21 years old, a female brought me out. She kissed me, and I thought, "Whoa!" All at once I felt very, very comfortable, and that led to my first gay relationship.

As a victim of childhood sexual abuse, she knew that sex with men could be enjoyable, but she also felt it was "no big deal." However, when she had sex with a woman, life suddenly seemed more congruent:

> I don't want to say that because I was a victim of incest, I became gay. That isn't it. I think it was always latent.

Richard   Richard didn't come out until he was nearly 30 and engaged to be married to a lovely woman. Although he looks back now and believes that he did have some crushes on guys in junior and senior high school, he was so disconnected from understanding what homosexuality was that he couldn't make the connection:

> Certainly there were a lot of feelings I had denied for many years and had kind of written off as, "Oh, I'm just really progressive and open-minded." And then when a guy hits on you, you're like, "Oh, my gosh! This is really exciting!" (laughter) So after being with a woman for 6 1/2 years—whom I loved and was going to marry, thinking all along that this is nice, this is really nice—experiencing what it's really like to feel that sexual excitement and passion was really eye-opening. I finally discovered what people were excited about! The next morning I woke up and went, "I've just had this epiphany—this revelation about what is exciting and who I am." So it's a fun memory to look back on.

Tip 2: Radically Accept Your New Identity and Life Difficulties

Accepting a New Identity

Once the idea of a new sexual identity becomes a possibility, a simultaneous process begins when that realization is accepted into the core of a person's being. More than one person interviewed said they needed to look into the mirror and say aloud, "I am a homosexual" until they accepted it. For those who found this revelation relieving, the process was shorter than it was for those who were afraid of the realization. Interestingly enough, not one person in my survey regretted the self-discovery of his or her homosexuality. Instead, all participants were more concerned with how others were going to receive them after this news was shared.

Self-acceptance for a sexual minority is a gutsy but life-affirming response that requires nothing of anyone else but everything from the individual. It is based on a need to take control of one's own life in spite of the potential objections of others. Dr. Janis Abrahms Spring (2004) talks about using acceptance as a road to healing. Although no person is responsible for the reactions of others, each queer person is responsible for creating a fulfilling and congruent life:

> Your freedom—perhaps your only freedom—is in deciding how to survive and transcend the injury [of others.] Don't underestimate this freedom: it's enormous. With it comes the power to decide how you're going to live the rest of your life. As you take the task of healing into your own hands, you empower yourself and make peace with the past. (p. 53)

Richard

When Father Alex began preaching sermons about respecting homosexuals as copartners in the gospel, Richard felt that he had been given permission to examine his own sexual feelings, which to this point had been subordinated to fit the expectations of others. It was during this time of self-reflection that he met his first boyfriend:

> Even though I had repressed my homosexual feelings for many years, I think I benefited because I was raised with a religious background in a very loving family. I spent my first 29 years really believing that I was a special creation of God and that I was a worthwhile person. So then at age 29 I never really doubted it. I remember thinking, "Okay, I'm gay, but now I don't know how I feel about that."

He began to feel okay about being gay because his priest had been courageous enough to talk about homosexuality as another way to be a human being, and as a result his coming out process was fairly short:

Because I was very secure in myself and in my faith when I finally came to the realization that I was gay, I thought, "Okay, this is who I am. So now it's time to move forward and deal with this part of my life."

Sam

For many years, Sam identified as being heterosexual. After 10 years of marriage he began to explore his feelings about homosexuality and, through a process of sexual experimentation, concluded that he really was gay:

> There was probably a time of about 2 or 3 years between the times I started to identify myself as being homosexual and the time I actually came out of the closet that became very difficult because I was married at the time. Once I honestly realized I was homosexual, I shared that with my wife, and we realized that being married was not the most appropriate situation for us. So there was not a whole lot of closet time. But there was sort of a transition period when I started to think, "Wait a minute! Am I really gay?" to a realization of, "You know, I really am." For the first 37 years of my life, I did not identify myself as being gay but straight. Although I had homosexual leanings and homosexual tendencies, naively I thought straight people had the same yearnings and feelings but just dealt with it. I figured it was just part of being a man. So I never really saw myself as being gay, but then I didn't know anyone who was gay either. This process of learning what homosexuality was and accepting that part of myself accelerated my coming out process.

Accepting Life's Difficulties

I have always loved the opening lines in *The Road Less Traveled* (Peck, 1978), and it seems appropriate to quote at this point:

> Life is difficult. This is a great truth, one of the greatest truths. It is a great truth because once we truly see this truth, we transcend it. Once we truly know that life is difficult—once we truly understand it—then life is no longer difficult. Because once it is accepted, the fact that life is difficult no longer matters. (p. 1)

It is well documented that people often have a very difficult time telling family members that they are gay, lesbian, or bisexual. Some radical acceptance has to do with more than self-identity because people also must reconcile with the realization that life is not fair and that some people may intentionally cause you grief. Radical acceptance helps people get past the ideas that someone needs to rescue us from our difficulties by helping us to adapt to life's difficulties. Lucy had a particularly poignant perspective on this.

Lucy: Theological Insight Helps

> [My partner and I] have this young female friend who identifies very clearly as Christian and just can't seem to reconcile how really awful things keep

happening in her life. It's very frustrating to watch. You see, she is a fundamentalist who has faith in an omnipotent God, and she thinks he should come in to renew her life completely. It's very hard to see her struggle with these things, which would be so much better if she just sort of accepted that shit happens! I personally think "shit happens" is a very powerful, spiritual statement. It's like, "It's not our fault; God didn't do this. Shit happens—move on!" I really like that expression.

Mark: Sometimes You Have to Deal With Difficult Things

Mark beautifully articulated how to make peace with the complexity of his gay life:

I found wonderful people affiliated with the campus ministry at the university I attended and other progressive Catholic circles, so it was kind of going inward and going outward and that all really helped me come out. By my early 20s I felt really settled with my identity. This is who I am. This is fine. This is not uncomplicated but that's how life is, and this is not at all inconsistent with how I understand what it meant to try to live as a Catholic man—a Christian man with a sense of conscience. Sometimes you have to deal with hard things, and this is what I got.

Debra: Now I Have This to Deal With

Debra has been a faithful Christian all of her life but didn't realize she was gay until she was in her mid-30s. A year later, she became extremely distraught when the relationship with the woman who inspired her response ended. Although coming in to herself did bring the relief of a new self-awareness by helping her make sense of previous marriages that never clicked, she now found herself ready for some heated conversations with God:

I felt dumped, bereft, alone, and I was angry at God and thinking, "Now I have to deal with this [too]," [on top of] all the other growing-up, developing issues that I had been struggling with. Yet my spirituality didn't change. Coming out probably reinforced my spirituality. I drew further on it, because my identity was my genesis with God. I joined the church at the age of 8, going forward as a little kid, thinking, "Well, why wouldn't I?" I never questioned my faith. Faith has been my gift.

Debra didn't come out in society until she was nearly 50. After 10 or more years of a growing self-awareness and increased spiritual growth that enlarged her self-confidence, she began to come out to her staff at work by mentioning her partner rather than choosing to live with more secrets. What she discovered was that many people already knew her situation and were a lot more comfortable about it than she had been. As her development continued over time, she came to accept that although her life had been far from easy, it was her responsibility to transcend difficulties by creating her own beauty and harmony.

Tip 3: Learn to Adapt to New Ways That Engage Life

For some people, coming out was like being shot out of a cannon. They had no idea what was really happening to them. Because things happened so fast and were accompanied by such intense emotions, they were often not sure they could make it through to the next day. One of the key ingredients for creating a more grounded experience in coming out is the confidence in one's ability to have the freedom to choose when and where to disclose this information.

To avoid a full-blown, debilitating crisis, it may be helpful to realize the differences among *stress, crisis,* and *system overload*:

> Stress occurs when there is an imbalance (perceived or actual) between what is actually happening—the stressors—and what a person feels capable of managing. Crisis occurs when the stress exceeds the ability to effectively handle the stressors. We all have different levels of tolerance—breaking points—beyond which we are no longer able to cope with the situations. When too many things hit us all at once, when stressors pile up, system overload sets in. (Ahrons, 1994, pp. 78–79)

When people know their feelings are normal and that the chaos of a specific self-disclosure will most likely be temporary, they can reduce the intensity of a crisis. By reminding oneself that this current crisis will pass, individuals can plan to accomplish fearful tasks and move on. When people can plan and thus feel more in control of their emotions—even for a day—then system overload can be avoided: "The way out of system overload is adaptation. Adaptation requires change—restructuring or reinventing some portion of life, changing the way stressors are perceived or managed, learning new skills and finding new resources" (Ahrons, 1994, pp. 78–79).

Richard: Accepting and Adapting, Moving On
Richard realized after he came out that he would have to leave his home in a small Idaho town because he didn't feel it would be a safe place for a gay man:

> Because I was very secure in myself and very secure in my faith and had come to the realization that I was gay, I thought, "Okay, this is who I am, so it's time to move forward and deal with this part of my life." [This] meant that I needed to

find an exit strategy for getting out of [my town]. It was a very hostile place. So 4 months after I had my first homosexual experience, I was out of the closet to a few people at church. I couldn't be out at work, but I started making plans for coming back to Seattle. (Interviewer: You knew at that point that you needed to leave?) Oh yeah. As soon as I finally came to the realization that I could look myself in the mirror and say, "I'm gay," I knew I had to leave because there's no way I could become the person I needed to be in this environment.

Bob: Coming Out Helped Me Accept Responsibility

Most queer people I interviewed felt that coming out was not only a necessary part of their personal development but also created an opportunity for taking responsibility to a new level. As Bob reflects:

I think coming out of the closet [represents] two things that are very interconnected: One is taking responsibility for who I am, and the other is that I am no longer responsible for who you are. Especially in terms of parents, I am no longer responsible for being the person you think that I am, now it's up to you to decide how you are going to react to that. On this side, I understand the power of coming out, because it is reclaiming, "This is who I am! But this is not all of who I am." That helped me move on. But when I was in the closet, I was trying to hide and be how others wanted me to be, which warped too much of my energy. I was just done; there's no other way to say it.

Many parents do not take this initial information well. Both Jim and Rick said that although their parents were some of the first people they told, this act of self-disclosure did not bring anyone in the family closer together. In fact, it did just the opposite, and, as a result, relationships remained strained for years.

Adaptation means confronting negative thoughts that once paralyzed people from moving forward. Obsessions with injustice, rejection, or poor self-images distract people from the business of living well and can often cause stress-related health problems. By accepting and adapting to the current situation one is facing, there must be a refusal to be reinfected with shame or resentment. One client sat in my office for weeks with his eyes tightly closed because he couldn't face his overwhelming life situations. However, as he began to open his eyes for even a few minutes each week, he also found the ability to deal with one obstacle at a time.

Rick found that when he looks back at where he's been he is amazed to see his progress:

I'm still working on that; it's still very hard to do, but progress is being made. One of the things is that I have learned in the new life that I have is that I don't have to have it all right now. I've got all the time in the world, and whatever happens is going to happen. All I do is show up and do what's in front of me, and I move forward. A little later I look up and say, "Wow! How'd I get here?" But it's just taking that next step day by day and doing what is in front of me.

One of the ways Jeff was able to reengage with life was to get involved in community service. His Alcoholics Anonymous (AA) sponsor suggested that he find a church and start volunteering in some way so that he could begin to see beyond himself. For several years he had looked out his windows at the beautiful gothic spire of Seattle's First Baptist Church:

> When I was first diagnosed with HIV, I used to watch the spire at night when it was all lit up and think there was some hope in that architecture. So one day I said to [my partner] Rick, "I'm going to check this out." This was February 11, 2004. The service wasn't too God heavy, dictatorial, or dogmatic, but it was loving and kind and full of all different kinds of people, including gays and lesbians. It all felt so normal—like a cross-section of my community. I came home and said, "That was easy!" But I didn't have a job and couldn't hold a job at that point. I was still too new [to sobriety], but I could volunteer somewhere. So I started working on the "Spire" mailings [First Baptist Church's newsletter] every Tuesday morning and began meeting people in the church. I still do that. I came home and told Rick about it and saw that the next week a gay pastor was going to be speaking about Jonathan and David and homosexuality in the Bible. We just had to check this out. As he talked about his own healing witness, we both sat there in church, held hands, and cried. We were overwhelmed by what we were hearing. [Previously, I felt like I didn't matter to God, and he had turned his back on me, but now] it felt like, "Finally, God is witnessing me now, and it's okay. I'm fundamentally okay!"

Tip 4: Make a Plan to Avoid Crisis Events

The plan should be a good one, because it seems that once a person declares his or her sexual orientation to others, this information is seldom erased from people's memories. Even if it is done during a phase of self-exploration, this becomes permanent information that can generate a variety of responses from others. Although no one can predict how someone else will respond to an outing, it would be wise to try and minimize potential chaos by understanding that coming out is a process that deserves making plans that fit a person's unique life situations.

Deciding Who to Tell

Deciding who to tell first is often a key question asked. Several studies have shown that parents are rarely the first persons in whom gay youth confide. Typically, most youths come out to their friends before risking their declaration with family members.

> An Internet study by!OutProud! (1998) "of nearly 2,000 sexual minority youths between the ages of 10 and 25 (mean 18 years) revealed that youths were most likely to have disclosed to their best friend (76%), friend at school (66%), and friends outside of work or school (61%). Far behind were mother (49%), brother or sister (38%), and father (36%). In other studies, around 10% of youths first disclosed their sexual orientation to a parent, and when this occurred it was almost always the mother. The father was rarely the first person a youth told, although the initial disclosure can be to both parents simultaneously. Only 2 in 194 youths first disclosed to their father in one study." Savin-Williams (2001, p. 32)

According to other researchers (D'Augelli & Herschberger [1993], Dube [2000] and Savin, Williams [1998]), the first recipient is nearly always a same-sex peer. Three quarters of community support group youths and college gay or bisexual men first came out to a friend. In three quarters of these cases, the friend was of the same sex, usually a best friend orsomeone the youth was dating or had dated. All youths had disclosed to a friend, but less than half had told a parent. A more recent study provides the first indication that the initial person may be another sexual minority youth, perhaps because other same-sex attracted youths are now visible and hence available to become recipients for first disclosures." (Savin-Williams, 2001, p. 33)

However, the prospect of telling one's parents is always a milestone event that looms heavily in a queer person's soul. Sometimes coming out to a parent is accomplished in as little as 3 months after telling a friend, and for others this news is not shared for years, depending largely on how the queer person believes his or her parents will react.

Also according to Savin-Williams (2001), p. 29:

> 93% of college gay men reported that coming out to parents was a "somewhat" to "extremely troubling" event for them …. Although coming out to parents ranked second to worries about AIDS among these support group youths, college gay men ranked it first, just ahead of terminating a close relationship. The fact that half of the college men characterized disclosing to parents as "extremely troubling" corroborates the view that until this event takes place it remains a central concern in the lives of many sexual minority youths.

Deciding When to Tell

When people consider the prospect of telling someone else about their sexual identity, most fear the worst. However, statistics show that most people are relieved when they can let their guards down to begin living a life that is more authentic. In my survey, 33% of respondents came out immediately with little or no negative effect. They also were the people with the greatest support from nurturing families or friends. Others took their time in sharing their good news with others for a variety of reasons. A full 19% said that their coming out to others took 2 to 3 years; 10% took 10 years. Another 10% took up to 15 years, largely because they were expecting very negative outcomes once this news was shared by a parent, and 3% have chosen to remain in the closet indefinitely. Of those I interviewed, 6% said that they exploded out of the closet before they were ready by someone who betrayed their confidence.

What Can Happen When There Is No Plan

Sometimes an unplanned disclosure can work out surprisingly well. If the connections are very strong and the individuals are secure in their own identities, this kind of news may not shake the relationship that much. Similarly, if parents have already been wondering if their son or daughter is in a queer relationship, they have already had time to process what this might mean to them before they ask. With the shock value greatly diminished, unplanned disclosures may work out fairly well.

Jeff: Well, Dad Asked

> My parents got to ask me [if I was gay] (laughs)—which is not the way I wished it could have been. But I was dropping as many heavy clues as I could. That conversation was August 5, 1985, when I was about 20. I already had a boyfriend and was living with him, [calling him my] "roommate," which didn't feel good but I felt like I needed to stay in hiding. So one day my father called on the phone and said, Your mother and I, well we were wonderin'…. We saw the situation with that one bedroom there, and you're living with—a guy—and, uh…."
> It just went on and on, and then I just said, "Dad, are you asking me if I'm gay?" (big laugh) And he said, "Well, uh—yeah." So I said, "Yes I am." He said, "Well, I just want you to know, we love you, and it doesn't matter. But we just want to ask if you are being kept against your will? Are you involved in drugs?" I said, "No, I'm happy!" And he said, "Well, okay, your mom's kind of quiet and is kind of upset about this." (laughs) Then he said, "So what I'd like to do is come out and talk to you directly. I don't want to have this conversation on the phone; I'd rather come out and see you," which sounded good to me. So in the awkwardness, he asked me what I was doing at the moment. Well, my partner and I were going off to a dinner party, so I replied that I was making a big fruit salad. So, I said, "I'm making a big fruit salad." There was this long pause of silence, and then we both just laughed!

At other times, however, disclosure of one's sexual identity may result in a complete system overload, which seems largely to be due to shock value and feelings of betrayal. If no one is prepared for this information, the results can be explosive.

Thomas: Exploded Out

Thomas always knew he wanted to be a pastor. But when he was in divinity school at age 25, he found himself being very attracted to a male undergraduate and began a relationship with him. However, his heart's desires were leading him in two directions. Not knowing how to integrate his own feelings with his calling, he came to a point where he considered that his love interests must be running away from what God desired for him, which was to be ordained and serve at a church. He believed that if he kept faith with God's desires, then he would surely be cured of homosexuality. Once he graduated from seminary, he left his lover, was ordained, and served at a small church on the outskirts of Detroit, believing he was doing the right thing.

However, he couldn't shake his feelings for this young man, and to make matters worse his church's music director kept asking to have a pastoral conversation about his own sexual orientation. Thomas says he felt trapped because in either situation he couldn't have integrity:

> If I were authentic with him and said, "This is my struggle too," that felt like a betrayal of what I was trying to do in being there [to be cured of his homosexuality]. If I didn't say that to him, then I was also not being truthful with him. And so under those terms, I felt like I didn't have enough integrity to be a minister.

So he left his clergy position and returned to Chicago to live with his former lover again, only to feel like he was living another lie because he couldn't tell his parents what was going on in his life. Since his father was a minister in the same denomination that had ordained Thomas, he felt that not telling the truth might be the better way to honor his father. After signing a contract to work for a conservative Christian college in Michigan, the following happened:

> I understood my life story at that time to be [that of] the [biblical story of the] prodigal son: If only I would give all this up I could go back. So I told the guy I was living with that I was going to get my life right and work in the Baptist college. He said, "If you leave me, I will write to the school and tell your parents," which he in fact did. And so everything exploded at once. The school withdrew my contract, and my parents sent me to a Christian psychiatrist; it was a nightmare. It could well have been the end of my life, except that I couldn't see adding that pain to my parents at that point.

The main issue for Thomas was personal integrity. There was no way for him to be authentic in either situation. He had to pretend to be someone he was not, or he had to put what he knew to be true about himself into the sin category, which meant that the only way to deal with it was to cut part of himself away:

> The downside of that was the way it forced me to deal with my sexuality as a category of sin that was being held against me. On the other hand, I could never really feel saved, which was the ultimate thing, right? I could never truly feel that there was any sense that God could save me from this. Because the sin category was filled with my sexuality, there wasn't room for anything else.

Although many people have shared their coming out experiences as liberation, Thomas remembers only pain and despair, because something precious was taken from him, which tipped him into system overload:

> It meant losing everything. I mean, the world couldn't be the same after I told my parents, "Yes, this person was right about me," and I could never go back into that world again and serve a church. Even though that was where all my friends were and where I had been successful, I had no idea of how I could ever be engaged in ministry again. The first task of coming out was integrating my sexuality and spirituality. Then I realized that coming out meant the integrating of my whole self with issues as they related to a community, like how I would be involved in a faith community as a gay person. I felt like I'd been called to ministry. I'd been trained. I loved all things religious. How was I going to integrate that part of my experience as a gay man in a religious community? What is the vocation part of that? This continues to be an ongoing struggle. How do I function in my vocation as a career? I can never be assured that one job is going to follow another.

Currently, Thomas is a content and well-loved pastor in a gay-friendly church in the Seattle area. But even today, as he tells of how he lived through this crisis, he knows his options would be limited if he ever chose to leave his current parish.

Tip 5: Find Social Support and Use It as a Buffer

One of the crisis events that may occur as a new identity is accepted is the profound sense of being utterly alone. It can be all too easy to lose sight of reality when obsessive thinking turns to isolation. To get outside themselves, people need to seek the company of caring friends or family members who remind them that they are not freaks or worthless human beings but are instead cherished parts of humanity. Straight friends can be of great help, meeting for lunches, taking walks in the park, or sharing meals or movies together to reinforce a person's sense of acceptance and normalcy.

Contacting the Tribe
At some point, the need will arise to have friendships within the tribe (i.e., gay community) who can assure them that their new feelings, attractions, and fears are very normal:

> We enter the tribe alone and naked, without previous personal history. And yet our own history is part of the history of the tribe. It is part of the tribe's nature that it can recognize our private, gay past—a past which seems as personal and private to us as our secret dreams and fantasies—and see it as a continuation of its own.... Contact with the tribe will be an ongoing part of a gay identity. It may be the strongest aspect of a gay personality, and the most misunderstood.... What is important is that the need to connect with this tribe is universal with us, and the denial of it is dangerous to gay men, I believe our very mental health depends on it. (Brass, 1999, pp. 180, 184, 185.)

Finding the "True Friend"
Especially helpful is someone from the gay tribe who is not a sexual partner but who becomes affectionately known as the "True Friend" (Brass, 1999), p. 183). He or she may be the perfect mentor to help a person in the art of coming out and in adapting to gay life because this person has already had this experience and can help make connections to others who understand. There are times a newly out person may feel like a pressure cooker needing to let off some steam. The true friend may provide the release for such moments while giving the advice one needs to avoid exploding out in frustration and anger. There is tremendous power in being listened to and in having one's pain and confusion held and honored by one who has been there.

Consider Creating a Network of Safety
People use many different ways to come out, but the following story illustrates one of the more creative ways—and it turned out to be an exceptional gift for an entire congregation.

Brett
Although Brett had wondered for years if he might be gay, it wasn't until after his divorce at age 39 that he had his first sexual relationship with a man and settled his orientation questions once and for all. As he told his story with a twinkle in his eye, "I went off to Boston and came back gay." However, just knowing his sexual identity wasn't his chief concern. Brett is also a devoted father whose daughter was young at the time, and he wasn't sure how he was going to negotiate his life on her behalf.

As he flew home from Boston to Seattle, he wondered what to do about church, where both he and his daughter were well known. He decided that since this particular church was quite rooted in social justice issues, he might find a way to appeal to the desire to fight oppression in their community. After forming a support group made up of members of the gay tribe, his pastor (whom he had come out to), and some close friends, he organized his congregational family around the idea of making their church a place that would support gays and lesbians. To his great delight, they all agreed that was one of the directions their church wanted to take:

> So although these were broad-minded people, I suspected that I might have to find someplace else if it didn't work. But I had this confidence that there was a chance. Then we had the whole political thing, and the church became a reconciling church. I took the risk, and it worked out! It was always a great place to take my daughter and for her to know, "My dad is gay, and everybody likes him." We had friends. Once when she was about 7, we were leaving church one day, and she said, "We have a lot of friends, don't we, Dad?" I almost cried about that, because that was exactly what I wanted for her. They provided that all the time for her growing up, even through high school. It seemed like she always had the confidence that it had to be okay to have a gay dad. She's always treated me that way, and I think it's the church that was a sounding board. Every other Sunday [that] we went there, through all those years, we always had friends who loved us and treated her well. Other gay people were there [and] were also treated well, and it was just wonderful. That was why I risked it and pursued it. I was glad it worked out so well for us, and, as a result, I've never had a coming out crisis.

Tip 6: Avoid Reacting to Others' Reactions

Some people will feel emotionally compelled to come out so they can stand arm in arm with others who are experiencing queer injustice. Even though Bob's coming out was on his terms, he did not work from a predetermined plan that might help all parties work through difficulty. Reactive moves usually end with predictable consequences.

Bob: I Couldn't Stand It

Bob had been hiding his sexual orientation for nearly 10 years until he had his "conversion" moment at his sister's wedding:

> What triggered my own disclosure was thinking about my brother's coming out years earlier and being able to witness my parents' response. I didn't really see it until my sister's wedding when we all came home. My father wouldn't even look at him—wouldn't even be in the same room with him—and I realized that the

only reason I was there was because I was living under this pretense. Seeing how he was treated and feeling that it was so wrong, I knew I couldn't allow him to be treated that way and not me. I knew what the response was going to be. But it was too exhausting. I was just done. There's just no other way to say it.

Although Bob's father failed over a period of years to find a better way to demonstrate his care for his sons, this is not usually the case. Most family members, after their initial reaction, eventually return to work out a new way of being in relationship with their adult children. Although many parents may never initiate a discussion about their child's sexuality, their actions of continued inclusion and love should not be denied.

One thing that may be helpful is to realize parents may need some time to respond positively to their son's or daughter's announcement of being gay. Whereas the queer person has usually had a great deal of time (sometimes years!) to process and accept his or her identity as a sexual minority, it can often come as a shock to those who are being told for the first time, and they will most likely react a bit poorly. In fact, it probably would be unusual for any of us to react calmly the first time we hear shocking news of any kind.

Although the person coming out wants others to accept his or her new self-awareness instantaneously, that may not be possible due to the full range of socially constructed ideas and emotions surrounding homosexuality. However, by making room for some less than positive reactions, a gay man can also practice giving to others what he wants for himself. By accepting and honoring those feelings of shock or betrayal in others as a moment of acute honesty and intimacy, it may be possible to separate the offending reaction from the person with whom they cared enough to share this news. By not perseverating on the reactive moment, the person who is coming out would do well to begin remembering all the times of shared history in this relationship and try to weigh the good against the bad.

The point here is to try to see the person who has rejected a loved one's new identity more objectively. Such a task asks people to be on their guard against seeing everything in black and white: "When we are unable to hold an 'ambivalent view' we demonize or deify people. Choosing sides feeds the illusion that we see things more clearly, but the opposite may be true" (Spring, 2004, p. 53).

For example, parents who respond poorly are most likely not rejecting their gay child standing before them but are facing their own fears and losses. They may need to go through a process of grieving the loss of their heterosexual dreams for their child. The fantasy of a Norman Rockwell life has been shattered, along with the marriage to the girl next door and future grandchildren who were to bring joy to their old age and carry on family legacies. It may also confront their religious teachings that have referred to homosexuality as an abomination in the eyes of God. They may not know how to deal with their perplexing emotions and the contradictions they feel between their intense love for their children and the fear that God might reject them for all eternity.

However, when people bring their best selves to the table and consciously choose not to be reactive, healing can occur over time if people remain connected enough to talk about their feelings and different life experiences.

Jeff

When Jeff's mom learned that her son was gay, she did not handle the news well. However, by viewing his mother in the greater context of their life together, he knew she would eventually come around:

> My mother was upset. She was menopausal, which made it worse. She had a hard time, and for a few months it was hard for me to be at home with her. As long as I've lived on my own I've lived in the heart of the city somewhere, so I would see [my parents] quite frequently. But for a while it wasn't okay. There were times when I could come home for 20 minutes, and my mom would say, "I need you to go now." That was hard, but I believed it would pass, and it did—it passed quickly. And now my parents and I have a relationship today that would not be what it is without having had a conscience contact with these experiences and a conversation about what we felt and what was hard. Now they know my life. I have no secrets from my family or my parents."

Tip 7: Make a Plan, but Be Flexible With the Results

Mark, a psychoanalyst who found my questions very intriguing, recalled coming out to his parents as a progression of many things. At first glance, his story appears to follow a model plan: becoming aware of his gay sexuality, taking time out in the closet to reflect on his emotional and spiritual life, finding wonderful people in his church to be his mentors and to provide social support, as well as making a logical plan of how to disclose his sexual identity to his parents. However, even the best-laid plans need to be flexible.

Mark: My Parents' Reactions Surprised Me

> I'm sure part of the reason I was drawn to psychoanalysis was that I had a very complicated mother who is no longer with us. She was a sociology professor and a converted Catholic, who was very involved with the Catholic worker movement.

It was started in the 1950s trying to take some particular views on how Jesus lived and then to apply those to working with the poor in urban centers. She was very involved with that stuff and presented herself as a very progressive Catholic. So I thought that when I came out to her it would be no problem. I think I was 18 or 19 at that time, but it turned out that it was a problem for her. She was not happy at all. She wanted me to be a priest and told me I could never tell my father because he'd be too ashamed. So it was difficult- with her. At first, I kind of believed or was so stunned by how she responded that I didn't say anything to my father for a year or two. But once I moved and began to integrate the pieces much more, I thought, "This is ridiculous." So I came out to him. And he was as my father typically is with these things: He was at first saddened, because the only template he had to think about what it is like to be a gay man was that it was going to be a terribly lonely, painful, and horrible existence. But I was already having so much fun I said, "That's clearly not the case! So I really appreciate that you think I may have a terrible life, but let me reassure you things are going to be fine!" So slowly, over time, I just kind of assimilated and incorporated these pieces of my life. I had a partner for 13 years, and he was as much a part of the family as anyone else, and my father liked him a great deal and was very accepting. They had a very close relationship. In fact, they were both sad when my partner and I ended things because they liked each other a lot. My dad's back east [now], and my mother died 3 to 4 years after I came out so she and I never really had a chance to work through it. But my father and I have, and that's been very nice. Subsequently, along these lines—my brother is also gay and was a Jesuit for 8 years. He came out only after my mom died, which tells you something about her power! But all in all, I would say that I have been surprised by many wonderful things since the time I first came out.

Tip 8: Take Your Time

Lucy: I Needed to Take My Time With Mom

Lucy came out in the early 1970s in the context of the women's movement in a progressive college town where her sexual identity didn't have to be a secret. Although she married a man, later divorced, went through a bisexual phase, and dabbled in many different spiritualities, the biggest issue in her life was how to tell her mother that she was a lesbian. Lucy, knowing her mother would react very poorly, decided to take her time in disclosing this kind of vulnerability. So she waited nearly 20 years and today is glad that she did.

Mom, of course, handled it very poorly. However, if I had come out to her when I first came out, I would not have been emotionally able to handle her reactions. So I think being closeted with my mother was the right thing to do, because by the time she reacted I was so comfortable with who I am that I knew it was her problem. Although I wasn't closeted in the rest of my life, that particular piece of the closet was actually good for me.

I heard several similar stories about taking the time necessary before disclosing such personal information. There was the young woman who held off telling her parents she was a lesbian for 4 years after her self-discovery to avoid unnecessarily inflicting more chaos in their lives. Yet she knew that when she was ready to come out she wanted them to be among the first to know. Another woman waited until her mother's 80th birthday before she volunteered that her "friend" of 23 years was actually her life partner. Her mom's reaction was actually quite lovely. In this case, the anticipated fear of her mother's reaction was not what stopped her disclosure, but rather it was her own internal homophobia. For a variety of reasons, including her work as a public school teacher in a small community, she had compartmentalized and withheld this part of her life in many situations. However, by taking her time to arrive at a place of increased self-confidence and not wanting this deep bond of love and trust between mother and daughter to be hindered any longer, she was able to share this intimate moment with her mother. Since that time she has experienced an increasing amount of disclosure in other areas of her life as well.

Therapists and other onlookers often believe their clients should come out as quickly as possible so their client's sexual identity can be fully realized and assimilated. This may largely be due to hidden agendas or anxieties of therapists who just want their clients to move on with their lives. It can be quite tiresome to sit with a client for extended periods of time without seeing the movement that would validate our own expertise. Being encouraged to come out faster or more completely than a particular person is ready to do may also be found in segments of the gay community. While this may be posed as something that would greatly help a closeted individual, those who are already out may have an agenda in their support: They can feel less isolated in their own lives. We all need to be mindful of our agendas when encouraging others to disclose their truths. Because this process is always more complex than meets the eye, queer people need to be able to share intimate news when it best suits their unique situation.

Tip 9: Make Room for Differing Amounts of Being Out

There is a social perception that one is either in the closet or out rather than allowing for gradients between the two positions. Current thinking in many White populations is that it is healthy to come out, and unhealthy to live a closeted life; however that may not be true in other cultures. Some people believe their sexual orientation is a much more private matter. Choosing not to come out does not necessarily mean they suffer from lack of pride or are buried in shame. There may be other situations surrounding their lives that would make this an unwise decision.

Culture and Ethnicity May Regulate Disclosure
I think it is imperative to make the effort to try and understand cultural meanings that are different from your own. Some of the studies I have read about have suggested that disclosure in some ethnic groups can disrupt important alliances within the family and the extended community. Informal norms such as "don't ask so they won't tell" may allow families to maintain and accept family members who are gay or lesbian without having to address the issues directly. Loving actions might speak in a more supportive way than any coming out party could possible do given cultural norms (Savin-Williams, 2001, p. 95).

Often the pressure is not to come out because the ethnic community is more homophobic than the dominant culture. Therefore, it is important for therapists to recognize what disclosure or nondisclosure means to individual clients and to refrain from basing judgments about client's emotional health or comfort with being lesbian, gay, or bisexual on how out they are and how many people they have disclosed their sexual identity to. Perez et al. (2000) pointed out:

> In Latino culture, overdisclosure often is not allowed (Green, 1997). African American LGB's [sic] may have an easier time than others because within their culture gender roles are more flexible and families rarely reject their children outright (Green, 1997). In fact for some Black families, coming out means being "taken in" (A. Smith, 1997). The Black family may reject the idea of a gay or lesbian identity, but fully accept the gay or lesbian person as a member of the Black community. The heavy emphasis on marriage in American Indian culture may preclude coming out. (Green, 1997, p. 167)

Unfortunately, information from studies is still lacking on what it means to come out in ethnic or other minority groups, and even less is written about the physically disabled clients or others who are dependent on others for bodily functions.

Once again, people need to be viewed within their social constructs. Teachers are often more closeted than in other professions due to public fears about the influences of homosexuals on children. Ministers, of course, are going to be more guarded, knowing that disclosure will most likely result in the loss of their professional career and calling. Married people who discover later in life that they are more gay than not must weigh the effects of their self-awareness on the lives of their spouses and children. I know some very brave and centered parents who have chosen to be very discreet in disclosing information about their sexual orientation to avoid harming their families. While I'm on this subject, let's not forget that Dr. Alfred Kinsey reported that most people's sexual orientation falls within a 6-point grade (Wikipedia). Just because a person possesses a greater degree of homosexual orientation does not mean that he or she will act on it. Sexual orientation and sexual behavior are not always in sync. Again, because we are multifaceted beings, we need to be allowed the dignity and respect necessary to wisely navigate the complex choices that best fit the totality of our lives—in our own style, in our own time.

Tip 10: Integrate Spirituality Into All Parts of Your Life

While it often seems easier to walk away from oppressive religions that cannot find room for gay spirituality, many people make the mistake of rejecting all things spiritual and end up cheating themselves out of the fuller human experience. Although they wish it could have been different, most people I surveyed said they had to forge their paths of self-acceptance and spiritual wholeness by themselves. This concept of "religious individualism" takes place on many fronts in a culture that stresses people find spiritual individualism over congregational or community support. Jodi O'Brien's (2004) research on queer Christian identities found religious individualism evident in many ways:

> Individuals experience an awakening of both religiosity and homosexuality that is very personal and profound. This awakening ushers in a sense of contradiction and a desire to somehow integrate themselves into the system of meaning from which they now feel outcast. Interviewees describe this period of initial struggle as very lonely and painful. There is a sense of insurmountable shame and alienation. The path to resolution is a solitary one. (pp. 186–187)

Three Similar Paths

O'Brien (2004) found three ways that religious gays and lesbians converge while creating individual forms of resolution in our current society.

Flight Away From Religion

Many coming out stories include denunciation and flight from their religious backgrounds. Some may not see good in any form of religion for a while. Yet it's not that they are against all things spiritual but that they are opposing a system of meaning that provided no place for their most authentic selves. These reactive expressions may be part of the process of internally reshaping one's sense of self and identity rather than letting that be done by the external authority of a religious teaching: "For many individuals this is a painful and alienating process that involves not only casting off an entire system of meaning and belonging, but forging a new (non-Christian) ideology" (O'Brien, 2004, p. 187).

Accepting the Teaching That Homosexuality Is an Affliction

While attending a recent American Association of Marriage and Family Therapy (AAMFT) annual conference, I wandered into one of the poster sessions and engaged in a conversation with student researcher Daman Reynolds, who conducted a study titled "Reconciling Gay and LDS Identities" (2007) that illustrates this particular position.

When asked how interviewees had come to view their same-sex attraction in light of Latter Day Saints (LDS) doctrine, the following sample of responses from Reynolds's (2007) study sounded all too familiar:

> I don't believe God "made me this way" or that He condones same-sex sexual or romantic relationships. I believe that problems related to this issue are simply one additional manifestation of what it means to live in a fallen world.

> I don't believe I am gay. That label is damaging and inappropriate. I believe I have been given an affliction, and that if I endure it well, I will receive complete restoration on Christ's timetable or at the resurrection.

> Acting on it is a sin. I hate it. It is hard not to hate myself because of it.

> The way it is now with me, I wish that it wasn't against God's will. I wouldn't be alone.... So I stay in the church because it's the right thing to do and I do want to be in the church, but at the same time, I am not happy at all.

Although these responses are from people of the LDS religion, you could poll homosexuals in many Christian denominations and find the very same responses. Many Evangelical churches feel they are progressing because they have moved from seeing all aspects of homosexuality as base to separating the categories of sin (e.g., sexual behaviors) from the non-sin (e.g., sexual feelings and orientation). In such instances, the struggle to be a good Christian would revolve around the battles of maintaining a life of gay celibacy. However, a person reentering these circles often assumes a self-image that bears an affliction and thus continues to wear a cloak of shame that causes a great deal of inner turmoil. These are often the people who seek a therapist or are referred by a church leader for reparative therapies that promise a cure for the gay malady. For those whose "cure" doesn't take, there is often a great deal of self-judgment for not being a good enough Christian or for lacking enough faith "to move mountains" (see Matthew 17:20). If healing for homosexual desires can't be found, people are often encouraged to remain closeted if they are to remain an active part of the congregation.

*Maintaining Both a Strong Spiritual Identity
and an Open Lesbian and Gay Identity*

A third response to spiritual individualism, however, is an increasing number of Christians and Jews who maintain both a strong religious identity as well as an open and proud lesbian, gay identity. Many gay Christians are creating a unique response to their predicament: Consider the following statement made by Brian in an interview conducted by O'Brien (2004)

> Healthy living means finding ways to throw off the guilt. It's not just the guilt of feeling like you've betrayed your family and friends and their expectations of you. It's the guilt that comes from messages all around you that you don't belong. That you're an aberration. Until one day you start to get it and say, "Hey, I'm here. I'm doing okay. I must belong." When you figure that you have courage to walk away from the church and realize the problem is them. They are not big enough to let you belong. (p. 187.)

Another Option: Learn to See Each Part of Coming Out Through a Spiritual Lens

Because many gays, lesbians, and bisexuals have such an aversion to Christianity, they may find the previous option enticing in its ideology but feel no desire to identify as a gay Christian. So, in addition to the three typical responses, I propose a fourth possibility: seeing all things as spiritual and incorporating into one's basic humanity the idea that

God is not distant, removed, and judging but is continually present in all things and is loving in every moment of our lives. I am not talking about pantheism, where all things are God, but panentheism, where the spirit of God is present in all things. This is the way of ancient Native American spirituality and is also found in the very roots of Celtic and Eastern Christianity.

Phillip Newell's (2000) devotional book *Celtic Benediction* exemplifies this by beginning each day with a simple prayer of opening the senses to such a possibility; "Be still and aware of God's presence within and all around." (p. 1) This makes every challenge, every argument with God and others, every new discovery of an authentic self to be a place to encounter the spiritual side of life.

By combining our previous definitions of spirituality as whatever connects outside our petty little selves to others or to the Divine, it may be possible to see each of the 10 helpful hints for coming out as moments to integrate spirituality into one's life:

1. Be aware of your best self and honor what you find: To be aware and honoring of one's best self could be a way to acknowledge the mysterious way each of us has been created and the freedom to live with authenticity.
2. Radically accept your new identity, life's difficulties, and other people: To radically accept oneself may be a way of honoring the Creator's image and purpose of each unique life as a present waiting to be unveiled to the world. To wrestle with God is an ancient and honorable way of spiritual growth.
3. Learn to adapt in new ways that engage life: To move beyond isolation by finding creative ways to reengage with the world is moving beyond radical acceptance to giving one's spirit feet for action.
4. Make a plan to avoid crisis events: Who needs more crisis events? Trying to find peaceful, thoughtful ways of intentional, centered living can certainly engage one's spiritual practices.
5. Find social support and use it: Social support might become one of the key pieces of gay spirituality, because it only comes alive when a person reveals something of his or her core with others.
6. Avoid reacting to the reactions of others: The ancient Hebrews taught that living in God's realm meant we were to turn our swords into plowshares for peace (see Isaiah 2:1–5). One of the goals of true spirituality is to become agents of peace and healing in this world. But sometimes the toxic waste inside our hearts prevents us from responding in wise ways: "We must be willing to pull the swords out so that our hearts can heal" (Gundrum, 2007). By transforming swords that caused us such misery

into plowshares for good, we can learn to live at peace with others. We must take responsibility for our own responses while learning to accept our collective humanness.

7. Make a plan but be flexible with the results: Eastern spiritual practices such as mindfulness have to do with remaining calmly focused by honoring the present moment for what is rather that what is hoped for. If being a calm presence in the midst of constant change isn't a chance to practice spirituality, I don't know what is.

8. Take your time with Mom and others: If God has "all the time in the world," why not follow the Divine example?

9. Make room for differing amounts of being out: Accepting others is to honor the unique life and spirit of each person we encounter. By putting aside our own agendas, we also disengage our own judgments of others. To stop internal and external judging is to reach outside the self for the power to stop such insanity. It also goes right along with the idea that "mercy triumphs over judgment" (James 2:13).

10. Integrate spirituality into all parts of your life: "Be still and be aware of Gods' presence within and all around" (Newell, 2000). Lead by example that being both homosexual and spiritually minded is not only possible but undeniable true.

Repeat all 10 steps. Coming out is a not a one-time event but a lifelong opportunity to practice your spirituality.

Tools for the Therapist

Therapists must not become impatient when clients do not come out as fast or as completely as we would like. It is important to honor the process and respect the great courage it takes for a person to stand outside social norms and be counted as different. Therapists need to check their own anxieties on this topic so they can tune into the wishes of their clients.

The therapist's office can be a great place to help clients prepare to come out to significant people in their lives by crafting letters to distant parents, planning conversations with loved ones, slowing down the process to determine who to tell and when; while this is all happening, the therapist should make sure clients have enough social and emotional support to sustain them. It is also important to educate clients who desire to come out to be patient with those receiving this news for the first time. Giving loved ones time to process this kind of news can make a big difference in how an entire family will respond.

It seems that how well a person psychologically adjusts "to coming out has some relationship to a client's acceptance or rejection of the illness model of homosexuality as well as to their response to oppression" (Perez et al., 2000, p. 165). If people are always fighting the idea that they are living under the affliction of same-sex attraction, they are going to have a tough time adapting to their new life. Therapists also must continually rebuff the medical model (or illness model) to help their queer clients envision and adapt to a positive gay life:

> The medical model views the source of the problem as an atomistic, concrete pathogen (e.g., a bacterium or carcinoma) located within the patient ... effective psychotherapy requires the establishment and maintenance of a therapeutic relationship strong enough to provide the safety and trust needed for the client to stay engaged with painful emotional material. (Hunsberger, 2007, p. 614)

7

The Search for an Inclusive Theology

A Presentation of Fish

The scientists who are sharing the truck
know it is impossible: the desert
too choked by heat and sediment, by silt
and pumice, there could be no lake here,
no clear water, but still the truck lurches
to a stop and they are told they are stopping
for fish. What is lost in translation? The Aita
men jump from the flat bed and sprint west
across the hardpan, until they shimmer
into the horizon, while the Aita women
stay and preen their children's kinky hair,
copper—tinted, and the Americans crawl
under the truck, the only shade there is,
flat bellied and playing cribbage, anxious
to be moving again. Foolishness,
but the day becomes low and angular
and loping spots ripple back
into existence. Proud, the men return
with a kite of sticks; tilapia pinned
on the points and one bangus fish,
eel-like and so long it takes two to carry,
fish pulled from sand, their eyes
still clear from the catching.

DAVID SYNDER

Like scientists, who cannot conceive someone could find a fish dinner in
the desert, many people have not been able to fathom that there is such

a thing as a gay, lesbian, or bisexual person of faith. Even for people who have come to understand that homosexuality is far more complex than they once believed, there is still a troubling theological gap when it comes to making room for gay spirituality. Their mentors taught that homosexual behavior is a sin, yet when they get to know gay people who seem to be more like themselves than not, they are puzzled and often feel a need to find exceptions to that rule.

It reminds me of a scene from *The Candidate* (Michael Ritchie, 1972), an award-winning movie in which Robert Redford plays a politician entering a campaign solely to gain a platform to speak against issues of injustice that have fueled his passions. Hoping to raise the moral consciousness of his fellow Americans, instead he is unexpectedly elected to the U.S. Senate. Never expecting to win the election, he turns to his colleagues and says, "What do we do now?" The movie ends with this question still unanswered.

Life often presents us with information and events we never imagined possible, leaving us to recreate life and meaning in the wake of new discoveries. What was once known to be impossible has now been shown to be reality, causing us to ask Redford's question many times in our lives: "What do we do now?"

Gay spirituality was once thought to be an oxymoron. Yet this book is full of collected stories from gay Christians, Mormons, Buddhists, pagans, Universalists, and New Agers. The spiritual life of gays, lesbians, and bisexuals has become a present reality. It should be obvious by now that sexual orientation does not need to preclude one's spirituality.

Assimilation: Looking Beyond Diversity

To this point I have been able to identify my place in society as an able-bodied male, middle-class American Caucasian, son, brother, friend, lover, husband, father, businessman, gardener, pastor, therapist, teacher, poet, author, Christian, Republican turned Democrat, and college graduate with a couple of advanced degrees. But during my lifetime I have noticed that the boundaries around all of these definitions have become more permeable with increased opportunities to make and maintain connections across barriers that were once nearly impervious.

Although we have progressed in acknowledging and even celebrating diversity, most of society is still in the process of learning how to assimilate it. However, when we discuss the intersection of sexual diversity with traditional models of faith we are often at a loss for knowing how to cross boundaries that will honor spirituality in the gay, lesbian, bisexual, and transgender (GLBT) community. Some people silence this discussion because they are too afraid to look at the potential breadth of their own sexuality. For many, it just doesn't fit into the categories that were previously ascribed to morality. Christians and Jews and Muslims may have difficulty making room for it because it doesn't fit traditional understandings of their sacred Scriptures. Therefore, gay spirituality is often negated or, at best, is viewed as a spirituality that is not legitimate because of strongly held beliefs based in theologies having to do with works righteousness, purity codes, or the fear of Divine retribution.

C. S. Lewis pointed out that "our first knowledge of punishment often precedes our first knowledge of having done anything wrong." (Brown-Taylor, 2000, p. 46) Like Adam and Eve, who were originally innocents exploring the delights of the garden of Eden, (Genesis, Chapter 3), sexual minorities are often merely exploring the territory of their own souls and end up becoming outsiders, segregated by the judgments or biases of those who have not stopped to consider what it must be like to walk in someone else's shoes.

The student rebellions of the 1960s brought a freedom of self-expression that led our society into many new arenas not considered possible in former decades. Later, the Reagan era of the 1980s initiated a counterrevolution that grew into a "rigid theology of what they believe is unassailable moral and political superiority" (Brokaw, 2007, p. 125). It seems that we still need to learn a valuable lesson. Separation that maintains racial, ethnic, religious, and sexual differences may create comfort zones and a sense of pride for belonging to a particular group, but it does not prepare us for a world where assimilation is becoming much more highly valued.

Contrary to many opinions, learning to assimilate does not mean that a person must surrender his or her ethnic pride or cultural, religious, or sexual identity distinctions. Instead, assimilation is about finding common goals, new standards of conduct, tolerance, and increased empathy. It is a way to challenge prejudice and hypocrisy. Tom Brokaw (2007), in his most recent book, *Boom!,* believes that the 21st century is going to need a great deal more of this than in times past:

> As a society, we are still inclined to cling to our old racial and cultural landscapes, fenced in by insecurities, biases, ignorance of others and intellectual laziness. The danger is that the American landscape then breaks up along the fault lines of anxieties that only continue to develop and deepen.
>
> Too many individuals and organizations are ready to help that destructive, divisive process along because of their own narrow views or for their own power.

They do not have the commonwealth welfare, as Thomas Jefferson described it, in mind, (p. 336).

However, there are some shining examples of how these boundaries are being crossed. In 1993, the White House under Bill Clinton helped initiate a new policy with the military known as "don't ask, don't tell." Rather than helping sexual minorities like Clinton had intended, it actually hindered careers in the Armed Forces and drove people further into the closet. Shortly after that, General Colin Powell was asked to be the commencement speaker at Harvard-Radcliffe University, which quickly set off a protest by gay and lesbian students refusing to attend a ceremony that honored someone who had been intimately involved in the policy they felt was personally demeaning:

> During one of the luncheons honoring Powell, a man wearing a top hat, tails, earrings and buttons denouncing the policy went up to General Powell and said, "I look forward to the day this issue no longer divides us."
>
> Powell, with four stars on his shoulders and an array of medals across his Army uniform, surprised the young man by embracing him with both arms, saying, "So do I and I hope that day comes sooner rather than later."
> News of this encounter took the anger out of the air and created a sense of community across a barrier that in the good old days, we would not even have acknowledged. (Brokaw, 2007, p. 500)

Thanks to the continued development of scientific research and a growing appreciation for the wide variance in human beings, there are abundant opportunities for profound change in the dialogues about the things that divide us and the attitudes that govern our lives. It may be hard to confront these issues, and it is certainly going to be uncomfortable at times, but we must talk about these matters so that we can make room for personal truths in each other's life experiences.

We Need to Talk About Theology

Single-strand theologies that insist there is only one acceptable version of truth cause problems for people who want to talk about the intersection of homosexuality and faith. What is needed is the development of languages and theologies that can assimilate the findings of scientific research so our spiritual and intellectual developments are more harmonious. However, it is not unusual for faith systems to be rather slow in adapting to societal changes, because emotionally laden beliefs are extraordinarily strong and resistant to change.

Over the past 5 years, a group of colleagues and I have led several national and local seminars that promote structured dialogue among people of differing perspectives on the topics of religion, homosexuality, and marriage. Our model for discussing this topic is based on the Public Conversations Project, which allows us to guide groups into a structured and respectful dialogue. Whenever personal beliefs are shared, it is a joy to watch people listen intently to another person's beliefs that differ greatly from their own. One of the outcomes of this process is often hearing a participant say, "I have never thought of it that way before. Thank you for sharing," or, "I've never had an honest discussion with someone like you; it has given me a lot to think about." Although we never purposefully guide participants into discussions about theology, this is usually at the front of most discussions.

What Is Theology?

The word *theology* was originally a Greek term, and it is best translated to mean "god-talk." It was originally used in Greek society to describe people's discourse about the gods. In later centuries, Christians adopted its use when referring to theories of God's identity and God's presence in our world.

Most of our ideas about theology come from the people who have mentored us (e.g., our pastors, educators, and family members) and whom we have come to know and trust. Although theologians and preachers may provide us their own theories about sin and salvation, we do not invent the realities those words describe:

> Long before there were preachers, churches or even organized religions, there were essential human experiences of community and alienation, of connection and dis-connection to the divine. You can find paintings of those experiences on the walls of prehistoric caves and hear richly symbolic stories about them that pre-date written language. Different wisdom traditions give different names to those experiences and offer different understandings of them but the experiences themselves are the realities that give rise to all the theories definitions. (Brown-Taylor, 2000, p. 42)

As you read this, I'm hoping that you will be thinking through your own theological framework and tracing the path of your own perceptions of homosexuality. My own spiritual background has its roots in Wesleyan theology (modeled after John Wesley), which holds that good theology should always be supported by the four pillars of Scripture, church tradition, personal experience, and the inner promptings of the Spirit. Many of my changing perceptions are due to how my own spirit has been moved by personal life experiences of those I have encountered, which means that I have to constantly reevaluate my understandings of the Scriptures when new information is revealed.

Pastoral Theology

As I open up this theological discussion, I must first admit that I certainly do not claim to know the mind of God. I also feel a need to declare that I view myself as a pastoral theologian rather than a systematic one. This means that I am most interested in the pragmatics of how my theology will affect the lives of the people I have encountered and served over many years. My chief concern lies with those who have felt cut off from their faith because someone else told them that their way of being human (and gay) has put them outside the circle of God's love. I know too many people who have felt the undertow of judgment, shame, and consequences of being considered a lesser human being by others who seem content with simple answers. Many sexual minorities live with a deep internal anguish stemming from personal rejections and fears simply because they have been honest about being different from straight society.

My own concepts about who God is and what it means to live in vital relationship to the Source of Life continue to be works in progress. I expect this to continue until the day I die. While the allure of simple "tried and true" answers may provide people a temporary escape so they won't have to ponder the difficult questions of how to apply their faith to new situations, it doesn't take long before rigid and outdated beliefs become riddled with exceptions to the rule. Even though human and divine systems are both complex and beyond our full understanding; we must continue to try to find languages that will work for us.

Postmodern Society Seeks New Languages for Its Spirituality

According to the most recent Gallup poll, 95% of residents in the United States continue to believe in God (Princeton Religion Research Center, 1985). However, many have stopped going to church, where the language they hear about God or the form of worship they encounter does not match their lives or the hunger of their hearts. What seems to be cresting the wave of spirituality today is the creation of individual worldviews, beliefs, practices, and languages from various sacred and secular traditions. Brian McClaren

(McClaren, 2000) suggests that what is needed is a "new systems approach to [church] program[s]—an approach that anticipates change." (p. 42) He refers to a new movement for people of faith, which he calls "The church on the other side" (p. 43), which will need to provide a key role in our culture as a place of arbitration for opposing views of Scriptures and social issues. Younger generations are much more interested in relational dialogue that seeks to understand the diverse applications of spiritual wisdom rather than hearing and preaching formalized, dogmatic sermons. By doing so, those associated with this conversation are attempting to acquire a new spiritual language that better describes the world as they understand it.

For example, one of my lesbian interviewees raised in a conservative Christian home currently finds Buddhist philosophy more compelling than the imperatives of Christian dogma. Her transformative devotional life consists of meditations using the martial art of healing known as Chi-Gong (Qigong). Another woman who was raised as a Christian described her evolving spirituality as reality based, whereas she tends to think of Christianity as too full of magical thinking to be useful for her. She has felt that Earth-centered religions like Wiccans and Gaia suit her best.

Some men and women have added new ways of linking their GLBT sexuality and their spirituality through The Body Electric, which employs a type of Eastern tantric sexuality that focuses individuals on the supreme flow of sacred life force, creating a transcendent state that often results in an increase of inner peace and self-acceptance.

One of the gay men I interviewed, who was raised with very strict Jehovah's Witnesses, found not only sobriety but also a wonderful healing community in weekly Alcoholics Anonymous (AA) meetings. Although he belongs to a progressive Christian church, he often wishes that the church could find a way to be as relationally transparent as his AA community.

For 90% of the people I surveyed, they seemed to be seeking some kind of salvation that would transform their way of being in the world so that their lives would be characterized by peace, meaning, maturity, and gracious acceptance. While everyone could name things that impeded their spiritual growth, no one referred to those as sin.

Redefining Sin

Although most people of faith have known about the concept of sin since they were very young, they may not have had a useful understanding of it when it comes to the social and spiritual dilemmas of life. In the Victory Heights view of the world from the late 1950s and early 1960s, churches and Sunday schools taught that the definition of sin was missing the mark of "God's plan for your life." (Campus Crusade tract, 1968) Variant sexualities were definitely off the mark. This meant that people's improper choices or rebellion against traditional or socially accepted ways of being could put them at risk for being excluded from God's plan of salvation. If you disagreed with literal interpretations of Scripture or did not abide by proper codes of conduct you were probably living on shaky ground.

Other words associated with sin include *damnation, penance, iniquity,* and *transgression*—words of fear from former eras when human relationships with God were laced with guilt, blame, and retribution rather than loving-kindness and grace. Those words were never very helpful in making ethical or even moral decisions that spoke to the heart. Instead, those discomforting words of judgment often seemed to rob the joy of life from people while making others into religious neurotics who became fearful of stepping outside their religion's specific codes of conduct. As often happens with things that make us too uncomfortable, we not only avoided them but eventually also quit using them altogether. However, as the 1960s began to emphasize individual freedoms and as the counterrevolutions of the 1980s focused on the protection of social privilege, we grew into a culture that became more focused on the individual while overlooking the social sins that oppressed our marginalized neighbors.

Because of my own youthful privilege and my religious culture's emphasis on individual salvation, I wasn't very aware of social sins until I became the pastor of a small suburban church whose community was made up of a large percentage of disadvantaged people. When I went to court with a young mother fighting for custody of her child, I saw firsthand how those with more money received lawyers with greater skills and resources than the poor, who had to rely on the State defender's office. As I heard the stories of bright, young people who had grown up in generations of financial and emotional poverty, I saw how impossible it seemed for them to go on to higher education because they had to spend so much of their energy on survival and recovery from abuse. When people were fired from decent jobs because they didn't have reliable transportation, or when we discovered that they needed a permanent address to obtain needed social benefits, our congregation many times felt the burden of trying to meet those needs. That was when I learned how abusive family systems can pass the tome of violence on to the next generation. I also heard how a "good

Christian family" attempted to steer their son away from homosexuality by threatening to have nothing to do with him if he "chose" to be gay, and I witnessed the effect of others who were so overcome with fear and judgment that they turned their own children out on the streets when they contracted AIDS. More and more hurting people began to find our congregation, and I had difficulty handling my own stresses. To say I was overwhelmed is putting it mildly.

Barbara Brown-Taylor (2000) described a similar discovery during her pastoral training education:

> Those powers did more real harm to people's spirits than we could begin to repair in our six or eight hours a week. They sucked the hope right out of people. They taught people not to trust. Worst of all, they treated human beings like trash, until the human beings began to believe them. Most days, all we did was bandage them up and send them back out on the streets, so that they could get chewed up all over again. (p. 19)

Unfortunately, much of our current society continues to overlook these kinds of social sins and chooses to focus instead on individual sins like homosexuality. My guess is that poverty, crime, oppression, degradation, and wrongful exploitation of the earth are too overwhelming for most people to handle, so they shift their attention to an enemy who seems safer to attack. Like the evolution of sexual and social mores, sin is often determined by whatever a particular group disapproves of with a wide variation due to economic status, creed, and ethnicity: "Selective Bible passages may be offered to support a group's definitions, but there is little awareness that God's values may turn out to be different than their own" (Brown-Taylor, 2000, p. 22).

Most of our definitions of sin have originated from social constructs. Take the theology of original sin, for example. Jesus was raised as a Jew who would have had no concept of original sin. That construct didn't come along until the 4th century A.D., when Saint Augustine turned the tale of Adam and Eve into an explanation for how the human race often chooses evil instead of good. (Brown-Taylor, 2000, p. 47) Those who disagreed, like the highly educated Roman-Celt Pelagius who believed in natural sanctity, were condemned as heretics. (Bradley, 2003, p. 52) This archetype has led many Christians into the belief that sin is primarily the disobedience of individuals.

Even in our lifetimes we have seen concepts of sin change. A sin in the late 1940s might have been wearing makeup or a gold ring, going to the movies, or playing cards. These ideas stemmed from Pauline texts suggesting that Christians should not be worldly but spiritually minded. Today, proponents of ecospirituality would tell us that our blatant misuse of the earth is one of our greatest sins and that being worldly minded is a virtue. Similarly, most people have known about the sins of pride and self-aggrandizement but have not paid enough attention to the sins of self-negation whereby our insecurities and low-self esteem have cut us off from the source of life and our God-given place in community. When you think about it, there are probably thousands of ways to turn away from the Source of Life.

For Jews, concepts of sin and salvation were more about how to follow the Torah in the here and now rather than worrying about escaping Hell's fires. To this day, Jews find the Christian focus on the world to come more than a little irrelevant. They are much more interested in assisting God in healing humanity in the present. Buddhists believe that enlightened life is about pursuing truth, so one might say that their concept of sin would be ignorance about the true nature of reality. For a Buddhist, salvation is a matter of waking up. If a lesbian Buddhist wakes up, should she not take the path that will lead her life into something that is most congruent and loving?

Rather than dropping the idea of sin altogether, we might find a new use for it by redefining it as: whatever turns you away from the source of life and makes you feel dead inside. Nearly everyone has done something that has made him or her that way. I can still remember at 13 how ashamed I was of myself when my friends and I stole some candy bars from the corner variety story. Because I experienced the life-robbing force of taking something that was not mine, I went back the next day when my buddies were not present to secretly put that candy bar back into its rightful place. I was able to mend that breach in my relationship with myself and the store owner that day; unfortunately, some of my adult sins were not so easily repaired.

Most likely, each of us has embarked on a spiritual path that consists of turning away from former toxic ways of life that no longer work to seek out something new that promises a more peaceful, meaningful, and abundant life that is connected to God. This to me is the essence of the Bible's salvation message. Many sexual minorities get sidetracked by the toxins of other people's noninclusive theologies when they begin to believe that they do not deserve a better and more abundant life. If they internalize the belief that their own way of being true to themselves is so reprehensible or unacceptable to God and others, they may lose all hope of salvation. At this point, the mistreatment of homosexuals becomes a social sin rather than an individual one, and the unintended consequences for our civilization can turn to monstrous bigotry.

So Is It Sin?

When it comes down to the question of homosexuality being a sin, it may be best to review our basic definition of sin. Does loving behavior shown toward a partner of the same sex constitute evil? Is it destructive? Is it abusive? Is it malicious? Or is it life-giving, renewing, and inspiring?

Maybe we should ask a gay man what it feels like to find solace and comfort in the arms of his lover or a lesbian how much life she gains when her girlfriend touches her tenderly.

Walt Whitman described this deep contentment:

> When I heard at the close of the day how my name had been
>   receiv'd with plaudits in the capitol, still it was not a
>   happy night for me that follow'd;
> And else, when I carous'd, or when my plans were accomplish'd
>   still I was not happy;
> But the day when I rose at dawn from the bed of perfect health,
>   refresh'd, singing, inhaling the ripe breath of autumn,
> When I saw the full moon in the west grow pale and disappear
>   in the morning light,
> When I wander'd alone over the beach, and undresing, bathed,
>   laughing with the cool waters, and saw the sun rise,
> And when I thought how my dear friend, my loved, was on his
>   way coming, O then I was happy;
> O then each breath tasted sweeter - and all that day my food
>   nourish'd me more - and the beautiful day pass'd well,
> And then the next came with equal joy - and with the next, at
>   evening, came my friend;
> And that night, while all was still, I heard the waters roll slowly
>   continually up the shores,
> I heard the hissing rustle of the liquid and sands, as directed to
>   me, whispering, to congratulate me,
> For the one I love most lay sleeping by me under the same cover
>   in the cool night,
> In the stilllness, in the autumn moonbeams, his face was
>   inclined toward me,

And his arm lay lightly around my breast - and that night I was
happy.

Walt Whitman, When I Heard at the Close of the day (Whitman, 1900)

When we describe something that is life-giving, loving, and
restorative—if our intimate relationships make us more alive, grounded,
and connected to our souls, the souls of others, and in closer affiliation with a loving God, then in my opinion we are obviously not talking
about sin.

Developing Adequate Theologies for Contemporary Life

Although many former beliefs about sacred literature have proved to be
inadequate for the current era, the spiritual value of biblical texts has
been relevant for nearly 3,000 years and continues to inspire faith today.
However, as I stated in chapter 1, each generation has the responsibility
and privilege of finding the right language, allegories, and interpretations
that will make the message the most relevant for its time.

New Knowledge Necessitates New Interpretation of Scripture

Scriptural Interpretations Have Changed With the Times

The Bible has been quoted and copied more times than any other book
in human history. Since the invention of the printing press in 1453, it has
also been printed more than any other text, has been translated into 1,200
languages, and continues to sell millions of copies around the world each
year. Make no mistake: Scripture still matters a great deal to most people
of faith.

For centuries, the Bible was the plumb line of truth. Because most people were uneducated, it was usually interpreted by clergy trained to view
Scriptures through lenses that would support their various religious institutions. It was the final authority, and because no science was its equal,
new discoveries were not welcome to contradict its lessons. During the
"Burning Times" from the 14th to 17th century, 50,000 to 100,000 victims
were burned at the stake for heresy, showing that it was not safe to challenge the status quo.

Religious education in the past taught people to believe what they were told. If priests interpreted the Genesis account of the world being created in 7 days as being literal, then people believed it to be so. This belief continues today, according to some studies suggesting that 70% of Americans still believe in a literal translation of the biblical book of Genesis. (Genesis, 1:1–2:4) However, there are biblical scholars who have come to realize that the Genesis story was never intended to provide a scientific explanation but was intended to convey a loving God's message of salvation through many different stories that are rich in the language of spiritual analogy. (Stevenson, 1967, pp. 25–33)

There are some other problems with our traditional interpretations of the creation story. For instance, most Sunday school lessons teach that we are all descendants of one man and one woman who lived in a garden on the banks of the Euphrates River. Modern archeologists are now finding the oldest human fossils in central Africa. Linguistic experts have learned that the Hebrew word for Adam, *adamah*, is the same word for Earth (as in "those who emerged from the earth"). This would make the creation story not about one man and one woman but about greater humanity created in God's image, who at times will make wrongful choices and have to live with the consequences. As we read through Genesis, we also come across the story of Abraham (Genesis), who shows us that even men of incredible faith can be flawed with deception because they do not fully trust in God's provisions, yet as we follow his story we can see how his faith evolved with his life experiences. Obviously, human beings have continuously learned to adapt their beliefs and to create new theologies over time to make room to assimilate new information. Like the storyteller's art in Native American folklore, we need to know that regardless of the accuracy of the facts, an essential truth can always be found within the story.

Finding an Adequate Purpose for the Bible

Inadequate Views

Although many former views of the Bible's purpose have come and gone over the centuries, there are still some inadequate ideas that may pose a problem for those seeking a way to honor the faith of gays and lesbians.

Rather than believing that the Bible is the manual of moral guidance (which condemns believers who live correctly to assume a self-righteous attitude in life while burying others in shame for failing to live up to the code of a particular sect), we need to find a better way to cherish its spiritual treasures. Similarly, by believing that one of the main purposes of the Bible is to impart spiritual information to us that we wouldn't otherwise know (which gives a platform to false prophets who possess "special" revelations that are usually misguided insights about the future), we need to discover an additional way to see its literary value.

Those who want to continue using the Bible as a reliable textbook of history, science, and cosmology have to look only at the example of the Italian astronomer Galileo to see some problems here. Galileo defended the Copernican theory, claiming that the earth revolves around the sun, instead of holding the popular biblical view of his day that the earth was the center of the universe. He was eventually led into one of the world's most famous trials by the Roman Inquisition, where he was charged with heresy, threatened with torture, and forced to recant. He lived the remainder of his life under house arrest and died with people still believing in a revolving sun in 1642. A full 300 years later, in 1967, the Catholic Church formally acknowledged he was right. One must realize, however, that this closing of the mind to known facts continues today. I once had a parishioner who refused to believe in the theory of an ancient earth and Jurassic animals of huge proportions because dinosaurs were not mentioned in the Bible! I found it interesting that he did, however, believe the platypus, zebra, and giraffe exist.

Some people like to see the Bible displayed on their coffee table because they believe it to be a source of protection shielding them from evil. I suggest they might find another way to combat the cost of homeowners' insurance. For those who believe that the Bible's purpose is to provide proper dogma of our belief systems, I would suggest another reading of James 2:19, which tells us that "even the demons believe—and shudder" pointing to the fact that belief and faith are two different things. Dogmatic faith does not change people's lives for the better; it only "makes them rigid and un-teachable. It is not biblical" (Stevenson, 1967, p. 24).

Many secular views seem inadequate to people of faith as well, like those that cast the Bible into the category of religious history with other ancient books of philosophy. This perspective takes the stance that the stories of the Bible are merely a collection of folklore from ancient Israel whose value would be like that of Homer's *Iliad* and *Odyssey*, which does not give any credit to its ability to inspire faith in God for people today.

A More Acceptable View

It is necessary to realize that the central thrust or purpose of the Bible is to illuminate the way of salvation. However, I also realize that the term *salvation* has largely lost its meaning for contemporary thinkers. Because salvation implies that someone is lost or needs to be saved, when modern people hear it they feel like asking, "Who is lost?" or "Saved from what?" In a society that has MapQuest available on every laptop computer, people don't often feel lost. We have become self-sufficient, mobile people, much too busy to ponder the feelings of existential angst. However, if we redefine the Bible as a book containing stories and histories of how people have continually found meaningful spirituality in their lives for more than 3,000 years, it suddenly becomes something that sounds universally relevant.

It is imperative to realize that the Bible often speaks of its central message through the language of analogy, where the text is meant to bear a likeness to something else. Some of the analogies found in the language of redemption and sacrificial blood atonement are a bit lost on this generation. Although the main idea of these analogies is of washing something clean in a way that goes deeper than ordinary soap and water, verses such as Hebrews 9:22—"the law requires that nearly everything be cleansed with blood, for without the shedding of blood there is no forgiveness"— tend to confuse and repulse people rather than attract them to sacred texts, especially if they are taken literally.

When we redefine the salvation analogy as a walk with God that provides a person with a *new beginning*, or a *renewed life*, it seems less locked into archaic terms and more applicable to our lives today. Similarly, when we use the biblical analogies of salvation being about *healing* and *reconciliation*, the use of sacred texts becomes much more germane and leads people to discuss their desires for being in relationship with the Divine.

Paul Tillich (in Stevenson, 1967), for example, defined sin as *estrangement* and *strained relationships*, which also speaks to the contemporary mind because we live in a time of estranged and alienated people "at sixes and sevens within themselves, estranged from one another, and haunted by a sense of God's absence. In the notion of salvation as the restoration of relationships we have another idea singularly timely in the present setting" (p. 31).

Another biblical analogy of salvation that might be more relevant for today's mind is one of *growth* and *maturity*. Although *maturity* is only mentioned a few times in Paul's letters in the New Testament, it is a very powerful theme that every postmodern mind can grasp. People are ripe to discuss concepts of growing up and becoming mature. People may not refer to themselves as sinners who need saving, but most people will admit that their occasional immaturity could use some improvement so they can become their best selves.

Being *connected* with God is also a useful analogy that speaks to the postmodern mind. Many people today who feel spiritually blocked in urban life have found that returning to nature evokes something spiritual inside them. Consider a woman walking through a verdant forest path replete with singing birds and scurrying squirrels, and she looks up to see the sun's rays caressing the path like fingers from heaven. Here she feels the innocence of nature and the mindless instinct of being a part of something greater. She doesn't have to think deeply but only to breathe in something wonderful. Suddenly she feels relaxed and connected to all of life. She might later describe this moment as something spiritual, because it unleashed a force that connected her to a power or presence greater than herself.

However, to make use of our spiritual moments involves choice. Whereas a squirrel may "know" God without thinking, men and women have the ability to choose whether they will ignore such moments or use them for Divine connection.

Because there are many creative ways God brings renewal to the soul, we have to ask ourselves a very important question if we are going to make room for other people's theologies, especially for those who are sexual minorities. Whereas the question for traditional believers has been, "Is your God big enough to enlighten the path in the forest?" the better question for this discussion is, "Is your God big enough to love someone in that forest who is a lesbian?" Seeing God with a big "G" will allow traditional people of faith believe that God has the ability to woo people to himself in his own way without the assistance of creeds, public confessions, or a socially acceptable sexual orientation. Life gives us many, many unanswered mysteries to ponder, but one thing we should always acknowledge at a core level is that no one should have his or her way of connecting with a loving God reduced by the judgment of others.

Taking a Fresh View of Biblical Inspiration

Deductive Theory

Many people have used deductive logic to explain how the Bible was written. Some have assumed there is a direct cause-and-effect relationship between God's voice and the words on the printed page. They have thus deduced that when God spoke in ancient times it was a faithfully recorded verbatim. When applied to the Bible, this kind of deductive logic often flows into the following beliefs:

1. Whatever God utters is errorless (inerrant).
2. The words of the Bible are God's utterances.
3. Therefore, the words of the Bible are errorless (inerrant).

Thus, the process of having written Scriptures becomes a passive process whereby human beings have been receivers of God's revelation: What God told them they wrote down immediately and without error. This goes along with the bumper sticker that reads, "God said it. I believe it. That settles it."

Deductive theories attempt to base their arguments for inspiration of the Bible on externals, categories of "objective" data that carry considerable sway despite the faith experience of the reader. However, one of the major problems accompanying a dictation theory is that it is inconsistent with the theology of free will. If man and God wrote the Scriptures concurrently, there is also room for the free activity of human writers. God cannot perfectly control the biblical writers without removing their freedom. Therefore, a more harmonious or dynamic understanding of inspiration seems more consistent. It is much more likely that the Bible was not dictated by an external source but that people were inspired by their spiritual encounter with the Spirit of God and then were moved to pass this information on to others through verbal and written forms so that the following generations could share in their wisdom and life-enhancing experiences.

Inductive Theory

The inductive method (i.e., the scientific method) begins with observations and facts and then draws from the findings a few powerful theories about how something might work. If new facts are evident later on, then the idea or theory must be changed or abandoned to properly reflect the data. Inductive logic allows for much more room to consider the validity of gay spirituality.

By taking a more scientific and historical view of the Bible, we begin to recognize that it has no one single ideology, author, or editor. Although some fundamentalist views have distorted many of its messages by claiming divine authorship or a particular viewpoint, they seem to overlook a few very important facts. There is no fundamentalist viewpoint that is consistent from cover to cover. The Bible originated from many different sources and was composed from variant movements and sects, which is why the biblical texts at times can be contradictory.

For example, the first five books of the Old Testament are largely about things that occurred before written language. Furthermore, they came from at least three different sources. The "J" source, or Yahwist tradition, claims that from the beginning of human history people referred to God as Yahweh. There is also the ancient "E," or Elohim, accounts, which refer to God as "the strong one" but can also be used to describe "the gods," since *elohim* can also be used in the plural. The "P" source, which came from the Priestly community, was mostly concerned with maintaining the religious stories and traditions of the priesthood.

In the creation and flood stories, from Genesis 1 and 6, respectively, both "J" and "E" sources are often combined into the same chapters by some unknown editors. Having two sources for the creation story also explains why Genesis 1 and Genesis 2 seem to tell the same story in two slightly different ways. Anthropologists have also found that the creation and flood stories of Genesis are extremely similar to other folklore from ancient Mesopotamia, which means that Adam, Eve, and Noah were not necessarily Israelites. Could it be that these stories were meant to represent all mankind instead of being stories of a specific people?

Complexity increases when we realize that the verbal stories about Abraham (who is credited with inventing monotheism) occurred some 2,000 years before Christ and were probably not written down until the first fall of Jerusalem in 587 B.C. Genesis stories are the base accounts not only of the Christian Bible but also of the Torah and the Koran, which makes Abraham the biological and spiritual father to 12 million Jews, 2 billion Christians, and 1 billion Muslims. The emerging interfaith movements are quick to remind us that all three religions lay claim to the same God. The point of all this discussion is to show how simple answers about the Bible are often flawed when we begin to look into them at a deeper level.

Wesley believed inspiration was present not only in the persons who were inspired to write the original stories but also when current believers read the ancient texts and find fresh interpretation for their lives. This just happens to be an approximation found in many of my interviews where gay Christians were in effect saying that after deeper reflection on Scriptural principles they were inspired to reclaim their spirituality. The Wesleyan view of inspiration reflects a cooperative, redemptive, interpersonal process where Scriptures continue to function as a means of grace to all readers through the ages. From this particular point of view, it appears that the purpose of spiritual revelation in creation, history, and the conscience of humanity both work to bring us into a relationship with God.

Reviewing the Process of Canonization

It wasn't until the 4th century that the Christian Bible as we know it today came into existence. However, it wasn't until 1546, at the Council of Trent, that protestant church leaders voted to accept the 66 books of the Old and New Testaments as the authoritative canonical books. The term *canon* was a metaphor the early church fathers used to refer to the rule of faith for church doctrine that was derived from the Greek word that can be translated as "straight rod" or "ruler." Since that time, the list of Scriptures that the church considered to be inspired came to be called the canon. Professor Larry Shelton (1992) explained (p. 31).

> The process of determining which writings to include in the canonical collection proved to be an enormous task. Both the Jewish and Christian canons developed over many centuries as a result of specific historical situations. In Israel, the principal of canonical authority was established with the giving of the law through Moses (Ex 24).Other authoritative utterances, documents, and collections developed as Israel journeyed through enslavement and liberations in the exilic and post-exilic periods. The saving actions and revelations of God were interpreted, recorded and collected. The testimonies of faith and the prophetic critiques and values became a collection of written documents that eventually attained a three-fold division into Law, Prophets and Writings. The process of formal canonical collection seems to have begun in the seventh-century Judah during the reign of Josiah (622–609 B.C.). The rediscovery of the book of law led Josiah to acknowledge the written law of Yahweh as the highest authority over Israel.

Old Testament Canon

The Old Testament canon became more developed during the Babylonian Exile (586–539 B.C.). As Israel's religious system had been forced to move away from the temple in Jerusalem, her priests and scribes worked to reshape the identity of the Israelites to fit their faith to the reality of their captivity. Out of necessity the Jews became "a people of the book" (Shelton, 1992, p. 32) so they would have something that would be indestructible, flexible, and portable. The word of God increasingly became identified with the written Scriptures when they returned from exile:

> The concept of inspiration began to be understood not only as a gift bestowed upon the living prophets, but as an attribute of the sacred writings as well. Following the Exile, prophetic activity decreased and the dynamic element of inspiration became more closely associated with the books that mediated God's word to his people. (Carpenter & McCown) p. 32)

Two other major events forced the Jews to become a people of the book. Not only was Christianity finding new interpretations of Jewish scriptures, but the destruction of their sacred Jerusalem temple in 70 A.D. also left them with few options. As they moved from their sacred lands to coastal cities, they learned new ways for their faith to survive the loss of religious institutions. By 90 A.D., the Jewish council reached a consensus on the content of the 39 books of the Old Testament canon that is very similar to what the Christian Scriptures are today.

New Testament Canon

The selection process of the New Testament canon was also the result of a long process of deciding which books of the church that had been circulating for decades were to be regarded as authoritative and inspired faith and practice for the Christian community.

The process of identifying the canon of Scripture began with an informal identification of the writings most edifying to the church. Gradually more criteria were applied so that by 200 A.D., 21 of the New Testament books had been accepted into the canon by general consensus of church leaders.

During the 4th century, Jerome and Augustine acknowledged 27 books of the canon, and their opinions were validated by decisions rendered at the Councils of Hippo (393 A.D.) and Carthage (397 A.D.). These councils thus adopted what had been considered for decades to be inspired works by witness of the Christian community. They proclaimed the witness of the apostles that God's revelation had culminated in the life of Jesus Christ, were universally taught throughout the Christian church, and believed to be written under the inspiration of the Holy Spirit:

> Canon is thus not just a list, but the shape of the way the sacred writings work in the life of the church. James Sanders and Brevard Childs have interpreted the

concept of canon on two major bases: They are interested not only in the process of collecting the Scriptures, but also the shape and form of the interpretation and use of the Scriptures in the church. Canon thus becomes a hermeneutical concept that interprets Scripture both in its historical context and as it continues to function in the community of faith. (Carpenter & McCown, 1992, p. 33)

Over the centuries, many theologians have continued to believe that the Bible is indeed something more than ancient stories and legends. It has been called the Living Word—not only because it was written under the inspiration of the Holy Spirit but also because it continues to inspire faith for believers in each generation. Today, many faith communities are taking a second look at former interpretations of these Scriptures as well as their potential misunderstandings about homosexuality and are trying to find new ways to become more inclusive of gays and lesbians in their worshiping communities.

Seven Things to Consider When Creating a "Biblical" View of Homosexuality

1. **There is no word for *homosexuality* in the Bible.** It does not exist. Although homosexual behavior has probably been around as long as humankind, the Bible hardly mentions it. Jesus grew up in Nazareth, which was only 3 miles from the Roman city Sepphoris, which had Roman baths, Greek gyms, and temples where homosexual behavior was probably known to occur. However, nowhere in the four Gospels does Jesus ever mention homosexual behavior. There are no direct teachings one way or another, neither are there any indirect inferences. Jesus must have had a different opinion from Americans who seem to be alarmed when gay people in their communities come out of the closet to claim their equal rights.

2. **Homosexual behavior is never the main topic of a text.** It is always included as part of something else, such as intended rape, idolatry, obsolete purity codes, or, as in two New Testament references, maintaining an inclusive religion that is based in grace for everyone. Furthermore, these texts are problematic because even when they appear to be rather cut-and-dried at first glance, it is not easy to determine their simple meaning. We don't know enough of the context or how the common language was used to make certain a decree that would exclude a sexual minority from the assembly of believers.

3. **Biblical authors did not understand homosexual orientation.** It wasn't until midway through the 20th century that human science began to understand the concept of sexual orientation. Previous to that time, the

accepted view was that homosexual behavior was considered to be a sign of mental illness or depravity. Similarly, those who were inspired to write the Scriptures didn't understand how some people's primary attraction could be for their own gender while others would be attracted to someone of the opposite sex. When people declare that the Bible condemns homosexuals, the best rebuttal is, "The Bible really doesn't address that question." The idea that homosexuals cannot be people of faith is, in my opinion, complete fallacy and goes against the idea that salvation is a matter of the heart for all people.

4. **Jesus embraced two known sexual minorities of his day.** Jesus welcomed prostitutes who were a condemned sexual minority. When challenging the self-righteous members of the dominant religious system he said, "Truly, the tax collectors and prostitutes are going into the kingdom of God ahead of you" (Matthew 21:3; Luke 7:35–50). The other sexual minority group Jesus welcomed was the eunuchs—men who either were unable to perform sexually with women or who had been castrated. We don't know a lot about these people, because the term *eunuch* seems to be used at times as a general term to describe those who are sexually different from the norm. Eunuchs were not allowed on the temple grounds because of their physical flaws (Leviticus 17:17; Deuteronomy 23:1), yet in Isaiah 56:1–8, they are promised everlasting names for being faithful to God. Probably one of the more interesting verses about this group is found in Matthew 19:7–12: "Some are eunuchs because they were born that way; others were made that way by men.... Those who can accept this should accept it." If a man could be born a eunuch, which was presumably a physical defect on his genitals or perhaps someone with hermaphrodite physicality, it certainly is possible that a person could be born as a homosexual. Acts 8:26–40 tells the story of Philip explaining an inclusive gospel with the Ethiopian eunuch. Although these verses are obviously speaking from Jesus' countercultural perspective, these Scriptures demonstrate that sexual minorities have full access to salvation and vital spirituality.

5. **Literal application of Scriptures to contemporary moral issues can be dangerous.** We have to look no further than the issue of slavery to understand this point. Since the Emancipation Proclamation we have disagreed with an aspect of biblical morality. The Bible never condemns slavery. Rather, it accepts what is considered a social norm and only provides guidance for slave owners to treat their slaves well. (i.e., Colossians 4:1, Ephesians 6:5–9, Philemon v 15–17)(Similarly, Paul suggests it is immoral when women do not cover their heads (I Corinthians 11:5, 6). If we try to convert a literal translation of the Bible into current society, then what are we to do with passages like Deuteronomy 25:11, "If two men are fighting and the wife of one of them comes to rescue

her husband from his assailant, and she reaches out and seizes him by his private parts, you shall cut off her hand"? However, there are some verses about social poverty and oppression that we would do well to obey to the letter. (i.e., Deuteronomy 15:11, Psalm 82:1-4, James 1:27)

6. **Jesus and the writings of the early church condemn judgmentalism** (Matthew 7:1–5, Romans 2:1, Romans 14:4–13) Rather than judging others, we should be learning what it is like to walk in their shoes. The church and society in general have been very cruel toward homosexuals for decades. Jesus advocated the ethic of love, and, above all, we are to apply that concept to our values and relationships today rather than dismissing or ostracizing people who are different. John 9:1–5 (*The Message*, a contemporary translation of the Bible) describes Jesus encountering a judgmental crowd who asked him, "Rabbi, who sinned; this man or his parents, causing him to be born blind?" Jesus said, "You are asking the wrong question. You are looking for someone to blame. There is no cause–effect here."

7. **There is no single sexual ethic in the Bible.** It would be so much easier if there was one consistent sexual ethic in the Bible; instead it includes several injunctions on this topic. The Bible allows for polygamy and concubines while also insisting that people marry within their culture. There are also stories about sexual abuses such as incest, rape, adultery, and murder that fly in the face of the ethics of loving your neighbor as you would love yourself (Dueteronomy 6:4, 5, Mark 12:29–31). While these horrible crimes are not condoned, those facts seem to be of secondary importance in the story of how God's people preserved their heritage. In the Song of Solomon, it would appear that people delighting in their sexual escapades are not only unmarried but also seem to have no guilt about it. In the New Testament, Paul provides polar opposite views on whether to marry at all.

Instead of sexual ethics, the Bible reveals different sexual mores that often changed over the thousand-year span when the Bible was being written. Mores are the customs that are accepted by a given community. It is obvious that we would not agree with many of the sexual customs that the Bible allows today. Mores can change with startling rapidity, creating bewildering dilemmas for people. Even within one lifetime, we have seen changes in how people prepare for marriage. Today, more and more couples both in and out of the church are living together before marriage, whereas 40 years ago this was considered to be a scandalous moral problem. It is obvious that sexual mores are varied and evolving.

The very idea of trying to find a sexual ethic reveals the compartmentalization of our lives today. It also reflects how we are increasingly defining ourselves by our sexuality. The reality is that we cannot separate our sexuality from the rest of our lives. As whole persons, we are physical, mental, sexual, emotional, and spiritual beings: "The Bible only knows a love ethic, which is constantly being brought to bear on whatever sexual mores are dominant in any given country, culture or period" (Wink, 1979, p. 6).

Reinterpreting Scriptures That Clobber Homosexuals

Although many authors have tackled the "clobber" verses with a much greater passion and inexhaustible exegesis than I am willing to do, it is important to take a quick look at their contexts as well as in light of knowledge available at the time they were written. As I stated already, it becomes easier to see why many progressive churches find these verses problematic for making a clear stand against homosexuality.

Old Testament Passages

Genesis 19

The current idea that homosexual behavior is forbidden in the Bible can be traced to a few passages. Probably the best-known Bible story that comes to mind when the topic of homosexuality is mentioned is the destruction of the cities of Sodom and Gomorrah found in Genesis 19. When reading this text at first glance, popular opinion often sides with the idea that God destroyed this city because the men of Sodom tried to rape male angels who were visitors sent from God. So popular is that view that our own English language has even co-opted the term *sodomite* to mean someone who engages in unusual sexual practices, which today could be applied to either gender. The fact is that none of the other Old Testament passages that refer to the sin of Sodom mention homosexual offenses. Ezekiel declares that their sin was being haughty, arrogant, and not being concerned with the poor and needy (Ezekiel 16:49–50). Jesus apparently believed that Sodom was destroyed for the sin of inhospitality (Matthew 10:14–15, Luke 10:10–12).

Interpreting the moral of this story as a judgment against homosexuals is a fairly recent phenomenon. The common assumption that homosexuality was Sodom's downfall has come from other literature and social trends and literature of the past century.

Leviticus 18 and 20

Only two places in the Old Testament specifically mention homosexual acts: Leviticus 18:22 ("Do not lie with a man as one lies with a woman; that is detestable") and Leviticus 20:13 ("If a man lies with a man as one lies with a woman, both of them have done what is detestable. They must be put to death; their blood will be on their own heads").

The Hebrew word *toevah* translated as detestable in the New International Version (NIV) was interpreted as an *abomination* in older translations. It does not usually mean something that is intrinsically evil, like rape or theft, "but something which is ritually unclean for Jews, like eating pork or engaging in intercourse during menstruation both of which are also prohibited in these same chapters" (Boswell, 1980, p. 100). It is often used in connection with a description of temple prostitutes and the uncleanness of the Gentiles (*goyim*), as in *toevah ha-goyim*.

Leviticus 18 was written to instruct the Jews how to distinguish themselves from all the pagans around them. The verse about homosexual acts immediately follows specific prohibition to idolatrous sexuality in pagan temples: "Do not give any of your children (*seed*) to be sacrificed to Molech, for you must not profane the name of your God" (Leviticus 18:21). (I have emphasized *seed* here because ancient Israel believed that spilling a man's sperm (seed) amounted to murder of his unborn children.) "In the Greek, the Levitical enactments against homosexual behavior characterize it unequivocally as ceremonially unclean rather than inherently evil" and usually associated it with idolatry (Boswell, 1980).

To further this argument, I think it is interesting that both Jesus and Paul find this verse irrelevant when it comes to a person being seen acceptable in God's sight. Jesus and the apostles taught that it was no longer the physical violations of Levitical purity codes that would defile the souls of men and women but the infidelity of the human heart.

The reality is that we pick and choose which Old Testament purity codes we want to honor. If we were to keep the entire ethical codes from Leviticus, we would also be abstaining from eating pork, shellfish, and rabbit. Home gardens would never have any hybridized roses, and we would not be allowed to wear cotton jeans with wool sweaters at the same time. Men could not shave their beard, and women would never cut their hair. So why does homosexual behavior hit us differently from the others? Our response has been socially conditioned.

Although the use of Levitical comments about abominations may seem to carry a far greater weight than the proscriptions surrounding them to a modern reader, it is likely that the ancient world knew no such hostility to homosexuality. Furthermore, as Christianity spread throughout the Roman world, the Council of Jerusalem in 49 A.D. ruled that converts to the Christian faith no longer had to keep the requirements of Moses, including circumcision. The only things still requested of Christians were to "abstain from food sacrificed to idols, from blood, from the meat of strangled animals and from sexual immorality" (Acts 15:29). It can also be argued that these New Testament prohibitions were given not for moral guidance but to simply facilitate a proper interaction between Gentile and Jewish members of the Christian communities by encouraging the former to avoid behavior that might particularly offend Jews who still felt a need to adhere to Levitical principles.

"Scared Faithless"

Last year my wife and I attended a very moving spring concert of the Seattle Men's Chorus, where they performed "Scared Faithless." It was a gutsy concert featuring 200 gay men from all kinds of religious backgrounds singing about their life struggles in the areas where sexuality and spirituality intersect. One of the performances was a clever monologue written by Ames Hall. Joe Nadeau, artistic director of Heartland Men's Chorus, has permitted me to use as a way of demonstrating what it might be like if a different part of the Levitical code had the same amount of social prejudice against it.

> Oh, beloved, oh beloved. I come to you with a heavy heart and the word of God on my lips. My friends, there is amongst us a true abomination—an abomination condemned by God Almighty Himself. What pains my heart dear friends is that many of you here tonight in this very room have indulged in this evil practice. Some, I'm afraid, this very evening.
>
> Perhaps it's the coaxing of Satan that tempted you—he need not whisper in your ear—it is all around us. The corrupt liberal media gives its stamp of approval, fine moral folks turn a blind eye these days, and every filthy piece of advertising, television show, or moving picture gives it big "thumbs up" on this very abomination to God ... even, my friends, promoting it to children as normal and acceptable. Yea, even desirable—as part of their lifestyle. Turn with me now to the Good Book. I'll give you a few moments to pull out your Bibles.
>
> Turn with me, now, to the book of Leviticus, 11th chapter, verses 9–12:
>
> 9These shall ye eat of all that are in the waters: whatsoever hath fins and scales in the waters, in the seas, and in the rivers, them shall ye eat. 10 And all that have not fins and scales in the seas, and in the rivers, of all that move in the waters, and of any living thing which is in the waters, they shall be an abomination

unto you. So I tell you friends, God Hates Shrimp. That smell of drawn butter might as well be the stench of sulfur and brimstone to the righteous. Be ye
washed in the blood, not the cocktail sauce. God … Hates … Shrimp. Boiled,
fried, cocktailed or ettoufe, gumbo, scampi or butter-fried and stuffed, make no
mistake: Shellfish is Hell fish.

   Have you sacrificed your love of God for the seafood lover in you? Have you
been having an affair with Captain D and Long John Silver? For the road to Hell
is surely paved with oyster shells, my friends.

   Join with me now and drive out the evil abomination. Rebuke the lobster,
shrimp, prawn, and langoustine. Defy Satan's power as you turn away from the
mussel, the clam, the abalone, and the conch; crawdaddy, crayfish or mudbug,
Maryland, Dungeness, Alaskan King or blue—remember, beloved, those very
crab claws you dip in butter with a little garlic and a squeeze of lemon, with
those little cute forks, those, those might just be the same claws that will drag
you into the Inferno.

Although the Old Testament is actually silent when it comes to the idea
of gay sexuality, there are stories of intense love relations between persons
of the same gender, such as Saul and David, David and Jonathan, and Ruth
and Naomi. These love stories have in fact been celebrated throughout the
Middle Ages in both ecclesiastical and popular literature as examples of
extraordinary devotion, some with distinctly erotic overtones.

Another argument that needs to be addressed before we leave the Old
Testament is the topic of original creation. According to Genesis 1 and
2, God made sexuality exclusively for the union of a man and a woman.
Some would argue that if people are born gay, surely the Bible would
have included the story of Adam and Steve. But we have to return to an
inductive reasoning here. The Bible is not a book of science or sociology.
The purpose of the creation story was to account for the origins of the
human race and the production of named offspring: "One would no more
expect an account of gay love than of friendship in Genesis … neither had
and neither would contribute to the story of the peopling of the earth"
(Boswell, 1980, p. 105).

New Testament References

1 Corinthians 6:9; 1 Timothy 1:10
In the New Testament, three writings from Paul have been used to support
opposition to homosexuality as we know it today. In both 1 Corinthians
6:9 and 1 Timothy 1:10, two words have been translated as *homosexuals*
in the lists of unsavory kinds of people who will be excluded from the
kingdom of heaven.

The first word, *malakoi,* is a very common Greek word that occurs in other areas of the New Testament. It can mean soft, sick, weak, delicate, or gentle. In a moral context it could mean someone who is "loose," "lacking self-control," or "unrestrained."

> But to assume that either of these concepts necessarily applies to gay people is wholly gratuitous. The word [*malakoi*] is never used in Greek to designate gay people as a group or even in reference to homosexual acts generically, and it often occurs in writings contemporary with the Pauline epistles in reference to heterosexual persons or activity. (Boswell, 1980, p. 106))

The use of *malakoi* provides a great example of how the use of language and its interpretations can change over time. All throughout the time of the Reformation the traditional protestant interpretation of this word was "masturbation," and the Catholic Church continued applying that meaning until well into the 20th century. If this were an accurate translation, 98% of the men in our society would certainly be facing eternal damnation. Thank God the use of language can change over time! What is interesting is that over the past century there were no new translations of this word than were known previously. The only thing that has changed is a shift in morality and logic. Today you would be hard-pressed to find anyone who believed that masturbation would preclude a person from heaven's rewards. However, the condemnation has not disappeared. It has just been applied to a group that is an easier and more despised target, even by biblical translators.

The second word, *arsenokoitai,* is used only once in the Bible and is quite rare in Greek usage, but its application to homosexual behavior is more logical. A strict translation could be "men who have sex"—which again could be used to describe 50% of humanity—but what is not understood is how this word was actually used in Paul's era. The best guess is to assume that what Paul was describing was his rejection of male prostitutes who were used in pagan fertility temples at that time. Some language experts believe that this was the common usage of this term from Paul's time well into the 4th century, after which it became confused with a variety of words for disapproved sexual activities. (Boswell, 1980 , p. 107)

Romans 1:26–31
The remaining verse to examine is not one that is subject to great mistranslations, but it is not often looked at in its context:

> Therefore God gave them over in the sinful desires of their hearts to sexual impurity for the degrading of their bodies with one another. They exchanged the truth of God for a lie, and worshiped and serve the created things rather than

the Creator—who is forever praised. Amen. Because of this, God gave them over to shameful lusts. Even their women exchanged natural relations for unnatural ones. In the same way the men also abandoned natural relations with women and were inflamed with lust for one another. Men committed indecent acts with other men, and received in themselves the due penalty for their perversion.

There is no doubt that part of this passage is about homosexual behavior, but when seen in its greater context one has to wonder what Paul is actually describing. As with all letters preserved for us in the New Testament, we have only one half of a conversation. Although we have Paul's answer, we don't know the question or situation to which he is responding. This is at times problematic because we can only speculate as to how this applies to our lives today.

It appears that Paul is responding to idolatry and is censoring the orgiastic pagan rites that honor false gods. It seems reasonable that Paul is writing to warn his flock about the immorality of temple prostitution that would not only distract but would also condemn the very hearts of those he sought to save.

One needs to pay close attention to the wording Paul uses about what is natural and unnatural. Contrary to popular opinions on this verse, he is not talking about something against the created order of things, as in what we see in nature, but rather something that goes against the natural affinities of a person. If this is true, then it makes sense that Paul is writing about heterosexuals who are temporarily going against their own natural desires to have sex with people of their own gender. Furthermore, there seems to be a lot of excess energy in the surrounding verses where Paul goes out of his way to describe how much depravity surrounds him. This entire sermon could also be Paul's way of making a rather dramatic point of what happens to Gentiles who refuse to acknowledge God by rejecting Christianity.

Herein lies part of the problem in trying to make this passage condemn what we know about homosexuality today. When we are talking about making room for the spirituality of gays and lesbians, we are certainly not talking about people who are idolaters, murderers, liars, slanderers, or people without faith in God, as Romans 1:27–31 articulates. We are talking about God-fearing people who feel more comfortable or, to use Paul's words, "natural" when partnering with a person of the same gender.

Paul does not distinguish what he thinks about gay people from heterosexuals who engage in periodic homosexual behavior. In fact, the latter is probably how most Jews of his day perceived same-sex encounters. Furthermore, since no one had studied homosexuals as a distinct group of people until the 20th century, it seems quite reasonable to say that Paul was not discussing sexual minorities in this text but, rather, homosexual acts being done by heterosexual persons with temple prostitutes, which would certainly validate the argument of acting against their own sexual and spiritual natures.

Using the Bible and Science Correctly

Obviously, when it comes to interpreting Scripture in the postmodern era, we have so much more information before us than previous generations did that it makes articulating our views of God and of truth itself quite a challenge. It is possible to interpret the Bible as condemning all homosexual behavior. But it is also possible to reach a different conclusion based on the ethics of love, social justice, and equal respect for all who are different from the majority. So we are left with our own interpretations of our life experiences and the convictions of our conscience. The relation of the Bible to the word or mind of God is not as easy as it may first appear, and sometimes we get it wrong!

Therefore, when it comes to understanding the need to make room for gay spirituality in our theology, it seems obvious that we need to allow for the possibility that people often use the Bible incorrectly to support socially constructed norms. In a film series, *Saving Jesus From the Right,* theologian and author Matthew Fox (2008) stated that because biblical authors had no concept of an inherent same-sex orientation, people who try to make a biblically grounded case against it are treading on shaky ground:

> The Bible has no way to explain homosexuality any more than it did to explain how the earth is not the center of the universe, but instead we rotate around the sun! This is the same problem encountered in Galileo's day .... The church is trying to make the Bible explain science. This is not a matter of faith, but of science. Since 1950 we have discovered that 8–10% of the population of the world is gay in all countries. Science has also known that there are over 400 species of animals where some of them exhibit same sex bonding or sexuality. It is a matter of science, and it would be great if Christians would get over this and get on to things that matter.

Recognizing Our Framing Stories

After examining the ancient languages of these texts, one begins to realize that the greater opposition to homosexuality does not come from the Bible but from our socially constructed norms, prejudices, and fears.

As with most beliefs, our position on homosexuality is largely dependent on the stories we tell ourselves and perhaps even more importantly on what our particular group in society believes.

Because we are social beings, the groups we belong to have great influence over our thinking. Social systems such as family, church, and political party often frame our outlook in life. They tell us who we are, how we should act, and what we are here for. Brian McLaren (2007) renamed this concept our "framing story":

> If our framing story is wise, strong, realistic, and constructive it can send us on a hopeful trajectory. But if our framing story is dysfunctional, weak, false, unrealistic, or destructive, it can send us on a downward arc, a dangerous, high-speed joyride toward un-peace, un-health, un-prosperity, and even un-life. (p. 67)

As I think about gay spirituality, I realize it is going to necessitate some reframing of people's stories. Without altering our framing stories we will never be able to solve our dilemma with homosexuality. My hope for our churches and society at large is to adopt a framing story that allows each person, no matter what sexual orientation, to be free, respected, and responsible creatures in vital relationship with a benevolent, wise, and loving God. In such a story, we would choose to believe that our Creator and Sustainer, Source of all loving relationships, wants us to pursue collaboration and peace while mutually caring for one another. In short, such a frame would focus on the ethic of love to be evident in all human relationships, sexual or otherwise.

The Ethic of Love and Commitment

The greatest ethic of the Scriptures is the ethic of love. Whereas there are 5–6 verses that appear to speak against homosexual behavior, there are more than 600 verses that pertain to the ethic of love. Jesus declared that the sum of all the Old Testament Law could be summed in one overarching law of love. James 2:8 calls this the royal law: "If you really keep the royal law found in Scripture, 'Love your neighbor as yourself,' you are doing right." If we appeal for how to make room for gay spirituality on this basis we stand on extremely solid ground indeed. Paul also backs this idea up by saying that no matter the situation, "if [I] have not love, I gain nothing" (1 Corinthians 13:3).

Jesus offered a radically altered framing story for the spirituality of his day. He broke all the norms and ignored ancient laws that were no longer relevant. Perhaps the Evangelical movement has domesticated his image and message so much that they have not been able to see him for the radical change agent he was at heart and how he always spoke out against oppression. In other words, those who are opposed to the idea of salvation coming into the lives of socially oppressed sexual minorities should not expect to have Jesus back up their bets in Vegas!

Dr. Stephen Jones (2005), a progressive American Baptist pastor, wrote a great summation along these lines of thought:

> Sexuality is God given and life affirming. It is one of the most beautiful features of human beings. We are sexual beings. We rob that gift of dignity when we use sex as a tool for manipulation, violence or subjugation. We celebrate that gift when we practice our sexuality in mutual, affirming, committed and wholesome ways. I believe in the same sexual ethic for gays and straights. And I believe that we can all be proud of the gift of sexuality God has given us: heterosexuals, gays, lesbians, transgender and bisexuals. (p. 4)

Norman Pittenger (as cited in Sweasey, 1997, p. 151), a gay theologian, suggested that a way to know if the ethic of love was present after a sexual encounter was to ask the following question:

> Now that I am leaving this person, am I leaving a body with whom I had gratification or am I leaving a person with whom I have shared something of the joy of mutual existence, expressed in physical fashion? If you answer person rather than body, you can be sure that the act has been right and good—and I dare say in accordance with the purpose for God and his children. The Latin liturgy for Holy Thursday includes the splendid words, ubi caritas et amor, ibi Deus, "where loving care and self giving are found, there is God present." (Sweasey, 1997, p. 151).

Case Study: Three Generations

Consider the following two case studies that attempt to make room for gay spirituality across three generations in a conservative Christian culture.

One day I received an e-mail from a father living out of the area who asked if I could see his college-age son who appeared to be suffering from depression or some kind of anxiety disorder. He was worried because Jonathan had not been sleeping or eating regularly, was skipping classes, and seemed to be continually on the verge of uncontrollable tears. He knew that his son wanted nothing to do with any kind of Bible counseling, yet Dad hoped that there may be a therapist with a Christian background that his son wouldn't object to. I assured him that I wouldn't delve into spiritual discussions unless his son brought the subject up himself. My desire was to help him in whatever way that would work for him.

Individual Sessions With Jonathan

When Jonathan called to make an appointment, his pauses and intonations gave me a sense that there was more going on than what his father described. However, I didn't want to make any assumptions over the phone and was just glad that this young man was ready to see a therapist to find relief from his very distressing symptoms.

Jonathan was a handsome young man who, at 20 years old, had declared that he was fiercely independent. Although he was relieved that his father had found a counselor for him, he let me know that he really didn't need parents anymore. He wanted to be able to figure things out for himself. He had already seen a campus doctor who prescribed a low dose of sertraline (Zoloft; Pfizer, New York) a few days before our appointment to help quell his anxiety so he could make use of therapy.

As I went through his intake information and began to ask him about his depressive symptoms, I began to assess that anxiety was much more prevalent than clinical depression. When I asked him what area of his life was most distressing, he told me about a recent romantic breakup. Since he had not been specific about the gender, I simply inquired if this was with a man or a woman. He looked at me for a moment assessing how safe this conversation seemed and then said in a low tone, "It was a guy," and then began to cry: "I've never been in love before." As I asked him to tell me about what this relationship had meant to him, lifetime fences of self-protection began to lower with each word uttered. He said that he began "freaking out" immediately after this romantic breakup. What appeared on the surface to be a depressive episode was instead a closeted homosexual affair that ended badly.

At 20 he still had not told his parents he was gay. He reiterated once again that he didn't think it mattered because he really didn't need his parents anymore. Subsequent inquiries as to when and where he no longer needed his parents revealed that his distancing was a buffer he had created over many years to deal with his perceived fear of rejection by his family when they found out he was gay. In truth, he actually wished he could be closer to his family.

Jonathan had been emotionally distancing himself from his family for about 7 years, which coincides with the time he first believed himself to be gay. He kept this information to himself because he was certain that the conservative religion of his parents would not allow them to handle this news in a positive manner and would instead reject his gay identity as sinful. Attending a conservative Christian school made him feel that the only way to get along with his peers was to keep his sexual orientation in the closet. As a result, he had no allies or anyone else with whom he could share his growing internal truth, and he was not sure that his sexuality and his spirituality could coexist. When I asked him if he thought it was possible to be a gay Christian, he said he had never considered that but at this time really wasn't very interested in being a Christian and that he certainly wasn't into going to church.

Using a solution-focused approach, I asked him to imagine what he desired. If he could wave a powerful magic wand, what would he want to happen in his life besides finding true love? What would he want from his family? How did he see his life playing out after he graduated from college? As he began to imagine what he wanted, as opposed to what he feared, he began to realize that he wished his parents could join him in this journey of self-discovery. He already felt solid and content in his gay identity, and he just wanted the people he loved the most to be happy for him. At first he couldn't imagine telling his parents this news. A bit later he was ready to tell them in a rather explosive way by dropping the "homosexual bomb" on them and then prescribing defensive limits on how he would allow his parents to respond to his news. His plan reminded me of dropping an egg into sizzling frying pan; it seemed broken and runny just before becoming a charred mess.

I modified this by letting him know that he was the one in charge of disclosing his new truth in any way he wanted, as long as he did it with respect and allowed others time to adjust to what might be shocking news. By creating an incremental "outing" plan he began to explore the possibility of reconciliation.

Breaking each aspect into manageable parts I asked who in his family was most likely to best handle his news. He was not sure. Could he imagine his parents rejecting him? No. Did his parents know any other sexual minorities? Yes, his Dad did, but he didn't think his mother had ever talked to an openly gay person. Did Dad treat gays with respect? Yes. Could he imagine his dad honoring his son's feelings even if he didn't understand them? Yes. Would he disagree on what to do with a gay sexuality? Probably. How would Dad feel? Angry. How would his mother feel? Sad.

When I was able to ask if Jonathan was able to handle his parents' emotions for a while, I wondered aloud if his father would always be angry or his mother sad. He was uncomfortable with the idea that he might have to deal with his father's anger or his mother's sadness. He didn't want his parents to be upset or hurt, but more than that he wanted to have an honest relation with them. As he began to realize there was a process involved in coming out, he also began to work a parallel process for finding empathy for others who might disagree with his choices.

Jonathan chose to write his parents a letter that needed 3 weeks worth of editing to reduce the pent up anger he felt for being a silent and unknowingly marginalized minority within the family. Because a letter of such an intimate declaration has a high degree of being saved by a parent for many years, we continued working on these trial letters until Jonathan was able to acknowledge that he cared enough about them to let them into this very intimate and personal part of his life. When he could quit telling them how they could or could not respond, he was ready to enter into a different kind of relationship, and the letter was in the mail the next day.

Sessions Alone With Dad

Fortunately, without my knowledge, Jonathan's parents were also meeting with a counselor in another city who helped them craft a letter of response reaffirming that nothing could ever shake their love for their son and how they were going to be working on how to process this new information. I'm sure that they had to go through some trial letters as well to flush the hurt and judgmental toxins that needed to be expressed elsewhere. When Dad responded, he said that when he came to town within the next month, he wanted to continue this conversation with his son face to face.

Although the plan was to eventually have a family session for father and son when Dad came to town, I had obtained Jonathan's permission to first have a private session with Dad to help him process and accept the news that he had a gay son so that future relational counseling could be most effective. During this session Jonathan's father talked about his own grief—worrying about what kind of life his son would have as a gay man and how he feared how others may treat him in the future. He also expressed how this altered the dreams he and his wife had always imagined, where Jonathan would find a loving wife who would eventually bear their grandchildren. He also wanted to know what most every parent wants to know when they first discover their child is gay. Was there any cure, and what did I think about therapy designed to change a person's sexual orientation? When I told him that the American Psychological Association questioned conversion therapies as potentially harmful to gay and lesbian clients because they were attempting to fix something that wasn't broken, I explained my belief was that there is no cure when there is no ailment. Although some institutions claim to have helped many people recover from homosexuality, the reality was that although they might alter a person's sexual behavior for a time, they had little success in changing a person's natural inclinations, feelings, fantasies, or sexual dreams. It would be better to find a way to make room for imagining a healthy way for Jonathan and his family to live a full and inclusive life with his natural attractions with people of the same gender.

Over the course of the next 2 hours, Dad began to move away from his grief and bargaining into expressing his keen admiration for his son. As I coached him in future conversations and in ways he could interact with his son and his gay friends by entering their world as an honored guest, Dad walked out ready to have a pleasant dinner that week with Jonathan and two of his closest friends who were also gay.

In later conversations, Dad and I spoke about theological aspects of understanding homosexuality and about how, though not popular with his particular church's interpretation of Scripture, there were other ways to look at this from a biblical perspective. Dad admitted that he sent his son to me because was the most liberal conservative (or most conservative liberal) he knew and was someone he felt his son might open up to. Dad had suspected his son might be a homosexual previous to his son's declarations and really didn't know what to do with this possibility. As most boomer parents, he felt caught between his own generation's understanding that homosexuality is a complex issue with few simple answers and an older generation's teachings that homosexuality is a grievous sin. He concluded by telling me that he intended to become an expert on this subject and would spend the next year reading everything he could get his hands on to find the best way to support his gay son.

Relational Counseling

When I facilitated the relational session with Dad and son it was obvious that they were growing closer and more in sync. Although Dad would never allow anything to hinder his own relationship with his son, he still needed to find a way to honor his own beliefs that homosexual activity is a sin. Jonathan found out that an ongoing relationship with his parents was not only preferable but also unshakeable. He had never realized that it was possible to live with known major differences and still be deeply connected.

A year later, in a subsequent chance meeting, Dad told me that his son was doing wonderfully and that their relationship had only grown closer through this process. Because a formerly toxic secret had come out, the need for distance and defensive posturing was greatly reduced. What emerged instead was a united family with greater closeness and respect with individuals maintaining their separate beliefs about homosexuality.

Conversations With Grandparents

In a different family, grandparents from a conservative Christian background had to figure out a way to deal with their granddaughter's homosexual relationship. They had been seeing some signs that made them worry about their grandchild and asked her father if their fears of homosexuality were founded. They had been worried and praying about their loved ones for weeks, not knowing what to do. Clearly, they were disapproving of this situation because it went against their understanding of Scripture. They had been taught that if a person committed his or her life to Christ, such issues would be resolved when people turned away from sin. However, there was also an expectation that people of faith, who strive for righteousness, behave in certain ways and not in others. Previously the boundaries around sexuality seemed plain and simple, which worked fine when homosexuality was an abstract concept. But now that this was a family matter, it had become personal. They knew they had to choose a loving response if they were going to remain in relationship with the rest of their family. By the next time they saw their granddaughter and her friend they were warm and authentic in their affections of love for both young women.

When I later commented on how well they seemed to be doing in adapting to their granddaughter's homosexual relationship, they looked surprised that I would even comment: "Why, of course we will act in loving ways! Just because we don't agree doesn't mean that our capacity to love had changed. She is our beloved granddaughter, and we will love and pray for her until the day we die, just as we have every since she was born."

Although the previous scenario ends on a pleasant note, the story of how families continue the process of making room for each other's views of spirituality and sexuality will be unending. It will need to be revisited and sorted out in each successive generation. Hopefully they will each continue to leave room for mystery. Like the poem "A Presentation of Fish," the unexpected can often become a pleasant surprise. Families who weather the coming out process and allow room for difference while maintaining loving connections will usually find their future relationships with their adult children to be more centered and closer than either would have imagined earlier.

Three Necessary Ingredients to Make Room for Gay Spirituality

Reviewing the personal stories of gay spirituality contained in this book, I am hoping for a different outcome than the movie postscript from *Charlie Wilson's War* (Mike Nichols, 2007): "These things happened. They were glorious and they changed the world. Then we [screwed] up the endgame."

It's easy to hear great stories and quickly forget them when we return to our normal patterns of living. However, as we have seen, when other people's stories are assimilated into our own, everything changes. So in closing, I have three timeless words to describe how we could create a better endgame that would be personally relevant to each generation as it makes room for gay spirituality: faith, hope, and love.

An Expanded Faith

For the parents of gay and lesbian children, I would suggest they begin to expand their own version of faith. Most boomer parents have recognized the complexity of this issue within their own generation. They can't disregard it, but they may not know what to do with it or how to incorporate it into their language of faith. An expanded faith may mean that people will need to explore some different theological definitions of what sin and salvation are for today's modern society. Like the father in the first scenario, they may need to become better educated students of human science and the art of interpreting biblical analogies to allow their faith to make room for social justice issues that their queer children are facing. It can be life changing, for instance, if we no longer refer to Luke 15:11ff as the "Parable of the Prodigal Son" but rather to realize this is really the "Parable of a Prodigal Father," who, upon seeing his long-lost son's approach from a far distance, extends himself without reserve. As this story unfolds, "prodigal" refers no longer to the reckless wastefulness of the younger son, but the reckless excess of the father's love who lavishes grace and riches on the undeserving son (Nouwen, 1994, p. 111). The prodigal father has expanded his faith to incorporate the child who had to rebel against being locked into a box of tradition that didn't fit him and the older child who chose to remain isolated in self-righteousness. Learning to expand your own faith will allow you to become a success in living out the lifelong pursuit of unconditional love in your family.

A Search for Hope

For young queer adults who are recognizing the truth of their own sexuality at the deepest levels of their humanity, I would suggest they keep an expanded view of hope alive in their hearts: hope that it is possible to connect to a meaningful spirituality while also being true to their self and their natural attractions. Although the media in the last decade has been swift to high-light Christians who preach hate-filled messages aimed at gays and lesbians, the truth is that most people of faith are appalled when they see this kind of theatrics on TV that run contrary to their own beliefs. There are numerous communities of faith that will welcome and accept people who are queer. According to Welcoming Resources (http://welcomingresources.org), there are more than 3,500 Welcoming and Affirming Churches in America today. Although few denominations have full agreement on this practice, it is pos-sible to find a church that will affirm gay spirituality in various Presbyterian, American Baptist, United Methodist, United Church of Christ, Evangelical Lutheran, Catholic, Episcopal, and Metropolitan Community churches. Many Reformed Jewish communities have also become very progressive and inclusive of homosexuals. For those who do not desire to be affiliated with institutional religion, there are many alternative spiritualities that one could explore that would nurture a deeper connection with God and one's own spirit. Hoping for a spiritual life keeps seekers balanced and centered while they travel the road to wholeness and maturity.

People in the helping professions can walk with others who travel that road encouraging them to be the change they desire. Seek to be the revolu-tion that they wish to see in the world. By helping others become authentic persons of faith who are also gay, lesbian, or bisexual, you can spread your vision of what spirituality in a GLBTIQ person looks like so others can get beyond their stereotypes and see something positive. Remember, percep-tions always change when the abstract becomes personal. What if queer people of faith banded together, shared their insights, and encouraged each other not to be massaged into passivity or malformed by others who have no desire to understand their way of being in the world? What if these people decided to reframe their identity as something that is good and beautiful and true and overflowing with the Good News? I believe such a group would find that it would be worth the effort and sacrifice because they would become unique examples of life-changing good news and witnesses of hope that no person is ever excluded from the love of God. If ever there is a message needed at this time in our society, this is it.

Figure 7.1 Seeking inclusive communities.

Living Out Love

For Truman-era grandparents (those who grew up during President Truman's terms of office) who have become the pillars of the church and have always believed that a person of faith should live within the traditional guidelines taught by their predecessors, I would suggest they expand their concept of love. They may never have had a conversation with a homosexual who is out of the closet. They may have been taught to squelch all sexual feelings that do not comply with the traditional mores of their culture and do not understand why a variant expression of sexuality should be celebrated or authenticated by others. They were probably taught to interpret literally the five passages of Scripture used so often to cast homosexuality into the category of sin. So rather than fighting against what they do not understand or assuming that they have the corner on truth, I would suggest that they stick to something that they know a great deal about, which is to live and walk in love with nonjudgmental compassion. This is something mentioned more than 40 times in the Gospels alone. As older generations make room for loving all the diverse people in their families and communities with the love they have learned from decades of walking by faith, they will be living out the reign of God in their lives in a way that will inspire future generations to do the same.

Choosing attitudes and words that heal rather than destroy when encountering people who are gay, lesbian, bisexual, or transgendered will increase the possibilities for spiritual development in queer folk who desire to make meaningful connections in their lives. In considering appropriate words for this mission it would be hard to go wrong with the closing words of an inspired sermon: "These three remain; faith hope and love. But the greatest of these is love" (1 Corinthians 13:13).

Coming Home

In the latter part of the 20th century, behavioral science helped us understand sexual identity development in ways that were previously unknown, giving credibility to GLBT people who have often said, "I have felt this way since I was very young." We have read true accounts of the GLBT community's increasing desire for meaningful spirituality while also learning that theology and interpretation of Scripture have always found new applications for each new generation of believers. The time to acknowledge the spiritual life in sexual minorities has come, which means that our society and religious communities have the choice to do something positive and life giving with this information. It seems only natural that one of the most healing things we can do is to make it easier for people to come home.

This journey will, of course, be confusing at times, but like all of our paths in life, the way becomes clearer as we walk it. Where things first appear rather topsy-turvy, they usually right themselves when we choose to accept and enjoy the new discoveries along the way. *Choice* is the key word. As we choose to live out the ethic of love whenever difference is encountered, we will grant more people access to basic human dignity and spiritual well-being. The success of various homecomings, however, will depend largely on how much room and respect dominant social groups will allow the sexual minorities in their lives.

Consider, for example, the spiritual provocation of Mary Oliver's classic poem. (Oliver, 1986, p. 14.)

Wild Geese

You do not have to be good.
You do not have to walk on your knees
for a hundred miles through the desert repenting.
You only have to let the soft animal of your body
    love what it loves.
Tell me about despair, yours, and I will tell you mine.
Meanwhile the world goes on.
Meanwhile the sun and the clear pebbles of the rain
are moving across the landscapes,
over the prairies and the deep trees,
the mountains and the rivers.
Meanwhile the wild geese, high in the clean blue air,
are heading home again.
Whoever you are, no matter how lonely,
the world offers itself to your imagination,
calls to you like the wild geese, harsh and exciting—
over and over announcing your place
in the family of things.

MARY OLIVER, "WILD GEESE*"

A true homecoming allows people to find their unique "place in the family of things." It will be different for every person in the queer nation. Some may come home to themselves for the first time when they begin to internalize the fact that they need not to be fixed but to be understood. For this part of the tribe, coming home may mean to enjoy their sexual orientation by employing the ethic of love toward themselves and others, even if they continue living rather closeted lives.

For others, coming home may mean making a return trip to their faith communities so they can become the change they have been seeking. By practicing authentic love and acceptance that reaches out to others, they can begin to show the world that there is indeed such a thing as a gay Christian, Jew, or Muslim. Some, of course, will find that their particular

---

* "Wild Geese" from *Dream Work* by Mary Oliver. Copyright © 1986 by Mary Oliver. Used by permission of Grove/Atlantic, Inc.

house of worship may not welcome this idea, which might necessitate moving to a congregation that has learned to welcome and affirm the GLBT community with open arms. As this continues to happen on a grander scale, inclusion will no longer be just a word in a dictionary but a heartfelt reality.

Coming home for those not desiring to be affiliated with organized religion may begin by exploring other creative ways to enrich their spiritual lives so they, too, can connect with the spirit of a loving God. But let it never be said that the spiritual life is unavailable to people whose sexual orientation turns toward someone of the same gender.

Coming out, or coming home—today is the time to nurture your soul.

For the Therapist

Every person deserves a place of respect in the human family, but sometimes the only place a queer person finds that initial hope is in the office of a pastor or therapist.

Poems such as "Wild Geese" can be useful means for opening a person's heart to the possibility of having a unique and valued place in society. By sitting with the "what if" question, a person can begin to activate different solutions for living a congruent GLBTIQ life.

A good therapist is an informed one. To be of most help, a therapist working with queer clients not only should become acquainted with traditional biblical prohibitions against homosexuality but also should read differing views of Scripture that lead to acceptance.

A good therapist is also one who is well connected to community resources. Pointing a client to various gay-affirmative Web sites can offer broader interpretations of Scripture as well connections to more than 3,500 welcoming and affirming churches across America. It may be helpful to your clients to realize that there are also non-Christian forms of spirituality that are very supportive of the GLBT community.

Sometimes people need to be given permission to rewrite their theology so they can be liberated from past religious toxicity that prevents them from accessing their spiritual nature. By suggesting such a task, clients and therapists may be surprised by the variety of ways people can create a spirituality that is meaningful to them.

Psychotherapy is different from pastoral counseling in this regard. Whereas the latter may use one belief system by which all others are judged, a therapist must be able to honor the various belief systems that give meaning and empowerment to his or her clients. To do this, therapists must be able to step away from imposing their own beliefs on their clients by embracing a kind of interspirituality that honors and respects the beliefs of others.

In a recent church newsletter, Pastor Catherine Fransson (2008) described how she has learned to make room for people's various approaches to God that are different from her Christian roots by noticing how deeply connected they are to the beauty of the world around us. She said that they often manage to waken in her "images of God yet unnamed. There are more names of God than any of us will ever master ... and it is so thrilling to encounter God in ways yet unmet. [This is] good exercise for the soul."

It would also be useful to realize how one's own belief system has emerged from a particular culture and has been refined in each generation. This may mean the therapist will also have to rewrite some of his or her own theology to find a way that validates the beliefs that are different from their own so they can provide the most help for their diverse client load. Although this may require enlarging one's image of God, this does not mean that a therapist cannot honor his or her own faith. Perhaps the best way to do that is to see oneself as extending the hands of divine grace through the skills of compassionate listening to help people discover God in their own way. One Christian therapist I know lights a candle before her sessions to be reminded that regardless of what happens in a session, Christ's light and love is ever present. A Jewish psychologist I know often remembers her clients as she prays specific prayers for God's healing in the world. When the soul-shaking work of spiritual transformation can be given to the client, there is an accompanying need to let go of any forms of coercion so that the client may encounter the love of God outside the counselor's office in any way God sees fit. With queer clients, therapists can often encourage this developmental process with the mere suggestion that one should never negate his or her own spirituality.

As you have read this book, I am hoping that you found yourself thinking through your own theological framework and tracing the path of your own perceptions of homosexuality. Where did those ideas come from?

Have they changed over the past 20 years? What is your own sense of how God works in the lives of the queer people you know? As I stated in the beginning of this book, every generation's belief systems adapt to address the social and moral issues of their era.

Hopefully, you have found a way to embrace the possibility of gay spirituality so that many more people in this world can find that it is possible to be true to themselves while also being true to their spiritual nature.

Research Resources

Qualitative vs. Quantitative Research

Quantitative research involves using very objective structured questions with predetermined response options, whose results can be carefully measured and quantified into the hard science of numbers and statistics. However *qualitative research* is known as the softer side of science because it uses a much more subjective method of personal in-depth interviews featuring open-ended questions, and a moderator who seeks to explore people's perceptions, opinions, and feelings about a particular subject.

Because I was much more interested in people's stories and their interpretation of life events, I chose to use the more flexible qualitative method for my research. Qualitative analysis also involves the discovery of patterns and themes in a given set of data, and noting possible changes over time.

Participants

The 30 gay, lesbian, or bisexual people were chosen because they not only represented the sexual minority group in I was most interested, but also because they were also interested in participating in a study about gay spirituality for their lives, and had seemed to find a way of making peace between themselves and a belief system. Some of these people were friends or acquaintances of mine, but many others were friends of friends, or people that my professional colleagues suggested I contact.

Research Methods

Conversational analysis was employed using my therapeutic skill of intensive listening to the way people communicate while answering key open ended questions.

As I conducted, listened to, and transcribed each conversation, I listened for every nuance of a communication including the pauses, hems, and haws that often demonstrates a subject's emotional state. Semiotics were also used as I studied people's responses, listening over and over again for the signs and meanings associated with their words.

The data for this study were gleaned from a standard set of open-ended questions. (see below) These questions were aimed to explore queer people's responses on the subject of spirituality, namely what had they found most helpful or most hindering in their spiritual development.

Each interview was no more than 40 minutes in length, which made for a total interview time of 20 hours among 30 subjects. The interpretation time, including transcribing all of the interviews, took more than three months. I found that I needed to go over and over those same interviews listening for common themes and for a fuller interpretation of each person's story. Even as I was writing this book, I continued to go over certain sections of transcripts for clarity. I found it fascinating to hear many things I did not pick up when simply engaged in the art of conversation.

Interviews were conducted in many different places, from lunch dates and coffee shops to private offices and homes. My objective was to find the place a person was most comfortable and where there was a sense of privacy and confidentiality afforded.

Although I had intended all interviews to be done individually, three sets of partners wanted to participate in these interviews together. Sometimes I would conduct a complete interview in the presence of the other person and other times I asked each person one question, and then interviewed their partner in sequence. In each case, once I was finished with the formal interview, more conversations ensued about gay spirituality that were not recorded or designed to be part of this study. However, it can be said that participating in this study, often stimulated spiritual interest and deeper reflections for all involved. As I stated at the beginning of this book, I always left my guests feeling that I was honored to be the recipient of their sacred stories.

Survey Questions

The first set of questions was designed to show the demographics of my research.

Age:
Gender
Sexual orientation
Religious background (if any)
Current Spiritual affiliation (if any;)
The second set featured open-ended questions meant to facilitate the telling of stories about key aspects of participants' lives and belief systems.
When I say "gay spirituality" what comes to mind?
Please describe a time when your sexuality and spirituality were most in conflict, and the approximate age when this occurred.
What impact did "being in the closet" have on your faith?
What impact did "coming out" have on your faith?
Have you ever had the experience of your spirituality and your sexuality being in sync? If so, what was your age when this occurred?
As a person of the GLBTQ community, what has most inhibited your spiritual growth?
As a person of the GLBTQ community, what has most encouraged your spiritual/emotional development?
If there is a purpose for gay spirituality in our world today, what would you say that could be?

Survey Results

Number of participants: 30
Gender: 18 men, 12 women
Sexual orientation: 50% gay men, 30% lesbian women, 18% bisexual men, 18% bisexual women
Average age of coming out 24.5 years of age (ranging from 1959–2004)
Those of participants raised in a religious home/culture: 93%

Percentage of respondents currently involved in spiritual practice: 90%

Percentage of respondents who do not practice spirituality: 10%

Ordained clergy or seminarians interviewed: 23%

Those reporting childhood sexual abuse: 13%

Themes Discovered

What most hindered a gay person's spiritual growth and development? (see chapter 4)

Personal reactions to others: 47%

Society's judgment and hatred of homosexuals: 30%

Self-destructive tendencies that were used to cope with shame and loss of hope: 20%

The Gay ghetto's intolerance of Christianity: 7%

What was most helpful for gay's spiritual growth and development? (see chapter 5)

Communities of acceptance, which includes family, friends, clergy, and therapists: 60%

Self-acceptance, learning to live for self rather than pleasing others: 33%

Developing one's own spiritual practices: 30%

References

Chapter 1

American Psychiatric Association, *Healthy minds. healthy lives.* Gay, lesbian and bisexual issues. Retrieved on July 23, 2008 from http://healthyminds.org/glbissues.cfm

Angelou, M, Retrieved on November 10, 2008, from http://www.Brainyquotes.com/quotes/authors/M/Maya_angelou.htm

Aponte, H. (2004, September 9–12). *Spirituality of therapists.* Paper presented at the American Association for Marriage and Family Therapy (AAMFT) seminar, Atlanta, GA.

Association of Welcoming and Affirming Baptists, October 1992. retrieved on November 11, 2008 from http://www.wabaptists.org/who_we_are/history.htm

Bridges, W. (2003). *Managing transitions.* Cambridge, MA: De Capo Press.

Carlson, T., & Erickson, M. (Eds.). (2002). *Spirituality and family therapy.* New York: Haworth Press.

Carlson, T., Erickson, M., & Seewald-Marqurdt, A. (2002). The spiritualities of therapists' lives: Using therapist's spiritual beliefs as resource for relational ethics. In T. Carlson & M. Erickson, *Spirituality and family therapy* (pp. 215–236). New York: Haworth Press.

Friedan, B. *The feminine mystique.* (1963). 2001 W.W. Norton Inc., New York, New York.

Dignity USA, Highlights of Dignity USA's history: 1969, retrieved on November 10, 2008, from http://www.dignityusa.org/history/1969.

Diagnostic statistical manual of mental disorders, (second edition) (1968). American Psychologcial Association, Washington, D. C.

Doughton, S. (2005, June 19). Born gay? How biology may drive orientation. *Seattle Times* (p.A:1,A:18).

Gay, lesbian, and bisexual issues, Healthy Minds.org. American Psychological Association, Washington, D.C., Retrieved on September 27, 2008 from http://www. heathyminds.org/glbissues.cfm

Gays in the military; give the law a name. (2007, July 24). The military personnel act of 1993. Retrievd on September 27, 2008 from http://www.cmrlink.org/HMilitary.asp?docID=300

Holt, S. (2004, July 17). Company to pay, change practices to end gender case. *Seattle Times*, retrieved on December 10, 2008, from http://community. seattletimes.nwsource.com/archive/?date=20040717&slug=boeingsettle

Lambert, M. J. (1992). Psychotherapy outcome research: Implications for integrative and eclectic therapists. In J. C. Norcross & M. R. Goldfried (Eds), *Handbook of psychotherapy integration* (pp. 94–129). New York: Basic.

Nouwen, H. (1992). *Life of the beloved, spiritual living in a secular world*. New York: Crossroad Publishing.

O'Hanlon, B. (2006). *Pathways to spirituality, connection, wholeness, and possibility for therapist and client*. New York: Norton, New York.

Savin-Williams, R. (2001). *Mom, dad. I'm gay. How families negotiate coming out.* American Psychological Association, Washington, D. C.

Schnarch, D. (1997). *Constructing the sexual crucible*. New York: Norton.

Stone Fish, L., & Harvey, R. (2005). *Nurturing queer youth*. New York: Norton and Company.

Sweasey, P. (1997). *From queer to eternity*. London: Cassell.

Time. (1966, April 8). Towards a hidden god. Retrieved Sept 27, 2008, at http:// www.time.com/time/magazine/article/0,9171,835309-1.00html

Wikholm, A. (1999). Summary, *1948, Kinsey publishers sexual behavior in human male*. Science and Medicine, www gay history, Retrieved on September 27, 2008, from www.gayhistory.com/rev2/factfiles/ff1948.htm

Wikipedia, Theology, Quotations, retrieved on November 11, 2008, from http:// en.wikipedia.org/wiki/theology

Wright, L. (1999, July–August). The stonewall riots—1969. *Socialism Today, 40.* Retrieved on July 27, 2008, from http://www.socialismtoday.org/40/stone-wall40.html

Chapter 2

Cohen, L. (1992). "Anthem," from the album, *The future*. Retrieved on September 29, 2008, from http://www.azlyrics.com/lyrics/leonardcohen/anthem.html

Ford, M. (2002). *The wounded prophet: A portrait of Henri J. M. Nouwen*. New York: Doubleday.

Laird, R. (1997, Winter). In memoriam to theologian/psychologist Henri Nouwen. *Record* (a newsletter of Evangelicals Concerned). Retrieved on January, 4, 2007, from http://www.ecinc/org/Records/rec_wnter97.htm

King, M. L, (1963, August 23). *I have a dream*. Retrieved on September 29, 2008, from http://www.boes.org.docs2mking01.html

Nouwen, H. (1994). *The return of the prodigal son, a story of homecoming*. New York: Doubleday.

Obama, B. (2006). *The audacity of hope.* Bethel, CT: Crown Publishing Company.

Reflections. (1996, November 11). *Christianity Today, 40*(13). Retrieved on July 23, 2008, from http://www.christianitytoday.com/ct/1996/november11/6td081. html?start=1

Sexual orientation and homosexuality. (2004). American Psychological Association Help Center. Retrieved on September 29, 2008, from www. Apahelpcenter.org/articles.php?id=31.

Stone Fish, L., & Harvey, R. (2005). *Nurturing queer youth, family therapy transformed.* New York: Norton.

Chapter 3

Bawer, B. (1993). *A place at the table, the gay individual in American society.* New York: Poseidon Press.

Blumenfeld, W. J. (1994). *Adolescence, sexual orientation & identity: An overview.* Retrieved on February 8, 2007, from http://www.geocities.com/ WestHollywood /Parade/9548/article_sexual_identity

Campolo, T. (2007, February 13). *Are evangelicals fixated on homosexuality?* Sojourner's archives. *God's Politics.* Retrieved on October 2, 2008, from http:// blog.beliefnet.com/godspolitics/2007/02/tony-campolo-are-evangelicals-fixated.html

Coleman, E. (1981–2). Developmental stages of the coming out process. *Journal of homosexuality,* Hawthorn Press, New York.

Cass, V, (1979). Homosexual identification formation; A theoretical model. *Journal of homosexuality,* Hawthorn Press, New York

Crain, W. C. (1985). *Kohlberg's stages of moral development, theories of development.* Prentice-Hall, New York pp. 118-136. Retrieved on July 25, 2007, from http://www.faculty.plts.edu/gpence/html/Kohlberg.htm

Dickinson, E. (1862). adapted from PoetryX, retrieved on December 16, 2008, from http://poetry.poetryx.com/poems/3560/

Kubler-Ross. E. (1969). *On death and dying,* Macmillan, NY. Retrieved on September 30, 2008, from http://changingminds.org/disciplines/change_ management/kubler_ross/kubler_ross.htm.

D'Augelli, A.R. (1995). Victimization of lesbian, gay and bisexual youth in community settings. *Journal of Community Psychology.*

Diagnostic & statistical manual of mental disorders. (second edition). (1968). American Psychologcial Association, Washington, D. C.

Elizur, Y., & Ziv, M. (2001, June). Family support and acceptance, gay male identity formation and psychological adjustment; A path model. *Family Process,* 40(2), 125–144. Retrieved on February 8, 2007, from http://www.blackwell-synergy.com/doi/full/10.1111/j.1545-5300.2001.4020100125

Genetics, environment shape sexual behavior. (2008, June 30). *US News and World Report*. Retrieved July 23, 2008, from http://health.usnews.com/articles/health/healthday/ 2008/06/30/genetics-environment-shap

Gorski, E. (2007, February 6). Haggard says he is 'completely heterosexual' *Denver Post*. Retrieved on February 8, 2007, from http://www.denverpost.com/portlet/article/html/fragments/print_article.jsp?articled=51649

Hetrick, E.S., & Martin, A.D. (1987). Developmental issues and their resolution for gay and lesbian adolescents. *Journal of Homosexuality*. Haworth , NY.

Kidron, B. (Director) (1995). *To Wong Foo, thanks for everything, Julie Newmar*. USA, Universal Pictures.

Lownsdale, S. (1997). Faith development across the life span: Fowler's integrative work. *Journal of Psychology and Theology*, 25(1) 49–63.

Lorde, A. (1984). *Sister Outsider*, The Crossing Press. Retrieved on September 29, 2008 from http://www.advocateweb.org.hope/quotes.asp

Newman. B., and Muzzonigro, P. (1993). The effects of traditional family values on the coming out process of gay male adolescents. *Adolescence*.

Parrott, L. III, & Steele, L. (1995). Integrating psychology and theology at undergraduate colleges; A developmental perspective. *Journal of Psychology and Theology*, 23(4), 261–265. Retrieved on February 8, 2007, from http://www.hope.edu/adedemic/psychology/335/webrep/faithdevel.html

Rosario, M., Rotheram-Borus, M.J., & Reid, H. (1996). Gay related stress and its correlates among gay and bisexual male adolescents of predominantly Black, and Hispanic background. *Journal of Community Psychology*.

Savin-Williams, R. (2001). *Mom, dad, I'm gay: How families negotiate coming out*. Washington, DC: American Psychological Association.

Stone Fish, L., & Harvey, R. G. (2005). *Nurturing queer youth*. New York: W.W. Norton & Company.

Weisman, J., & Babington, C. (2006, October 5). Aide: I told Hastert staff about Foley 3 years ago. *Seattle Times*, p. A1.

Wikipedia. Retrieved on September 29, 2008, from http://en.wikipedia.org/wiki/intersexuality.

Wing, K. A. (1997, September 30). *Adult faith development: current thinking*. Retrieved on April 21, 2008, from http://www.hope.edu/academic/psychology/335/webrep2/faithdev.

Wolski Conn, J., (ed) (1986. p. 226–232). *Women's spirituality; Resources for Christian development*; Paulist Press. Retrieved on Sept 29, 2008, from http://faculty.plts.edu/gpence/html/folwer.htm

Chapter 4

Carlson, T. D., & Erickson, M. J. (Eds.) (2002). *Spirituality and family therapy*. New York: Haworth Press.

O'Hanlon, B. (2006). *Pathways to spirituality*. New York: Norton and Co.

Washington post and the associated press. (2006, October 5). Public office, secret life, *Seattle Times* p. A3.

Wikipedia, Carl Jung. Retrieved on September 29, 2008, from http://en.wikipedia. org/wiki/carl_jung

Chapter 5

Campolo, T. (2007, February 13). *Are evangelicals fixated on homosexuality?* Sojourner's archives. *God's Politics.* Retrieved on October 2, 2008, from http:// blog.beliefnet.com/godspolitics/2007/02/tony-campolo-are-evangelicals-fixated.html.

Dickinson, E. *Hope is the thing that floats.* Retrieved on September 30, 2008, from http://academic.brooklyn.cuny.edu/english/melani/cs6/hope.html

Gallup, G., Jr. (1998). *The gallup poll, public opinion 1997.* Wilmington, DE: Scholarly Resources, Inc

Hanford, J. (1993). Is the faith of faith development Christian faith?, *Pastoral Psychology,* Vol 42, No. 2. Retrieved on September 30, 2008, from http:// www.springerlink.com/content/l31806040461440m/

Hardy, K. V. (2007, October 11). Strategies for healing strained relationships. *Race, reality and relationships.* Presented at the American Association for Marriage and Family Therapy (AAMFT) seminar for the Eikenberg Institute for Relationships, New York.

Hobbs, J. (2008, March 11). Pastoral ministry to gays and lesbians, climate of care. *Christian Century,* Chicago, Ill.

Kennedy J. F. Retrieved on November 11, 2008, from http://www.quoteationspage. com/quote/27085.html.

Lombardi, K.S. (2000, April 30). Helping clergy help the anguished. *The New York Times.* Retrieved on October 2, 2008, from http://query.nytimes.com/gst/full-page.html?res=9C05E6DD1130F933A05757C0A9669C8B63&sec=&spon= &pagewanted=2

Newell, J. P. (2002). *Sounds of the eternal, a Celtic psalter.* Grand Rapids, MI: William Eerdmans Publishing Co.

Nouwen, H, (2000). *Life of the beloved, spiritual living in a secular world.* Crossword. New York.

O'Connell-Higgins, G. (1994). *Resilient adults, overcoming a cruel past.* San Francisco: Jossey-Bass, Inc.

O'Hanlon, B. (2006). *Pathways to spirituality.* New York: Norton and Co.

Turnbull, L. (2007, September 1). Gwen Hall, 56, pastoral backer of gay rights. *Seattle Times,* B6.

Wesley, J., I felt my heart strangely warmed, Journal of John Wesley. *Christian Classics Ethereal Library.* Retrieved on September 30, 2008, from http:// www.ccel.org/ccel/wesley/journal.vi.ii.xvi.html

Chapter 6

Ahrons, C. (1994). *The good divorce, keeping your family together when your marriage comes apart.* New York: Harper Collins.

Anita the Christian Lesbian. http://www.sisterfriends-together.org/category/anita/

Blumenfeld, W. J. (1994). *Adolescence, sexual orientation & identity: An overview.* Retrieved on February 8, 2007, from http://wwgeocities.com/WestHollywood /Parade/9548/article_sexual_identity

Brass, P. (1999). *How to survive your own gay life.* New York: Belhue Press.

D'augelli, A.R., & Hershberger, S.L. (1993). Lesbian, gay and bisexual youth in community settings; Personal challenges and mental health problems. *American Journal of Community Psychology*, 21, 421–448; Dube' E.M. (2000). The role of sexual behavior in the identification process of gay and bisexual males. *Journal of Sex Research*, 37,123–132: and Savine-Williams, R. C. (1998) "... and then I became gay"; Young men's stories. New York; Routledge.

Evangelicals Concerned. http://www.ecwr.org/

Greene, B. (1997). Ethnic minority lesbians and gay men: Mental health and treatment issues. In B. Greene (Ed.), *Ethnic and cultural diversity among lesbians and gay men*; (pp. 216–239). Newbury Park, CA: Sage.

Gundrum, G. (2007, December 20). *What are we waiting for?* [sermon] Retrieved on December 22, 2007, from http://www.Seattlefirstbaptistchurch.org

Hunsberger, P. H. (2007, September). Reestablishing clinical psychology's subjective core. *American Psychologist.*, pp. 614-615.

Matthew Shepard Foundation, Matthew's Life. (2006). Retrieved on October 1, 2008, from http://www.matthewshepard.org/site/PageServer?pagename=mat_Matthews_Life

Newell, J. P. (2000). *Celtic benediction, prayers morning and might prayer.* Grand Rapids, MI: William Eerdman's Publishing Company.

O'Brien, J. (2004). Wrestling the angel of contradiction, queer Christian identities. *Culture and Religion*, 5(2), 186–187.

!OutProud! The national coalition for gay, lesbian, bisexual and transgendered youth and Oasis magazine. (1998, March). *!OutProud! Oasis internet survey of queer and questioning youth.*

Peck, M. S. (1978). *The road less traveled, a new psychology of love, traditional values and spiritual growth.* New York: Simon and Schuster.

Perez, R. M., DeBord, K., & Bieschke, K. J. (Eds.). (2000). *Handbook of counseling and psychotherapy with lesbian, gay and bisexual clients.* Washington, DC: American Psychological Association.

Reynolds, D. (2007, October). *Reconciling gay and LDS identities.* Poster presented at the American Association for Marriage and Family Therapy (AAMFT) National Convention, Long Beach, CA.

Savin-Williams, R. (2001). *Mom, dad. I'm gay. How families negotiate coming out.* Washington, DC: American Psychological Association.

Smith, A. (1997). Cultural diversity and the coming-out process: Implications for therapy practice. In B. Greene (ed.), *Ethnic and cultural diversity among lesbians and gay men* (pp. 279–300). Newbury Park, CA: Sage.

Spring, J. A. (2004). *How can I forgive you? The courage to forgive, the freedom not to.* New York: Harper Collins.

Sweasey, P. (1997). *From queer to eternity, spirituality in the lives of lesbian, gay and bisexual people.* London: Cassell.

Trujillo. C.M. (1997). Sexual identity and the discontents of difference. In B. Greene (Ed.), *Ethnic and cultural diversity among lesbians and gay men.* (pp. 266-278). Newbury Park, CA: Sage.

Wikipedia, Kinsey Scale. Retrieved on October 1, 2008 from http://en.wikipedia.org/wiki/Kinsey_scale

Chapter 7

Boswell, J. (1980). *Christianity, social tolerance, and homosexuality, gay people in western Europe from the beginning of the Christian era to the fourteenth century.* Chicago: University Press of Chicago.

Bradley, I. (2003). *The Celtic Way*, Darton, Longman, and Todd, London.

Brokaw, T. (2007). *Boom! Voices of the sixties, personal reflections on the '60s and today.* New York: Random House.

Brown-Taylor, B. (2000). *Speaking of sin, the lost language of salvation.* Cambridge, MA: Cowley Publications.

Campus Crusade for Christ. (1968). Have you heard about the four spiritual laws? *New Life Publications*, Orlando, Florida.

Fox, M. (2008). *Saving Jesus.* [Motion picture series] Living the Questions. Phoenix, Arizona.

Fransson, C. (2008, June 9). In my own words. *Spire* [Seattle First Baptist Newsletter], *71*(26). (Available from Seattle First Baptist Church, 1111 Harvard Ave., Seattle, WA 98122)

Jones, S. (2005). *What does the Bible (really) teach about homosexuality?* [pamphlet]. (Available from Seattle First Baptist Church, 1111 Harvard Ave., Seattle, WA 98122)

Keillor, G, (Ed.) (2002). What I heard at the close of day. *Good Poems*, Penguin Group, NY.

McClaren,B.D. (2000). *The church on the other side.*, Grand Rapids, Michigan: Publishing Hiuse Zondervan

McClaren, B. D. (2007). *Everything must change: Jesus, global crises, and a revolution of hope.* Nashville, TN: Thomas Nelson.

Nouwen, H. (1994). *The return of the prodigal son, a story of homecoming*, Doubleday, NY.

Oliver, M. (1986). Wild Geese. *Dream Work*. Altlantic Monthly Press, NY, NY.

Princeton Religion Research Center. (1985) *Religion in America*. Princeton, NJ: Author.

Shelton, R. L. (1992). Nature, character, and origin of Scripture. In E. Carpenter & W. McCown, *Asbury bible commentary* (pp. 19–38). Grand Rapids, MI: Zondervan Publishing House.

Stevenson, D. (1967). *In the bible preacher's workshop*. Nashville, TN: Abingdon Press.

Sweasey, P. (1997). *From queer to eternity, spirituality in the lives of lesbian, gay and bisexual people*. London: Casswell.

Wink, W. (1979). Homosexuality and the Bible. *Christian Century Magazine*. Retrieved on July 23, 2008, from http://www.bridges-across.org/ba/winkhombib.htm#hom

Whitman, Walt. (1900). In David McKay (Ed.), *Leaves of grass* (p. 126). Silverman & Co: Philadelphia.

Index